AN INTRODUCTION TO
COMPUTER-BASED
LIBRARY SYSTEMS

HEYDEN INTERNATIONAL TOPICS IN
SCIENCE

Editor: L. C. Thomas

RTL/2 Design and Philosophy   J. G. P. BARNES

Introduction to PASCAL   C. A. G. WEBSTER

Charge-Coupled Devices   M. H. ROSS

Computer Applications in Shipbuilding Technology   C. KUO

An Introduction to Computer-based
     Library Systems   L. A. TEDD

Analysis with Ion-Selective Electrodes   P. L. BAILEY

Analysis of Drugs of Abuse   E. BERMAN

Environmental Pollution Analysis   P. D. GOULDEN

Paper and Thin Layer Chromatography
     in Environmental Analysis   M. E. GETZ

Interfacing Computers with Laboratory Equipment   A. CARRICK

AN INTRODUCTION TO COMPUTER-BASED LIBRARY SYSTEMS

L. A. TEDD

College of Librarianship Wales,
Aberystwyth, Dyfed, Wales

LONDON · NEW YORK · RHEINE

Heyden & Son Ltd., Spectrum House, Alderton Crescent, London NW4 3XX.
Heyden & Son Inc., 225 Park Avenue, New York, N.Y. 10017, U.S.A.
Heyden & Son GmbH, Münsterstrasse 22, 4440 Rheine/Westf., Germany.

ISBN 0 85501 221 8

Printed in Great Britain by Galliard (Printers) Ltd, Gt. Yarmouth, Norfolk.

CONTENTS

FOREWORD xi

PREFACE xiii

Chapter 1   AN OVERVIEW OF COMPUTER-BASED
LIBRARY SYSTEMS 1

Introduction 1
Historical Phases of Development 3
Reasons for Developing Computer-Based Systems . 4
Arguments against Developing Computer-Based Systems 5
Whose Computer to Use? 6
Potential Problems of Computer-Based Systems in
Libraries 8
Costs of Computer-Based Library Systems . . . 9
References 9
Further Reading 10

Chapter 2   WHAT IS A COMPUTER? 11

Introduction 11
Computer Processing 11
The Computer 13
Input 13
Output 18

v

Backing Store 19
Main Store 19
Central Processor Unit (CPU) 20
Computer Systems 21
Computer Manufacturers 22
References 23
Further Reading 23

Chapter 3   COMMUNICATING WITH THE COMPUTER   . 24

Introduction 24
Information Structure 24
Programming 28
Programming in BASIC 31
Compilers 33
Operating Systems 35
Program Packages 36
References 36

Chapter 4   SETTING UP COMPUTER SYSTEMS IN LIBRARIES   37

Introduction 37
Feasibility Study 37
Systems Analysis 38
Implementation 40
Library Involvement 42
Staffing 46
Flow Charts 47
References 49
Further Reading 49

Chapter 5   MACHINE-READABLE CATALOGUING (MARC)   50

Introduction 50
History 50
Current Situation 51
Future of UK MARC 53
Uses Made of MARC 54
Software and Services 56
The MARC Record 58
Examples 60
References 63
Further Reading 64

Chapter 6   ACQUISITIONS AND CATALOGUING SYSTEMS   65

Introduction   65
Acquisitions Systems   66
Cataloguing Systems   68
Method of Processing   71
Bibliographic Record   72
Software and Services   74
Filing   75
Union Catalogues and Co-operation   76
Evaluation and Costs   77
Examples   81
References   85

Chapter 7   CIRCULATION CONTROL   87

Introduction   87
Input   88
Files   90
Processes and Output   90
Data Collection Devices   93
Method of Processing   99
Records   101
Software and Services   103
Evaluation and Costs   103
Examples   105
References   110

Chapter 8   SERIALS CONTROL   111

Introduction   111
Cataloguing and Listing   112
Accessioning   113
Subscriptions Control   115
Binding   115
Circulation   116
Method of Processing   117
Bibliographic Record   118
Software and Services   119
International Serials Data System   120
Examples   121
References   124

Chapter 9   COMPUTER-PRODUCED INDEXES   .   .   .   126

               Introduction   126
               Machine-formatted Indexes   127
               KWIC-type Indexes   129
               Indexes Generated by String Manipulation .   .   .   132
               Other Machine-generated Indexes   135
               Software and Services   137
               General Computer System   138
               Evaluation and Costs   139
               Examples   141
               References   144

Chapter 10   SELECTIVE DISSEMINATION OF INFORMATION   145

               Introduction   145
               An SDI System   146
               Search Methods   147
               Profile Construction   150
               Externally Produced Databases   152
               Software and Services   154
               Evaluation and Costs   157
               Examples   160
               References   164
               Further Reading   165

Chapter 11   RETROSPECTIVE SEARCH SYSTEMS .   .   .   166

               Introduction   166
               A Retrospective Search System   167
               Access   168
               Search Methods   170
               Software and Services   173
               Training and Instruction of Users   176
               Evaluation and Costs   178
               Future   181
               Examples   183
               References   189
               Further Reading   190

App. I   BINARY ARITHMETIC   191

App. II   GLOSSARY OF COMPUTER TERMS FOR
             LIBRARIANS   193

App. III   HOW TO COMPUTE A MODULUS 11 CHECK
             DIGIT   197

ACRONYM INDEX   198

SUBJECT INDEX   201

FOREWORD

The object of this series of monographs is the timely dissemination of essential information about topics of current interest in science. Interdisciplinary aspects are given fullest attention. The series aims at the presentation of new techniques, ideas and applications in sufficient detail to enable those who are not specialists in a particular subject to appreciate the applicability of the subject matter to their own work, and the bibliographies included in each monograph will guide readers in extending their knowledge of the subject to any desired depth. The depth of treatment of course makes them compact definitive books for the specialist as well. The series will from time to time include more general reviews of selected areas of scientific advancement, for which a somewhat wider readership is envisaged.

The series is to be priced at a level to attract the individual purchaser as much as the librarian. The topics and the depth of treatment should suit both the student and the research worker, academic or industrial. The range of topics in this series will eventually span the whole extent of scientific interests and the authorship will reflect the international nature of the subject matter.

An Introduction to Computer-Based Library Systems was commissioned for inclusion in this series to provide a background to the rapidly increasing use of computers both in library housekeeping applications and in information retrieval systems. Although written with the student of librarianship and information science in mind, this book will nevertheless be of value to those already using computers in library and information services. The three sections of the book cover an introduction to computers, from a librarian's viewpoint; computer-based library systems to control acquisition, cataloguing, charging, and the processing of serials; and computer-based information retrieval systems. It is written at a level which will not only enable the general reader to obtain an appreciation of the present scope and future potential of applications of the computer in libraries, but also, by virtue of its numerous descriptions of existing systems and its detailed references, serve as a handy reference compilation for specialist librarians and information scientists.

L. C. Thomas

PREFACE

The rapid growth of computer-based systems in libraries and information units provides for exciting developments in both the library and computer professions, and there is a very real need for suitable introductory texts on this subject.

This book is written to satisfy the need and is directed very largely at the student of librarianship and information science; however, I believe that the practitioner will also find that it contains useful information. In this role, the book has to be a snapshot of the situation at the time of writing. Most, if not all, the systems will develop and expand as time goes by. For the past three years I have conducted a 30-hour course of lectures and seminars for the International Graduate Summer School held at the College of Librarianship Wales, in Aberystwyth. The text of this book is based on material covered in that course.

The book divides into three sections. The first (Chapters 2–4) introduces computer systems from a librarian's viewpoint. The second section (Chapters 5–8) studies computer-based applications in library housekeeping procedures, and the third (Chapters 9–11) covers computer-based information retrieval systems. Terminology potentially unfamiliar to the reader is explained in a glossary of computer terms which forms part of the Appendices, and an acronym index is also included.

Many references to working systems in Britain and abroad are made throughout the text; inevitably the problems of geography have biased these examples somewhat towards Britain. I have tried wherever possible to indicate operational and development costs and associated dates to allow the reader to adjust for inflation.

I have received help from very many people when writing this book and I should particularly like to acknowledge the following practitioners: John Lamble of Bath University, David Buckle of BLCMP, John Davies of Blackwell's, Dick Denniss of Camden, Mr Brown of Cheshire County, Robin Clough of ICI, Nick Pond of INSPEC, Keith Williams of Liverpool Polytechnic,

Roger Summit of Lockheed, Keith Clennett of Oxford City, Guido Goedeme of the Royal Library, Brussels; Miss Kirkpatrick of the Rubber and Plastics Research Association and Richard Hudson of SWALCAP. Colleagues at the College of Librarianship Wales, have also been a great help, especially Lionel Madden who read through the manuscript and Mike Keen who checked the later chapters for accuracy. My family were also involved in the production of this book, especially my sister, Rosemary Davies, who typed the draft of the manuscript, my mother, Margaret Davies, who helped with the proof reading and my husband, Mike, who provided technical and practical support throughout.

Eglwysfach   Lucy A. Tedd
October 1976

CHAPTER 1

AN OVERVIEW OF COMPUTER-BASED LIBRARY SYSTEMS

INTRODUCTION

Computers are used in libraries to assist in the areas of housekeeping and information retrieval.

Housekeeping

The housekeeping procedures in a library are those which are necessary for the administration of the library. They can be separated into four broad areas.

(1) Acquisitions

This covers the selection, ordering and accessioning of items into the library's collection. Computers are used to send order slips and 'chasers' for unacknowledged or overdue orders to the booksellers, to produce lists of books on order, to keep account of the money spent, to produce accessions lists of recently acquired material, and so on.

(2) Cataloguing

This includes the job of describing, recording and displaying details of the holdings of the library. Computers are used to aid in the production and maintenance of catalogues. The quality of the information in the catalogue is still dependent on the cataloguer.

(3) Circulation or charging control

Computers are used in this procedure to keep account of items that are on loan from the library and to whom they are loaned. Overdue notices and notices recalling reserved books can be produced by the computer.

(4) Serials control

Items which are published periodically or serially, such as journals, conference proceedings, annuals or newsletters, need to be processed in a different manner by the library than items which are only published once. The majority of serials control systems which make use of computers do so to produce lists in various orders of the serial publications held by the library. More ambitious systems make use of the computer to assist in the control of subscriptions and in the accessioning of issues.

One international development which has had a big effect on library house-keeping procedures, especially on acquisitions and cataloguing, is MARC or Machine-Readable Cataloguing. This started in the USA in the mid-1960s as a machine-readable version of the catalogue of the Library of Congress. Now many countries all over the world are producing machine-readable records of their national bibliography in the MARC format.

Information retrieval

Computers are used for two broad information retrieval functions.

(1) Production of indexes

Computer-produced indexes, as other indexes, are manually searched. The computer can be used to format or generate the entries of the index. In the former situation the decision on the index entries is taken by human indexers and the computer is used to produce the index in various orders. In the latter situation the computer generates the index entries according to a prescribed set of rules.

(2) Searching files of documents

The computer can be used for running current-awareness searches as well as retrospective searches. In a current-awareness system the computer notifies the user of recently published documents, whereas in a retrospective system the computer searches a file of document details to answer a particular request.

One of the main influences in the rise of computer-based information retrieval systems has been the availability of large files of bibliographic records. These are frequently a by-product of the production of printed indexing and abstracting journals. In the 1960s the producers of these journals found that conventional techniques were inefficient for processing the increased number of serial publications, and so they began to use computer techniques. The bibliographic details of records can be used for computer-searched systems as well as for the production of the indexing and abstracting journal.

The most recent survey of computer-based systems in UK libraries was undertaken by Aslib in 1973,[1] when it was reported that 135 libraries were operating computer-based systems. Information about systems which will be operational on 1st July 1976 is currently being collected for a second edition of the directory.

The Library Automation Research and Consulting (LARC) Association in the USA has surveyed the use of computers in libraries all over the world. The survey for the USA reported on 506 libraries with computer-based systems in 1971.[2]

HISTORICAL PHASES OF DEVELOPMENT

The history of computer-based library systems can be divided into three phases.

Experimental system phase

In the early 1960s several libraries both in North America and in the UK began to experiment with using computers to assist in the processing of information. Several of these systems evolved from punched-card data processing systems.

In the UK the public libraries of Camden and West Sussex and the university libraries of Newcastle and Southampton are examples of libraries which were involved in the experimental phase.

Some of the systems developed during this phase failed for reasons such as:

the computer technology of the time was inadequate;

librarians were not sufficiently definitive in their requirements of the computer-based system;

computer people thought that they knew the librarians' requirements of the computer-based system;

it was thought that all the individual systems in a library should be simultaneously converted to being computer-based.

Local systems phase

Since the late 1960s many librarians have made use of the computer as a tool in the organization of the library's procedures. Most of these systems have been developed locally, either in an academic library, special library or public library.

Many of these systems are operating successfully. Some of the reasons for the success are:

the computer technology is improved;

the experiences of libraries involved in the experimental phase have been used;

there is better communication between librarians and computer people;

the systems are better designed and managed.

Most libraries with computer-based systems are in this phase of development.

Co-operative systems phase

In the 1970s there has been an increase in co-operation and resource sharing by libraries developing computer-based systems. In some cases more formalized library networks have been established.

One example of a co-operative system in the UK is the Birmingham Libraries Co-operative Mechanisation Project (BLCMP). Details of other examples of co-operation in UK libraries have been reported.[3] In the USA the Ohio College

Library Center (OCLC) is an example of a library network, and details of other networks are given in Ref. 4. BLCMP and OCLC are described in Chapter 5.

With the savings in cost to be gained from a co-operative approach to computer-based systems it is thought that most libraries will adopt this approach in the future. The problems to be considered and the decisions to be made when setting up a network are discussed in Ref. 5.

REASONS FOR DEVELOPING COMPUTER-BASED SYSTEMS

There are several reasons for developing computer-based systems in libraries and these will be described individually although they are often inter-linked.

To manage a process more rapidly, more accurately or less expensively

Many library processes can be reduced to clerical procedures of sorting, filing and sending notices. This tends to be routine and boring work which is subject to human error. The computer can be instructed to do these tasks and so the library staff can be released for more worthwhile work. However, there will be some routine and boring work associated with the computer-based system.

The computer can process information much faster than humans and can therefore help to increase the flow of work through the library.

Provided the information entering the computer is accurate, then the computer should process the information accurately. (There is a proverb in the computer world: 'Garbage in, garbage out'.)

If the computer-based system is well-designed and properly managed, it is often possible to reduce the operating costs.

To help overcome increasing library work loads

The increase in the amount of published literature over the last 10–15 years is probably well-known. One example is in the rise of the rate at which book titles are published. Figures given in Ref. 6 show that between 1880 and 1960 the average annual increase in the number of published titles was 2.8%, whereas between 1960 and 1969 the comparable figure was 7.8%.

In many situations, especially in the current economic climate, librarians are unable to recruit more staff to deal with the increase in work and so computer-based systems are used.

To offer new and improved services to users and library staff

With this increase in publications, some of the services provided for users are inadequate.

For instance, the users of an industrial library will wish to be kept aware of recently published articles. Such a need may be satisfied by a computer-based current-awareness service. Union catalogues as well as subset catalogues in particular subject areas can be produced to offer library users and library staff more information about the holdings of the library or libraries. More and better management information can be produced from computer-based systems. This can be used to aid decision making in the library.

These, and other examples of new and improved services, will be clarified in the text.

To make use of external services

Many organisations are now offering services in which the information is recorded in a form suitable for computer processing.

The British Library Bibliographic Services Division offers bibliographic details, in the MARC format, of recently published books in machine-readable form. It is thought that their printed publications, in particular their catalogue card service, will alter in the future and so libraries subscribing to these services may need to think about a computer-based system. Some booksellers also offer computer-based information services to aid a library in selecting, ordering and cataloguing books. Producers of printed indexes to the serial literature are also making information available in a machine-readable form.

As a solution in forming a common system when libraries merge

Many new libraries have been formed by the amalgamation of existing libraries in the UK during the past 14 years. In this situation a common processing system is required and many libraries have developed computer-based systems as the solution.

The local government authorities of London, England and Wales, and Scotland were re-organized in 1964, 1974 and 1975 respectively. This affected the public library service. In the academic library area polytechnics have been formed from previously existing technical colleges.

ARGUMENTS AGAINST DEVELOPING COMPUTER-BASED SYSTEMS

Over the years many librarians have objected to the rise of computer-based systems in libraries. One of the main papers on this topic was written by Mason in 1971.[7] In this paper he explodes eight 'myths' which he thinks that computer-enthusiastic librarians believe. Paraphrased, the points made were:

(a) computers do not make everything effortless;

(b) computer-based procedures do not usually save time over the manual procedures which are replaced;

(c) a computer-based system does not save money;

(d) it is not easy to implement the system on a new computer;

(e) it is not easy to transfer the programs for computer-based systems between libraries;

(f) it is not cheaper to share computer services;

(g) it is not easy to combine individual library systems into a totally integrated system;

(h) users will not receive a better service from a computer-based library system.

Several replies defending computer-based library systems were published.[8,9]

Although most of Mason's statements are broad generalizations, they do contain some truth. However, Mason blamed the computer itself for most of the problems rather than the people who manage and design computer systems. The designers and managers in the 1960s were not always fully aware of the potential problems inherent in computer-based library systems; some systems were oversold, some budgets were over-run and other systems were installed for the wrong reasons. Because of such facts many computer-based systems produced less than their expected benefits. Nevertheless, there has been a general record of success which should become better as the technology improves and there is better communication between librarians and computer people.

In the UK, Davison of the Scientific Documentation Centre has objected strongly to government-sponsored projects on computer-based current-awareness services[10] and Taylor has recently objected to the effect of computer-based systems on book selection policies.[11]

It can only be emphasized that a computer system is as good as or as bad as the human beings who design, implement and operate the system.

There are, undoubtedly, examples of unsuccessful computer-based systems in libraries but these are rarely reported in the literature.

One exception is the production of the British National Film Catalogue.[12] During 1972 to 1975 this catalogue was produced by computer as an experiment to test the feasibility of using a computer to catalogue non-book materials. It transpired that it took longer to prepare the information for input to the computer system than it did to run a manual system. Only about 3000 items are processed each year and it was thought that this small figure was one of the reasons for the failure.

WHOSE COMPUTER TO USE?

In Warheit's reply[8] to Mason's paper[7] one of the points made was that systems should be designed according to the resources available. One such resource is the computer and the amount of its time available to the library.

There are five possible answers to the question of whose computer should be used. In general, a library will only adopt one alternative, but there are situations where more than one alternative provides the best solution.

Parent body's computer

Most libraries operating computer-based systems use the computer of the parent body. In a public library this implies that the local authority's computer is used;

in a special library that the parent organization's computer is used. In university libraries the main university computer is often dedicated to teaching and research work and is not available for the more administrative type of work of libraries; a report on the computer needs for university library operations in the UK has been published.[13] Some university libraries share computer services with the general administration unit of the university.

Using the parent body's computer is normally a cheap solution. However, the computer (and the computer staff) are then not under the control of the library. This means that the library frequently has to compete with other departments within the organization for the necessary computer system resources.

Some libraries have been encouraged in the use of the parent body's computer because the computer was under-utilized. This situation soon alters as several departments begin to use the computer and sometimes the resulting service deteriorates. Departments are often allocated priorities in the use of the computer.

If the library is some distance from the computer centre there can be communication problems. These are solved either by a 'person on a bicycle' (or similar messenger service) or by installing a telecommunications link.

Library's computer

Some libraries are buying minicomputers to be used for special processes, such as circulation control, cataloguing or acquisitions systems, in the library. These are frequently linked, in some manner, to a larger computer outside the library. Minicomputers are described in the next chapter and their use in libraries is described, where appropriate, in the text.

Some of the libraries of the larger universities in North America carry out all their computer processing on their own computer.

This solution gives the library control over the computer (and the computer staff) which can have disadvantages as well as the obvious advantages.

Commercial computer bureaux

This is a common solution for libraries without a parent body computer. Bureaux, which sell computer time and other related services, exist in several countries. Some libraries use computer bureaux because the bureaux have particular programs available.

The British Library currently uses a bureau to produce the MARC information. Several libraries or information units make use of the Imperial Chemical Industry's (ICI) computer bureau for an information retrieval package known as the Agricultural System for the Storage and Subsequent Selection of Information (ASSASSIN).

This can be an expensive solution. However, a good service is normally offered.

Shared computer

Libraries can co-operate to instal a computer that will be used solely for processing their information.

In the UK, the three university libraries of Bristol, Cardiff and Exeter have formed a co-operative project known as the South Western Academic Libraries Co-operative Automation Project (SWALCAP). Assisted by a grant from the British Library Research and Development Department (BLRDD), they have bought a computer which will be used co-operatively.

In the USA, the OCLC system has its own computer which is shared between the participating libraries.

National computer

In some countries libraries make use of a national computer system.

The British Library has recently ordered a computer, which, when operational, will allow libraries throughout the country to access the centralized file of MARC records which will assist in production of their catalogues.

POTENTIAL PROBLEMS OF COMPUTER-BASED SYSTEMS IN LIBRARIES

In the past many of the problems of computer-based library systems have arisen from the poor communication between librarians and computer people. This has resulted in some badly designed systems which either do not reflect the requirements of the library or are inefficient and costly to operate. Both sets of personnel should be aware of this communication problem and should attempt to solve it.

Warheit's paper[8] refers to the need for making realistic plans and for using available resources. He indicates the need for a responsible individual from the staff of the library, who is aware of the potential of computer-based systems in libraries, to be in charge of the development of the computer-based system. This is therefore another potential problem if the library does not have such a person. Another potential problem highlighted in Warheit's paper is the frequent lack of available time and money necessary to develop the system. These resources need to be estimated accurately before starting a project.

The attitudes of the library staff and library users can also be potential problems. Staff may be afraid of losing their jobs with the installation of a computer-based system. Although job specifications change, it is very rare for a member of the library staff to be made redundant because of the introduction of a computer-based library system. Details of the education and training necessary for library staff and the guidance necessary for library users are given in Chapter 4.

Pflug describes some of the side-effects of introducing computer-based systems into libraries.[14] These effects are not always realized at the design stage and can present problems. One side-effect is on the work flow and volume of work in the library. The introduction of an information retrieval service using externally produced information often results in an increase in inter-library loans as users wish to see relevant documents that are not held by the library.

When designing a computer-based library system it is necessary to be aware of these potential problems so that they can be catered for in the final system. A survey of commonplace problems in library automation has been reported by the LARC Association.[15]

COSTS OF COMPUTER-BASED LIBRARY SYSTEMS

Details of the development and operational costs of computer-based library systems are rarely published. This situation is beginning to change as librarians and computer people are realizing the need for cost-effective systems.

One reason for this lack of information was that many of the early systems, being experimental, were funded by governments. This is still happening to some extent. In 1973/74, the Office for Scientific and Technical Information (OSTI), which is now the BLRDD, spent a total of £762 900 on grants and contracts concerned with computer-related library and information projects.[16]

Mason outlines four problems related to the costs of computer-based library systems.[17] These are:

(a) the open-ended cost of development;
(b) the unpredictability of operational costs;
(c) the lack of easily available costs of competitive manual systems;
(d) an unwillingness by some people to analyse fully the cost of their operations.

Details of costs, where available, have been included in the chapters on the various applications. Obviously these will change and so the date at which the cost applied needs to be taken into account.

A chapter on cost accounting in libraries is included in Ref. 18.

At Ohio State University, which operates a fairly sophisticated computer-based charging system, the operating cost for each item borrowed from the library is currently split equally between computer system costs and staff costs.[19] However, staff costs are continuously increasing whereas computer processing costs are decreasing. Figures from IBM included in Ref. 19 show that the cost of a computer obeying 1 000 000 instructions was $40 in 1955 and was estimated as $.08 in 1975. Similarly, the hardware cost of storing 1 000 000 instructions on a computer was $135 in 1955 and was estimated as $.50 in 1975.

REFERENCES

1. C. W. J. Wilson, *Directory of Operational Computer Applications in United Kingdom Libraries and Information Units*, Aslib, London (1973). ISBN 0 85142 054 0.
2. F. E. Patrinostro, *A Survey of Automated Activities in the Libraries of the United States*, The LARC Association Incorporated, Tempe, Arizona (1971).

3. J. Plaister, Co-operation in England. *Library Trends*, **24**, 417–23 (1975).
4. B. Butler, State of the Nation in Networking. *Journal of Library Automation*, **8**, 200–20 (1975).
5. B. Markuson, Library Network Planning. *Network*, **2**, 7–8 (1975).
6. D. B. Hokkanen, American Book Title Out-put—a Ninety-year Overview, *Bowker Annual of Library and Book Trade Information*, 1971, R. R. Bowker Company, New York (1971). ISBN 0 8352 0472 3.
7. E. Mason, The Great Gas Bubble Prick't; or, Computers Revealed by a Gentleman of Quality. *College and Research Libraries*, **32**, 183–96 (1971).
8. I. A. Warheit, When Some Library Systems Fail. *Wilson Library Bulletin*, **46**, 52–8 (1971).
9. A. B. Veaner, *Are Computer-Oriented Librarians Really Incompetent?* The LARC Association Incorporated, Tempe, Arizona (1971).
10. P. S. Davison, Selective Dissemination of Information: Past, Present and Future Development of SDI in the Long March to Becoming a Major Disseminator of Scientific Information. *Research in Librarianship*, **25**, 5–30 (1974).
11. N. Taylor, Dehumanized: the Worst Possible Time for Blind Ordering of Rubbish. *Library Association Record*, **78**, 17 (1976).
12. B. Davies, Catalogue and Computer. *British Film Institute News*, **23**, 4 (1976).
13. N. Higham, *Computer Needs for University Library Operations*, Standing Conference of National and University Libraries, London (1973). ISBN 0 900210 02 8.
14. G. Pflug, The Effects of Automation on Library Administration. *International Federation of Library Associations Journal*, **1**, 267–75 (1975).
15. F. S. Patrinostro, *A Survey of Commonplace Problems in Library Automation*, The LARC Association Incorporated, Tempe, Arizona (1973). ISBN 0 88257 073 0.
16. R. M. Duchesne, The Use of Computers in British Libraries and Information Services: an Analysis. *Program*, **8**, 183–90 (1974).
17. E. Mason, Automation or Russian roulette? in *Proceedings of the 1972 Clinic on Library Applications of Data Processing* (ed. F. W. Lancaster), University of Illinois Graduate School of Library Science, Urbana (1972). ISBN 0 85157 158 1.
18. R. M. Hayes and J. Becker, *Handbook of Data Processing for Libraries*, 2nd ed., Melville Publishing Company, Los Angeles (1974). ISBN 0 471 36483 5.
19. H. Atkinson, Personnel Savings Through Computerized Library Systems. *Library Trends*, **23**, 587–94 (1975).

FURTHER READING

R. T. Kimber, *Automation in Libraries*, 2nd ed., Pergamon Press, Oxford (1974). ISBN 0 08 017969 X.

S. J. Swihart and B. F. Hefley, *Computer Systems in the Library: a Handbook for Managers and Designers*, Melville Publishing Company, Los Angeles (1973). ISBN 0 471 83995 7.

P. H. Vickers, *Automation Guidelines for Public Libraries*, Her Majesty's Stationery Office, London (1975). ISBN 0 11 270269 4.

J. Wainwright, *Computer Provision in British Libraries*, Aslib, London (1975). ISBN 0 85142 069 9.

CHAPTER 2

WHAT IS A COMPUTER?

INTRODUCTION

Chambers's Twentieth Century Dictionary defines a computer to be: 'a mechanical, electric or electronic machine for carrying out especially complex calculations'.

The modern electronic computer is not only capable of vast quantities of calculations, but holds within itself the instructions that tell it which calculations to perform. These instructions are known as a program. Even some of the pocket-size calculators on the market today are capable of holding a program, though these are not normally referred to as computers. The increased availability of such calculators exemplifies the rapid rate of change of the technology on which a computer is based. When the electronic computer was evolved in the 1940s a large room full of valves was required to do what a computer on top of a desk can do today.

The term 'computer' covers a wide range of machines, from microcomputers, through minicomputers to large main-frame computers. Although the dividing line between these is ill-defined, it is important to comprehend the general range of capabilities implied by these terms. A library which instals a minicomputer to control its charging system cannot necessarily expect that same minicomputer to be capable of producing its catalogue using magnetic tapes acquired from elsewhere.

COMPUTER PROCESSING

As far as the librarian is concerned there are three ways by which information can be processed by a computer system.

Batch processing

In a simple system, jobs to be undertaken by the computer are processed one after another so that there is a linear flow through the system. This means that one job is finished before another is started. A more complicated batch system would involve the computer sharing its time between several programs. Batch processing can present problems for a librarian. First, there will be a time delay (sometimes appreciable and of the order of days) before the results are obtained. This means that in a batch-processed charging system it is impossible to answer immediately the question: 'Who has this book on loan?' Second, it precludes direct access to the computer and hence there is no interaction with the program or files of information.

Despite these restrictions there are many library tasks that are not affected; for example, catalogue production, production of order notes to send to booksellers and listing serials held by the library. For certain types of work, such as these jobs, batch processing is inherently more efficient than any other method of processing.

On-line processing

This method of processing was devised by some people who thought it would be good to sit at a typewriter, 'talk' with a computer and think that the computer was dedicated to processing their job. If there is more than one person 'talking' to the computer then it shares its time between each of them. This sharing of time (or time-sharing as it is known) is not normally noticed by the person sitting at the terminal as the computer is so fast.

Typical computer operations are measured in microseconds or nanoseconds (0.000 001 and 0.000 000 001 of a second respectively). Some impression of the smallness of a nanosecond can be gained from the fact that there are almost as many nanoseconds in a second as seconds in 30 years. On-line processing overcomes the disadvantages of batch processing noted above (delay of receiving results and lack of interaction). However, on-line processing might not be available to the library; for instance, the computer might not support on-line working or it might not be appropriate for the library to be connected (perhaps via the telephone network) all day to the computer.

Remote job entry processing

This is a linking of on-line and batch processing. An on-line terminal is used to enter a job into the queue of jobs to be batch processed by the computer. This saves the library from physically transporting the program or data to the computer centre. When the computer has completed the job the resultant files can be interrogated on the terminal. This method of processing is also dependent on the computer system and a means of connecting the library to the computer centre. Remote job entry processing still suffers from the delayed results inherent in batch processing.

THE COMPUTER

An analogy can be drawn between a computer and a clerical worker. The information in the IN tray is processed according to instructions; a calculator might be used or a file of records referred to, and the results placed in the OUT tray.

The basic units of a computer system can be thought of in a similar way (Fig. 2.1) and are generally referred to as hardware.

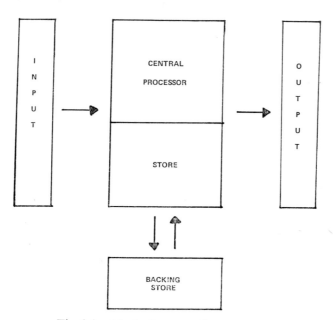

Fig. 2.1. Block diagram of a computer.

The so-called peripherals of the computer system are the input and output units and the backing store; they are partly mechanical and hence expensive and not as reliable as the purely electronic parts. It is usually the peripherals which are the most noticeable parts of a computer system and with which the library staff are mostly concerned. How is the information to be presented to the computer? How will the library receive output from the computer? Can the library use MARC tapes? The solutions to such problems will all be partly or wholly dependent upon the peripherals of the computer system.

INPUT

This is the means of transferring information (both instructions and data) into the computer system. Most machine-readable forms involve coding a character into a series of binary digits (these can be thought of as '0's and '1's and are known as bits).

01000001 is the code for the letter A. In the early days most computers had their own codes for characters and so inter-computer communication was difficult. The situation is becoming more standardised and the two most widely used codes are:

ASCII—American Standard Code for Information Interchange;
EBCDIC—Extended Binary Coded Decimal Interchange Code.

The media used for inputting information include:

Paper-tape

This is an old method and will be familiar to those who have used Telex machines or tape typewriters in libraries. Different widths of paper-tape are in use; common sizes have five holes or eight holes, representing the number of bits. Each character is punched as a pattern of holes across the tape. The word ABRACADABRA might be represented as in Fig. 2.2.

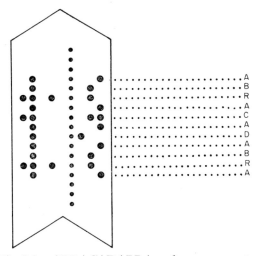

Fig. 2.2.   ABRACADABRA code on a paper-tape.

Paper-tapes are usually prepared away from the computer using a typewriter-like machine. To input the paper-tape to the computer it is passed through a paper-tape reader. This consists of a mechanism to move the tape, a light source and some photo-electric cells which produce an electric current if light shines on them. Thus, if a hole passes under the light there is a current and if there is no hole there is not a current.

Some computer charging systems accumulate information about issues and returns on paper-tape.

Punched cards

This is another old method of recording information. It was invented by

Herman Hollerith to aid in the processing of information from the 1890 US Census. The idea was given to Hollerith by Dr Billings, then librarian of the Library of the Surgeon's General Office (forerunner of the US National Library of Medicine).[1]

Punched cards operate on a similar principle to paper-tape with each of the 80 vertical columns capable of being coded to represent a character. Usually the characters represented are printed at the top of the card. An example of the punching for ABRACADABRA is given in Fig. 2.3.

Cards are punched using a special machine known as a card punch.

Punched cards are sometimes used in serials control systems and in charging systems to record the basic information about an item.

Magnetic tape

This looks like audio tape but is of a better quality. Conventional magnetic tape is half an inch wide. Individual, tiny areas of the surface are magnetised, each in one of two ways, to represent a '0' or a '1'. These bits across the width of the tape are used to represent a character, in a similar way to paper-tape. When using magnetic tape as an input medium it is necessary to know the number of tracks across the tape and also the density at which the information was recorded. The density is measured in bits per inch (bpi), with typical densities being 556 bpi and 800 bpi.

Magnetic tape cassettes (similar to audio cassettes) are now also being used to hold data. The Plessey Library Pen charging system (described in Chapter 7) records data about transactions on a magnetic tape cassette. Being smaller, these cassettes hold much less information than a reel of half-inch tape.

Half-inch tape is usually used when a large amount of data is transferred from one computer system to another. Libraries that subscribe to services supplying bibliographic information in machine-readable form usually receive this information on magnetic tape.

Paper-tape, punched cards and magnetic tape are the most common methods of transferring information to machine-readable form. There are advantages and disadvantages to each. Paper-tape is good for bibliographic work where the length of the record might vary, or where a wide range of characters is required. Computer operators, on the other hand, prefer to process punched cards and these are much easier to edit. Magnetic tapes are faster, which cuts down on computer time, but are more expensive to buy. Paper-tape and punched cards are both bulky and with current paper shortages are likely to disappear. However, many people have a preference for paper as they can see the holes and therefore 'read' the characters and so it will be some years before punched cards and paper-tape disappear.

If an on-line or remote job entry system is used, other equipment is necessary to communicate with the computer.

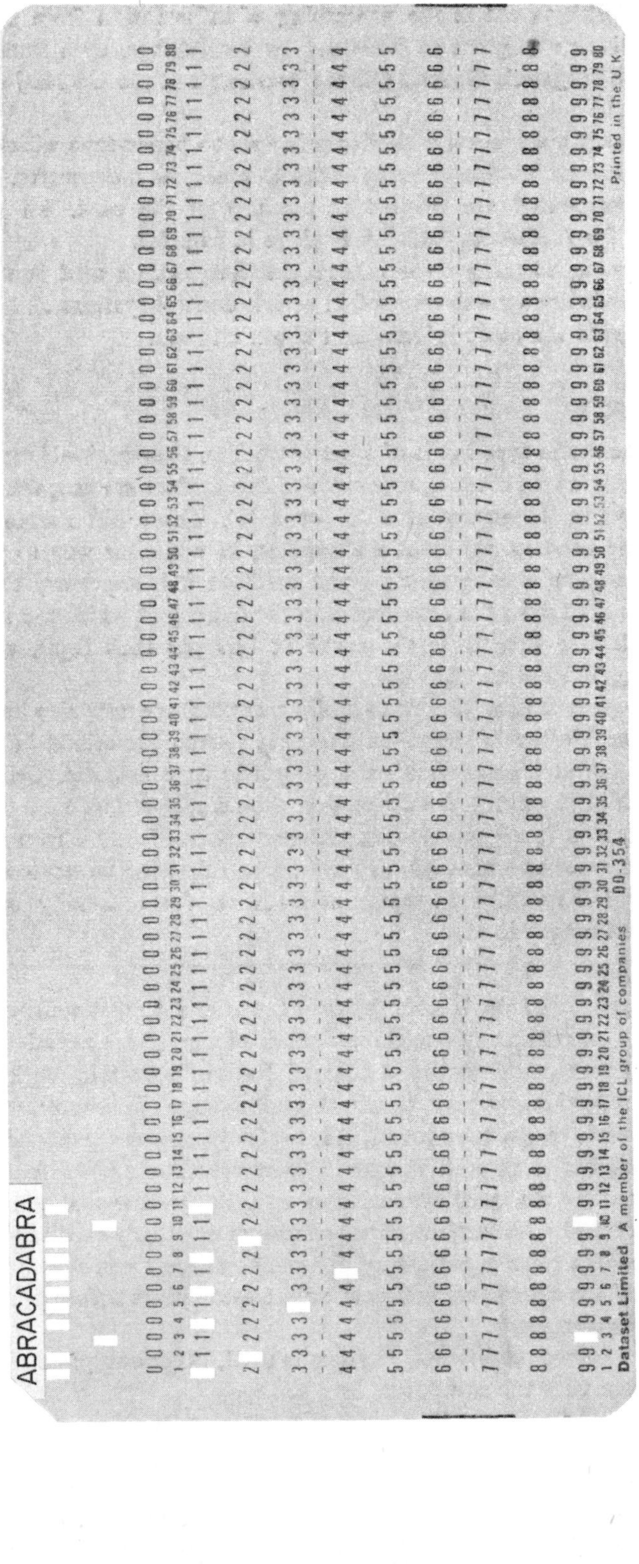

Fig. 2.3. ABRACADABRA coded on a punched card.

Teletypewriter

This consists of a keyboard and a printer on which are recorded both the characters typed by the user and the characters transmitted by the computer. A means of recording on, and reading the information from, paper-tape or magnetic tape cassette is usually attached. The basic machines are slow (a printing speed of 10 characters per second), noisy, but relatively cheap (about £700). There are faster (a printing speed of 30 characters per second), more silent and more expensive (about £2000) teletypewriters currently available.

It is worth noting that a Telex machine can be used as a teletypewriter. At least one computer bureau in the UK (Atkins Computer Services Ltd., Epsom, Surrey) supports this. It is slow (a printing speed of 6 characters per second) and noisy.

Visual Display Unit (VDU)

This can be used instead of a teletypewriter for on-line communication. It consists of a small television-like screen to display characters, and a keyboard. VDUs are frequently used by libraries for interrogating files and for adding, amending or deleting records in these files. The speed at which they operate is chiefly dependent on the speed of the telecommunications channel that links the VDU to the computer. This speed is usually measured in baud (where 1 baud is normally equal to 1 bit per second). Access using the normal switched telephone network might typically be at 300 baud (or 30 characters per second).

There are some other methods of inputting information which are not so widely used but are of interest to librarians.

Optical Character Recognition (OCR)

At present this cannot be used with ordinary handwriting or print. The text to be input is prepared on a typewriter using a special type-font. The two fonts currently in use are known as OCR 'A' and OCR 'B'. The typed pages are passed through a reader which can distinguish the various characters. These readers are not cheap and so a bureau is often used to record the characters on to a magnetic tape which can be used for processing.[2]

Computer Input Microfilm (CIM)

This is a rapidly developing technology which allows data on microfilm to be input to a computer system. The text must be prepared in a strictly specified format and the choice of type-fonts is limited. It is likely that the OCR 'B' font will be used. The CIM unit scans the film, identifies the characters and feeds this information to a computer for processing. At present there is only one true CIM device commercially available.

OUTPUT

This is the means by which the computer system can communicate results to the outside world and, where necessary, make the information readable.

Several of the devices discussed under 'input' are also applicable for 'output'. For on-line systems, teletypewriters and visual display units can be used as output devices. Information can also be output on magnetic tape, punched cards or punched paper-tape. Other forms of output include:

Printers

Line printers, as their name implies, print a whole line (of up to 132 characters) at a time on continuous stationery. The stationery normally used is single-sheet, low quality paper. Multi-part stationery, with interleaved layers of carbon paper, can be used to obtain multiple copies of the information being output. Continuous sheets of gummed labels, catalogue cards or post-cards can be used when necessary. Most line printers are limited to upper-case characters, although some do provide for lower-case characters. In some instances special printing mechanisms need to be designed. This happened for example, when the National Library of Egypt wished to produce its catalogue in Arabic.[3]

Speeds of line printers vary between 100 to 2000 lines per minute.

There is a rapid development of fast serial printers. These print character by character at speeds varying between 30 and 200 characters per second. Each character is usually formed from a matrix of dots. Serial printers are generally cheaper than line printers.

Computer Output Microfilm (COM)

COM includes output on microfilm (usually stored on cassettes) and microfiche. A COM recorder converts computer-produced information to microfilm in a single operation. The equipment is expensive, and so libraries normally produce a magnetic tape which is sent to a bureau for the production of the film or fiche. Special viewers are then required to read the information on the film or fiche, as it is usually reduced by 24, 42 or 48 times.

This is a fast, space-saving, economical and ecologically advantageous solution in situations where large files are to be output. A typical bureau cost for producing 1000 frames of film or fiche is £7.50, with a copying charge of 75p per 1000 frames.[2]

Computer typesetting

This is a more sophisticated form of hard copy output than line printer paper. Information from a computer is converted into fully made-up pages on photographic film. This is then used to make printing plates for offset litho printing. The pages can be composed and set to several designs, and several type-fonts are available. Thus a much higher level of typographical quality is obtained by this method. This technique is used for printing the British National Bibliography, many indexes and library catalogues. Some newspapers and books are also produced using this technique.

Again the equipment is expensive and so libraries use bureaux.

These methods of outputting information are discussed in greater depth in Chapters 6 and 9.

BACKING STORE

Information that is not currently being processed by the computer is kept on backing store. This can be magnetic tape, disc or drum.

A description of magnetic tape has already been given in the section on input. Information is written to, and read from, the tape by passing the tape over a device known as the read/write head.

A disc, which resembles a long playing record, can be magnetised on both sides. Discs are mounted on a vertical spindle which continuously rotates. Information is written to and read from the disc by read/write heads mounted on arms which move radially across the disc. Up to 11 discs may be mounted on a single spindle.

A magnetic drum is a rotating cylinder which is coated with a magnetic material. The cylinder is divided into tracks running parallel to each other around the circumference. Each track has a separate read/write head.

The method of accessing information on these devices differs; with magnetic tape it is sequential whereas with disc and drum it is random. To access some specified information on magnetic tape it is necessary to wind the tape forward or backward until the required portion of the tape is under the read/write head. With discs and drums the heads are moved directly to the required portion of the device. When processing information on-line, direct access is required and so magnetic tapes are not used. However, if a job requires sequential processing of records they can be adequately stored on magnetic tape.

MAIN STORE

Information currently being processed needs to be in the main store. This is made of devices capable of being in one of two states, thus signifying a '0' or a '1'. Bits can be grouped together to form a byte (or character) and further grouped to form a word. The word is the practical element used for storing and transmitting information in the computer. The decision as to how many bits there are in the word (the word-length) is taken by the computer designers (e.g. 8 bits, 16 bits, 48 bits, 60 bits).

A computer word can be thought of as a jam-jar, as in Fig. 2.4. Since the jam-jars must be accessed they need an address. Taking a mythical computer with a word-length of 8 bits, jam-jar 28 might hold 00001001. (This is equivalent to the decimal number 9 as explained in Appendix I.)

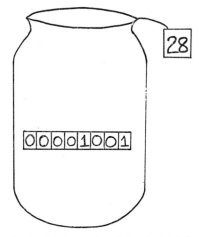

Fig. 2.4.   Storing the decimal number 9 in the 28th location of the store.

The size of the main store is often quoted when describing a computer system. Words as well as bytes are used as a measure. 32K words means approximately 32 000 words whereas 64Kb means 64 000 bytes. If the first measure is of a computer with a 16-bit word-length and the second of a computer with an 8-bit byte then the sizes are the same.

CENTRAL PROCESSOR UNIT (CPU)

This is the main part of the computer and consists of the control unit and the arithmetic unit. The control interprets the list of instructions that form the program and arranges for them to be obeyed. This function can be likened to the conductor of an orchestra who interprets the musical score and ensures that all the musicians play at the appropriate moment.

Instructions involving the arithmetic unit are of two types: arithmetic instructions and 'branch' instructions. The 'branch' instructions involve a comparison of two values, with a different branch of instructions being obeyed depending on the result of the comparison. Such an operation is at the heart of all sorting programs. The CPU is the fastest part of the computer system.

Example: Instruction 01011100 is to be obeyed.

Another function of the computer designer is to define the instructions that the computer can obey. In this example the first 3 bits (010) are to be an instruction code and the remaining 5 bits (11100 or 28 in decimal) an address. 010 might be the code to increment (or add one to) the contents of the address specified. Execution of this instruction adds 1 to the contents of jam-jar 28 (9) to give 10 and stores this number in jam-jar 28, as in Fig. 2.5.

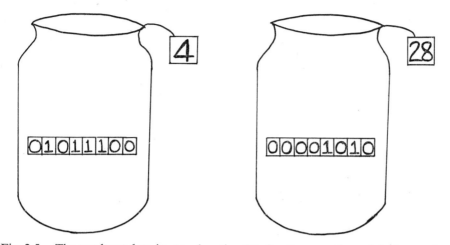

Fig. 2.5. The resultant data in store location 28 after the execution of the instruction in store location 4.

COMPUTER SYSTEMS

Any computer system will have varying amounts of the hardware described. A main-frame computer has typically a punched card or paper-tape reader (sometimes both), magnetic tape(s), disc(s), drum, line printer(s) and a control console which is used by the operators. If the software supports on-line working, then local or distant terminals may be attached. Main-frame computers vary in price depending on the size and speed of the main store, capability and speed of the processor, and number and capability of the peripherals. Their costs range between £50 000 and several million pounds.

Minicomputers were first introduced in the early 1960s. They are much cheaper than the larger, general purpose computers because they have limited peripherals and software. The word-length is typically 16-bits. Minicomputers are normally housed in compact cabinets and can even be placed on a desk. Little power is consumed, air-conditioning is not normally necessary and no special training is needed for operating the machine. Their costs range from £2000–£80 000. Minicomputers can be used in several ways:

(a) as a stand-alone system offering batch or on-line processing;

(b) as a front-end system (the minicomputer is used to control the communication between several on-line terminals and the main-frame computer, which is often referred to as the host in this situation);

(c) as part of a network. When several large computers are linked in a network, minicomputers are often used to control the telecommunications.

Librarians might encounter minicomputers in any of these situations. If used as a stand-alone system in a library then a magnetic tape is often produced by the minicomputer which is sent to a larger computer for further processing. The number of minicomputers used in library applications is increasing and examples will be referred to where appropriate in the text.

Microcomputers were introduced in the early 1970s. They consist of a processing unit and some store made on a very small 'chip' of silicon. The cost of such devices has dropped rapidly over the past few years and is currently about £20. To be useful as a computer system, peripherals and more store must be added which obviously increases the cost. The continuing development of such devices will create new opportunities for computer systems in libraries.

COMPUTER MANUFACTURERS

Computers used by libraries will be referred to throughout the text and it is necessary therefore to have a minimal grasp of some of the makers of computers and their products. There are many manufacturers and their products change rapidly as the technology advances. Table 2.1 gives brief details of some manufacturers whose products are used in library systems.

TABLE 2.1

Manufacturer	Range of computers produced	Example
Burroughs	Small–large	B1726 (small)
Control Data Corporation	Small–large	CDC7600 (very large)
Data General Corporation	Mini	Nova 1220
Digico	Mini	Micro 16
Digital Equipment Corporation	Mini–medium	PDP 11/40
Hewlett Packard	Mini	HP2116A
Honeywell	Small–large	Honeywell 125 (small)
Intel Corporation	Micro	Intel 8080
International Business Machines (IBM)	Small–large	IBM 370/165 (large)
International Computers Limited (ICL)	Small–large	ICL 2980 (large)
Texas Instruments	Mini	TI980A
Univac	Medium–large	9300 (medium)

One manufacturer not included in the table is Rank Xerox. They produced several computers until they withdrew from the market in 1975. Several libraries are still using their computers.

The majority of computer-based library systems in the UK use ICL or IBM computers. Both these firms manufacture a large range of software as well as hardware. ICL was formed in 1968 as an amalgamation of several UK computer firms. Their main computers are the ICL 1900 series, System 4 and the comparatively new 2900 series. IBM is easily the world's largest computer manufacturer. The 360 series and the more recent 370 series are their main products.

REFERENCES

1. F. B. Rogers, *Librarianship in a World of Machines: First Annual C. C. Williams Memorial Lecture at Peabody Library School*, George Peabody College for Teachers, Nashville, Tennessee (1966).
2. F. Robinson, The Uses of OCR and COM in Information Work. *Program*, **8**, 137–48 (1974).
3. A. R. Sabry and A. E. Jeffreys, The Catalogue Conversion Project of the National Library of Cairo: a Progress Report. *Program*, **9**, 78–83 (1975).

FURTHER READING

D. Carey, *How it Works: the Computer*, Wills and Hepworth, Loughborough (1971).
J. A. T. Pritchard, *Selection and Use of Terminals in On-line Systems*, NCC Publications, Manchester (1974). ISBN 0 85012 117 5.
J. Wainwright, Why Use a Minicomputer? Some Factors Affecting Their Selection. *Program*, **10**, 7–13 (1976).

CHAPTER 3

COMMUNICATING WITH THE COMPUTER

INTRODUCTION

When a procedure in a library is to be organised by a computer it is necessary to provide the computer with the following:

(a) the data, or information, to be processed;
(b) a list of instructions on how to process the data.

The choice of which medium to use to present the information to the computer is dependent on the computer system and the mode of processing. Possible alternatives were discussed in Chapter 2. The detailed instructions for processing the data will be written by a programmer. Library personnel will assist in the broad design of the system by helping to decide what information is to be processed and how this is to be done. Full details of this analysis are given in Chapter 4. This chapter will describe methods of structuring the information and how the instructions are given to the computer.

INFORMATION STRUCTURE

A typical computer file, like a manual file, consists of a number of records each of which consists of a number of items. In computer jargon the position of an item in a record is referred to as a field. In a library catalogue the file is made up of catalogue records each giving details of the author, title, publisher, date, etc. of a publication held by the library. The items in the record are made up of words, which in turn are made up of characters. In Chapter 2 it was shown how the character A is coded for entry into a computer system. The record, therefore, is presented to the computer as a long list of characters. It is frequently necessary to identify the fields of a computer record: for instance, to print a file in author order, to produce a list of books on order from a particular bookseller or a list of serials held by a departmental library. To a human being it is obvious that

JOE BLOGGS is a person's name. This is not obvious to a computer and so it is necessary to have a method of telling the computer where one field ends and another begins. There are several methods, which are best illustrated by an example. example.

EXAMPLE

The County Library of Gwynedd requires a computer file of its borrowers. The librarian decides to include the name, home town and number of each borrower.

Solution 1: Fixed Field Format

The length (in number of characters) of each field is specified along with the position of each field within the record:

borrower number	6 characters;
borrower name	20 characters;
town	16 characters.

The records for Mary Jones, number 21869 living in Tywyn and for Bryn Hepplewhite-Stevenson, number 8167 living in the town with the longest name in the UK, namely Llanfairpwllgwyngyllgogerychwyrndrobwllllantissiliogogo-goch, would be

```
21869MARY JONES            TYWYN
8167BRYN HEPPLEWHITE-STELLANFAIR PG
```

The first record has some redundant spaces whereas the second record has to be truncated, with the possibility in this case of annoying the borrower. Although it is difficult to estimate the optimum number of characters for each field, it is certainly easier for the computer to deal with a fixed field formatted record.

Solution 2: Variable Field Format

A character is defined to signify the start (or end) of each field:

@   start of borrower's number;
$ start of borrower's name;
*   start of town.

(Note—characters are chosen that are unlikely to occur in the record.) In this format the records would be

```
@21869$MARY JONES*TYWYN
@8167$BRYN HEPPLEWHITE-STEVENSON*LLANFAIRPWLL-
GWYNGYLLGOGERYCHWYRNDROBWLLLLANTISSILIOGOGO-
GOCH
```

This is much more attractive from the library view-point, but it necessitates a more complicated program.

Solution 3: Directory Format

The character position of the start of each field is specified by a directory at the start of the record as shown in **(I)**

This is a mixture of fixed and variable fields. It is a solution adopted by several libraries for dealing with bibliographic files.

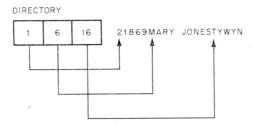

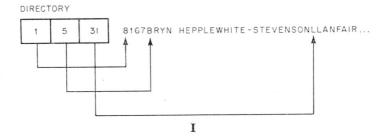

I

When deciding which fields to include in the record, the library staff must think of all the possible information which might be required from the system. This point will be clarified in later chapters on applications.

Having decided the optimum method of structuring the fields in the record, the method of organizing the records in the file must be determined.

There are basically two ways of accessing records from a file, namely sequential and random access. Sequential access implies that the records are accessed one after another or in sequence, whereas random access implies that all the records are equally accessible. The method of access required governs the file organization. Files are stored on backing store and this also governs the file organization: records on magnetic tape, for instance, can only be accessed sequentially.

For sequential access a sequential file structure is used. This is the simplest file structure; records are physically stored in some ordered sequence. For example, in a library charging system the file of books currently on loan might be ordered in ascending numerical sequence by book number. To check if any books are overdue, then all the records are accessed and this file structure is efficient. However, to find all books on loan to a particular borrower, then again all records are accessed and the borrower field checked. This is uneconomic unless the file is particularly small. If a reasonably high proportion of the records is required, for instance, the records of books returned during the day, then a sequential file could be efficient; the records of the returned books would be sorted into ascending numerical sequence and then be processed by one 'pass' through all the records in the file. An analogy can be made with adding cards to the author catalogue in a library. The catalogue itself is a sequential file, and it is common to sort the new cards into author order and have one 'pass' through the catalogue to insert all the new cards.

Random access files can be organized in several ways. Such files include not only the records but also an index of 'keys' or search elements pointing at appropriate records in the file. To access a particular element the computer searches the index, and not the records themselves, for the specified key and thus obtains the address(es) of the record(s) in the file. This is analogous to a library user consulting the author catalogue (now an index to the library collection) for the location of a book by a specific author. Often the records in the file are stored sequentially so that the whole file can be processed efficiently. Under these circumstances, the file is referred to as an indexed sequential file. In some cases, especially the on-line information retrieval systems described in Chapter 11, all possible items in the record suitable for searching are included in the index. The file is then called inverted; searching a specific key leads to a list of all documents containing that key.

Two examples of random access file systems are given to clarify these points.

EXAMPLE 1

The on-line order and invoice system operated by the booksellers B. H. Blackwell, Oxford.

The main book file can be searched by any one of four keys. Examples of the keys for accessing this book are given.

(a) Author/Title. The key is made up of the first 4 letters of the author's surname and the first 2 letters of the first main word in the title, e.g. TEDDIN.

(b) Title. The key is made up of the first 4 letters of the first two main words in the title, e.g. INTRCOMP.

(c) Author. The key is made up of the first 4 letters of the surname and the first 4 letters of the first name, e.g. TEDDLUCY.

(d) International Standard Book Number, e.g. 0 85501 221 8.

EXAMPLE 2

The on-line information retrieval system, ORBIT, operated by the System Development Corporation.[1]

The file structure contains at least three sections.

(a) *Index section*

This is an integrated file of all the directly searchable keys in the records. It is arranged alphabetically. Entries in the index for this book might include

COMPUTER SYSTEMS (DESCRIPTOR)
ENGLISH (LANGUAGE)
HEYDEN (PUBLISHER)
LIBRARIES (DESCRIPTOR)
LONDON (PLACE OF PUBLICATION)
TEDD, LUCY A. (AUTHOR)
1977 (YEAR OF PUBLICATION)

Each entry includes the number of records in the file indexed by that key, and a pointer to an entry in the postings section.

(b) *Postings section*

This consists of a list of all the addresses in the print file of the records containing each index entry.

(c) *Print file*

This consists of the records in the file inserted in a manner suitable for printing.

Examples of searching file structures such as this are given in Chapter 11.

As with most decisions, the cost factor must be considered when deciding on methods of file organization. Components of this cost include:

cost of updating the file (including amendments, deletions and additions);
cost of searching the file;
cost of the storage medium used;
processing costs.

PROGRAMMING

The list of instructions given to the computer telling it how to perform a particular task is known as a program. A problem arises when deciding what language should be used to communicate these instructions to the computer. English can be ambiguous and is often difficult to analyse. This is exemplified by the following sentences:

(a) Nothing acts faster than Anadin.
(b) Fruit flies like a banana. Time flies like an arrow.

Even when instructions are given in English some human intuition is required to understand them. The instructions on how to use some hair shampoo might be:

Wet hair;
Apply shampoo;
Rinse;
Repeat.

The instruction to stop is never given and so one would be continuously washing one's hair! This is what a computer would do until the shampoo, or more realistically the resources being used by the program were exhausted. Many programmers have blushed to find that their program contains just such a continuous loop.

English, therefore, is not a good language to use when programming. This has long been realized by others who require to communicate instructions. Compilers of knitting patterns have formulated a special language, as seen in Fig. 3.1. This has similar constructions to programming languages.

THE BACK

Using No. 10 or 11 needles cast on 83 sts and work
    8 rows in k1, p1 rib.
Change to No. 8 or 9 needles.
1st Row. S1, knit to end.
2nd Row. S1, p1, *k3, p1, rep from * to last st, k1
3rd Row. S1, *k1, p3, rep from * to last 2 sts, k2.
4th Row. S1, p1, *k3, p1, rep from*to last st, k1.
5th Row. S1, knit to end.
6th Row. S1, k2, * p1, k3, rep from * to end.
7th Row. S1, p2, *k1, p3, rep from * to last 4 sts, k1.
    p2, k1.
8th Row. S1, k2, * p1, k3, rep from * to end.
These 8 rows form patt.
Cont. in patt. Until work measures 6½ inches, ending
    on wrong side.

Fig. 3.1. An example of knitting pattern 'language' (reproduced by courtesy of Sirdar Limited).

Composers of music also use a special code which is interpreted by the musician when playing from the score.

Codes and languages are used by programmers when communicating instructions to the computer. In Chapter 2 there was an instruction 01011100. An instruction such as this, that is made up of bits, is known as a binary instruction. Although it is very easy for the computer to interpret, it is clumsy for human beings to use. To overcome this the address part of the instruction (11100) can be referred to by a symbol (perhaps B), and the instruction (010) by a mnemonic for the instruction (perhaps INC).

The binary instruction 01011100 is then written as INC B. It will be converted to the binary form before being obeyed and so have the same effect with 1 being added to the contents of the 'jam-jar' referred to as B. Instructions such as INC B are known as assembly language instructions. Because each type of computer has its own set of instructions the assembly language programmer is governed by the particular computer being used. This in turn implies that if an assembly language program written for one computer is needed by someone with another computer, then the program must be re-written in the assembly language for the other computer.

Assembly languages that librarians might encounter are:

BAL   on the IBM 360 and 370 series;
PLAN   on the ICL 1900 series;
USERCODE on the ICL System 4 series.

The computer's basic instructions are very primitive and so a fairly long assembly language program is usually necessary. It is easy to make mistakes when writing such programs. Such problems of using assembly languages are alleviated by using high-level languages. These allow users to write in a notation oriented towards their problems. High-level language programs are more concise and are much less dependent on the particular computer system being used than are assembly language programs.

There are many high-level languages. Examples of the instruction to increment the value of B are given for some of the most well-used languages.

ALGOL 60   Algorithmic Language 60
              $B := B+1$;
ALGOL 68   Algorithmic Language 68
              B *plusab* 1;
BASIC   Beginners All purpose Symbolic Instruction Code
              LET $B = B+1$
COBOL   Common Business Oriented Language
              ADD 1 TO B.
FORTRAN   Formula Translator
              $B = B+1$
PL/I   Program Language One
              $B = B+1$;

(Although these high-level statements correspond to only one machine-code instruction, this is not typical. Most high-level statements will correspond to many machine-code instructions.)

ALGOL 60 and FORTRAN were designed primarily for scientific work, although both have been used for library applications. COBOL was designed for business applications and is used by many libraries. PL/I is a very general language and has an extremely wide application area, which includes library applications. ALGOL 68 is suited to library work, but as it is a comparatively new language it has not yet been used for library applications.

Moving a high-level language program to a different computer requires some effort, but nowhere near as much as that required for an assembly language program.

Factors affecting the decision on which programming language is to be used are discussed later in the chapter.

Library staff, in general, will not be required to program. However, some information on writing a program is included here for any interested readers.

PROGRAMMING IN BASIC [2]

BASIC was designed to be an 'easy-to-learn' language which is suitable for beginners. It illustrates the nature of programming in a high-level language. A BASIC program is composed of a number of statements or commands each of which is numbered. The instructions are obeyed in numerical sequence, unless a branch instruction is obeyed, in which case the number of the next statement to be obeyed is specified in the instruction.

Some of the BASIC statements are:

INPUT   to read data from the outside world into the computer store. The words of the store are referred to by a single character,
e.g.   10 INPUT P
If 6 is read in from the input device then 6 is stored in P.

PRINT   to print the contents of a word of the store so that it can be understood by the outside world,
e.g.   50 PRINT X
If the value in X is 14, then 14 is printed by the output device.

LET   to do arithmetic and place the result in a word of store,
e.g.   20 LET D = 5
Place value 5 in D.
30 LET A = B $*$ C
Multiply the values in B and C together and place the result in A. If 6 is in B and 2 in C, then 12 would be placed in A.

IF   to compare two values and branch accordingly,
e.g.   40 IF X < 10 THEN 90
If the value in X is less than 10, then statement 90 is the next to be obeyed, otherwise it will be the next highest numbered statement.

GO TO   to specify the next statement to be obeyed,
e.g.   60 GO TO 100

REM   to write a remark to aid understanding of the program. This statement has no effect on the running of the program,
e.g.   200 REM THIS IS AN EXAMPLE OF A REMARK

END   to stop the program,
e.g.   605 END

Using these statements a program can be written to solve the following problem.

PROBLEM: An academic library has three categories of borrower: under-graduate, postgraduate and staff. All borrowers have been assigned 4-digit numbers starting with 7, 8 and 9 respectively. Calculate the percentage of items on loan to staff given the list of all items currently on loan.

Records in the list are of the form: borrower number, book number. The end of the list is signified by a borrower number 5555.

STRATEGY: The first stage in writing a program is to decide on the strategy of the solution. For this problem the following sum must be evaluated:

$$\frac{\text{number of items on loan to staff}}{\text{total number of items on loan}} \times 100$$

The numbers will be found by processing the list and keeping two counts; one to give the numerator and the other the denominator for the division.

DESIGN: The next stage involves a detailed design for the program. This can be described in several ways. A flow chart is one, and an example of a flow chart for this problem is given in Chapter 4. A list of step-by-step instructions can also be used, as below:

(1) make 'count of all loans' zero;
(2) make 'count of all staff loans' zero;
(3) read next record;
(4) if it is the end go to step 9;
(5) add one to 'count of all loans';
(6) if it is not a staff loan go to step 3;
(7) add one to 'count of staff loans';
(8) go to step 3;
(9) calculate the required percentage;
(10) print the percentage;
(11) end.

PROGRAM: The next stage is to translate the instructions into a programming language which in this instance is BASIC. Remark statements are added to explain the flow of the program.

```
 5  REM   L IS COUNT OF ALL LOANS
 7  REM   S IS COUNT OF STAFF LOANS
10          LET L = 0
20          LET S = 0
25  REM   READ NEXT RECORD
27  REM   B IS BORROWER NUMBER, C IS BOOK NUMBER
30          INPUT B, C
35  REM   CHECK TO SEE IF IT IS THE END
40          IF B = 5555 THEN 90
50          LET L = L + 1
55  REM   CHECK TO SEE IF IT IS A STAFF LOAN
60          IF B <9000 THEN 30
```

```
70          LET S = S + 1
80          GO TO 30
85   REM    CALCULATE THE PERCENTAGE
90          LET P = S/L * 100
100         PRINT P
110         END
```

TESTING: The next stage is to test the program on some suitable data. An example of this is shown in Fig. 3.2 along with the values held in the words of store throughout the program. This program was run using Atkins Computer Bureau.

The testing stage is also known as 'debugging' in computer jargon. Having been thoroughly tested the program can be used to process live data. Documentation of the program must be written so that it can be easily maintained (more details on documentation are given in Chapter 4).

COMPILERS

Before a program written in a high-level language can run on a particular computer it must be processed by a compiler. This is a program that translates from the high-level language into the machine-code for that computer. This is represented in Fig. 3.3.

As well as translating, the compiler checks the structure of the language to ensure that no illegal or potentially ambiguous statements occur in the program. If they do, then the job is halted after the compilation stage and the erroneous statements are printed out along with a message indicating why they are in error. The compiler is machine-dependent and so a program written in ALGOL 68 will need an ALGOL 68 compiler for the computer on which it is to run. Since compilers are fairly costly both to produce and to buy, it cannot be assumed that all computer systems will have compilers for all programming languages. Indeed, few computer systems will have compilers for all the programming languages already referred to in the text.

Compilers are written to specified language standards thus facilitating the movement of programs between different computer systems. Several compilers for the same language are sometimes available on the same computer. One compiler might be fast but lead to inefficient machine-code programs; this is useful when developing programs. Another compiler might be slow but produce highly efficient machine-code programs and thus be useful when a program is error-free and is being used for production runs.

The decision as to which programming language to use is not normally taken solely by library personnel. However, it is worth noting some of the factors involved in the decision.

(a) Available compilers.

```
!BASIC
>5 REM  L IS COUNT OF ALL LOANS
>7 REM  S IS COUNT OF STAFF LOANS
>10      LET L=0
>20      LET S=0
>25 REM READ NEXT RECORD
>27 REM B IS BORROWER NUMBER,C IS BOOK NUMBER
>30      INPUT B,C
>35 REM CHECK TO SEE IF IT IS THE END
>40      IF B=5555 THEN 90
>50      LET L=L+1
>55 REM CHECK TO SEE IF IT IS A STAFF LOAN
>60      IF B<9000 THEN 30
>70      LET S=S+1
>80      GO TO 30
>85 REM CALCULATE THE PERCENTAGE
>90      LET P=S/L*100
>100     PRINT P
>110     END
>RUN
18:21   JUN 23   RUNWBAA...
?7123,5890
?8234,45
?9067,4098
?9123,654
?7345,6091                ◄────────── DATA
?7248,609
?9834,6854
?7395,217
?8812,4765
?9881,5784
?5555,0                   ◄────────── END OF DATA
 40.0000                  ◄────────── ANSWER

 110  HALT
```

Fig. 3.2.   Testing the program.

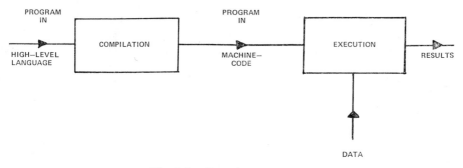

Fig. 3.3.   Running a program.

(b) Available store. Especially when programming minicomputers, the amount of store may be limited. However, buying more store is usually cheaper than the work involved in fitting in to the available store.

(c) Available support.

(d) Programming time. It takes less time (and is therefore less costly) to develop programs in high-level languages.

(e) Processing time. Assembly language programs are usually processed faster on the computer.

(f) Portability. If there is any likelihood of the programs being used on another computer system, whether at another library or when the current computer is replaced, then they ought to be written in a commonly available high-level language.

(g) Maintenance. Sooner or later all programs need to be amended or corrected. It is generally easier to do this maintenance if the programs are written in a high-level language.

OPERATING SYSTEMS

The compilers and the user programs form part of the software of a computer system. Another important part of the software is the operating system. Basically this is a set of master programs which supervises the running of all other programs through the computer. It also controls the input from, and output to, the peripherals and the compilation of programs. The capabilities of the operating system determine the possible methods of processing.

A very simple operating system might allow only one program at a time to be read, compiled, obeyed and the results output. A more sophisticated operating system might allow several programs to proceed in parallel, thus allowing better utilization of the computer's resources. Another operating system might allow one user at a time to interact with, or have on-line access to, the files. The most sophisticated systems allow many users concurrent on-line access whilst also processing batch jobs in the background.

A special language, known as the job control language, is used to communicate with the operating system. Commands such as loading magnetic tapes, loading the line-printer with special stationery, requesting that data be punched on to paper-tape and so on are included in the language.

The operating systems on the ICL 1900 series are known as GEORGE whilst on the IBM 360 and 370 series they are called OS.

PROGRAM PACKAGES

General purpose programs or program packages are also included under the term software. These are programs to solve general problems such as sorting and updating files, statistical analyses, etc. More specific packages for library applications also exist. Packages are produced and marketed by various organizations:

computer manufacturers;
software houses (firms specializing in writing software);
academic and research institutions;
national bodies;
other libraries.

A charge is usually made for the use of packages. This varies according to the complexity of the package, the number of users of the package, the degree of support provided and the type of supplier. Support provided might vary from nothing to extensive help which includes training in the use of the package, assistance in meeting particular problems and provision of updated versions of the package.

Program packages suitable for particular applications will be described where appropriate in the text. Factors affecting the selection of packages are given in Chapter 4.

When buying a computer system, which some librarians are now involved in with the increased use of minicomputers, some of the supplied software may be costed separately from the hardware. This is a manifestation of the fact that software costs are increasing while hardware costs decrease. Including purchaser's own software costs, about 90% of the expenditure on computer systems is now on software rather than hardware.

REFERENCES

1. *SDC Search Service: ORBIT User Manual*, System Development Corporation, Santa Monica (1975).
2. J. G. Kemeny and T. E. Kurtz, *Basic Programming*, Wiley, New York (1971). ISBN 0 471 46830 4.

CHAPTER 4

SETTING UP COMPUTER SYSTEMS IN LIBRARIES

INTRODUCTION

One of the features of a successful library computer system is the good communication between the library and computer staff. Cox *et al.*[1] outline some of the areas of misunderstanding that can occur between these two groups of personnel. Some of the points included are:

a lack of appreciation by each side of the work of the other;
the belief that a manual system should be automated in its current state;
a failure to realize that direct communication between the librarian and the computer specialist needs a considerable amount of groundwork.

There is a need for both formal and informal communication. Both groups have their own jargon.

For example, an audio-visual librarian uses the word software to refer to films, slides, tapes, and so on. This differs from the computer person's meaning of the word outlined in Chapter 3. A glossary of some of the computer terms useful for librarians involved in this subject is given in Appendix II.

In this chapter the feasibility, analysis, design and implementation stages are described in general and then the involvement necessary by library staff is discussed in more detail. All these stages are referred to collectively as the project.

FEASIBILITY STUDY

Before any computer system is installed in a library a formal study should be undertaken to ascertain the feasibility of the new system.

The broad objectives of the system must be defined by the library personnel involved. Constraints on the new system such as timing, financial, staffing or political constraints should be identified.

The first step in the feasibility study is to establish, independently of the present system, the information needs of the system. Data are gathered by questionnaire, interview and observation. Observation needs to be as unobtrusive as possible since people adopt different work patterns if they suspect they are being watched. (Robinson et al.[2] refer to a story of an observer who rang up at random intervals to ask what the subject was doing. The survey indicated that the subject spent 100% of his time answering the telephone.)

The next step is to obtain sufficient information about the existing system to enable comparisons to be made with a possible computer system. Forms used, sizes of files, method and frequency of processing, staff involvement, services to users and costs are features of the present system which need to be studied.

Using all this information it is possible to define the requirements of the system and to outline the necessary computer and manual operations. Potential benefits should be identified and costed, where possible. These benefits might include improved overall performance, more and better services to users, more management information, a flexible system with the capability of being extended.

Possible designs of the system are outlined and then costed. A rough plan of the project is made which includes staff requirements and timescales. The complications of implementing the system should be identified.

At the end of the feasibility study a report is presented to the library management who have to decide if the potential benefits are worth the cost involved. If it is decided that the costs are not justified, then it is possible that a more efficient manual system might emerge which could be implemented. If it is decided that the costs are justified, then the detailed analysis and design stage commences.

The formal feasibility study is important because it provides the right psychological environment for both positive and negative attitudes to be discussed. It also provides a calm environment for evaluation of the potential system before resources and reputations are committed.

SYSTEMS ANALYSIS

Systems analysis is defined by Chapman et al.[3] to be:

> 'the logical analysis of the present system; the evaluation of the efficiency, economy, accuracy, productivity and timeliness of existing methods and procedures measured against the established goals of the library; and the design of new methods and procedures to improve the flow of information through the system'.

Systems analysis does not have to be undertaken with a view to setting up a computer system. At Lancaster University Library, a group made use of systems analysis techniques to study the effects of managerial decisions in large-scale complex situations. A mathematical model of the library system was derived and input values varied to obtain optimum output measurements. A by-product of that analysis is a computer-based library management game.[4] Participants, in groups, decide the purchasing and loans policies of a given library for one year. The charging system is simulated and the performance measures for that year printed. Using this information the group can amend the policies for subsequent years and study the effects.

Bernstein[5] outlines several principles to be followed when planning a computer-based system in the library. These can be summarized as:

(a) obtain the complete agreement of the parent authority;

(b) appoint a project leader and a secretary;

(c) appoint a librarian or group of librarians to be involved in the detailed analysis;

(d) establish who is responsible for each part of the system;

(e) set up a plan so that individuals are aware of their workload throughout the project;

(f) compare time, financial and personnel aspects of the intended system with the old system;

(g) keep accurate notes during the analysis;

(h) exploit to the maximum the results of other libraries' work;

(i) conclude the analysis with a detailed report which librarians and analysts are obliged to follow;

(j) establish conditions for working off the backlog of information;

(k) familiarize library personnel with the working of the computer system.

These points will be amplified where appropriate in the chapter.

A library system can be described schematically as in Fig. 4.1. The management information required must be known at the design stage and will be a pre-planned by-product of the system.

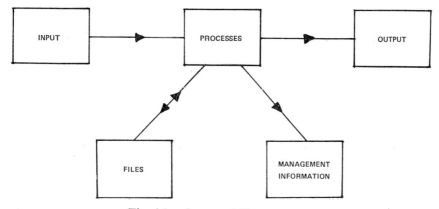

Fig. 4.1. A general library system.

As the definition implies, this stage involves the detailed analysis and design of the system. The analysis is a continuation, in greater depth, of the survey carried out in the feasibility study. Critical examination of the system is often based on the questions What? Why? How? Where? When? and Who? A detailed specification of the functions of the system being analysed is the outcome of this stage.

The system must then be designed and specified in complete detail. This is necessary both for the programming of the system and for the introduction of new systems in the library. Alternative solutions proposed during the feasibility study are investigated in greater depth. Sometimes computer models of the solutions are programmed and their working simulated. The most appropriate solution is chosen. Data gathered during the analysis are used to design record formats, file structures, processes and the input and output forms of the new system.

This stage may take several months as the design needs detailed discussion by all those involved. It is much cheaper to correct mistakes at this stage than when the system has been programmed. Regular meetings of the computer people and library people involved are necessary to report on the progress attained and the problems encountered.

The main outcome of this stage is a report specifying in complete detail the computer and manual functions of the system. This is frequently referred to as the system specification. The description of the computer procedures is frequently in the form of a flow chart (flow charting is described later in the chapter). The report must also specify work that needs to be carried out by the library before the system can be installed, e.g. converting files to machine-readable form or preparing the book stock for a computer-based charging system. This report is used by librarians and computer people to ensure concurrence of the specified and final systems.

When the system has been designed in depth a re-assessment of the costs and benefits can be made.

IMPLEMENTATION

The following stages carry on from the systems analysis.

Programming and testing

The aim of this stage is to design, produce, document and test a suite of computer programs that efficiently meet the requirements of the system specification. Decisions on programming language, methods of storage and processing would be made in the system design stage as timings and costings would be affected.

Apart from the working programs, the main output from this stage is the program documentation. For each program in the system this should contain:

(a) a brief description of its function;
(b) details of its specification and amendments;
(c) flow charts prepared by the programmer;
(d) a listing of the statements making up the program;
(e) data used to test it and the results of the tests.

It is essential for such documentation to be produced so that the problems of maintaining the programs are minimized. It is very likely that changes to the programs will be required and these might not be carried out by the original programmer.

Each program must be tested and then the whole computer system linked together and tested. Live data, if available, from the library should be used and the system demonstrated to library management. The non-computer procedures can then be added and the total system given thorough trials.

When the total system is finalized an operating handbook giving detailed instructions of both computer and manual procedures must be prepared.

Installation

Planning for the installation stage should take place well in advance and form part of the system design stage. Several methods of installation can be adopted.

(1) Complete changeover

The old system is replaced directly by the new system on a specified day. This is only possible if the system is simple and does not involve too many transactions or departments.

(2) Phased approach

The total system is divided into sections. Each section is installed individually and proved to work satisfactorily before another section is installed. Being controlled and gradual, this is a good solution for those systems involving a large number of transactions or those which do not have to be implemented within a limited timescale.

(3) Parallel running

Both old and new systems are operated in parallel for a period of time until the new system works satisfactorily. This is the solution often adopted for large and complex systems. However, there are some disadvantages; staff get frustrated at having to operate two systems and it is an expensive solution.

(4) Pilot operation

The system is installed in a smaller and less busy branch before being installed in the main library. In this way many teething problems can be worked out without involving too many staff and users.

The decision as to which method is best is very dependent on the individual circumstances of the type of system, the type of library and the time constraints.

Maintenance and development

However well designed and tested, the system will need alteration after running for a period of time. This needs to be recognized by the librarian so that appropriate budgeting can be made for programming during the year after installation. The library service itself might change, thus involving development of the system. This emphasizes the importance of a flexible system design and good program documentation.

LIBRARY INVOLVEMENT

So far the analysis and implementation have been considered from an overall viewpoint. There are many other factors that the library staff must consider during these stages.

Selection of equipment

Information regarding necessary equipment needs to be collected during the feasibility study so that the order can be placed during the system design stage. Details of manufacturers producing suitable products can be gathered from various sources, some of which are:

> computer year books and other publications;
> appropriate trade exhibitions;
> National Computing Centre (Oxford Road, Manchester, UK);
> other libraries.

It is often worthwhile to visit other libraries operating similar computer-based systems. This not only gives the library staff more insight into the equipment, but also gives them an opportunity to discuss the whole system and to crystallize their ideas.

Manufacturers producing suitable equipment need to be contacted and their products demonstrated. If possible, members of the library staff involved with the new equipment should be included in these discussions and demonstrations. For instance, the comments of the library assistants working on the issue desk are useful when selecting a data collection device, as are the comments of the cataloguers when selecting a COM film or fiche viewer.

The performance of the equipment needs to be checked to ensure that it can cope with the necessary volume of work. When comparing the costs of equipment from different manufacturers it is necessary to look not only at the capital costs but also at the maintenance charges and the maintenance service offered by the manufacturer. This is, of course, equally true when buying any machine.

Depending on the equipment, the length of the delay before delivery varies and might be as long as a year. This needs to be remembered when choosing the installation date. When the equipment arrives it must be tested and operators trained to use it before the installation stage. If a major computer system is to be bought, then a formal 'invitation to tender' approach must be adopted.

Selection of program packages

The above description of the systems analysis assumes a totally 'in-house' approach with the programs being written specifically for the library system that is being analysed. Other libraries may have installed similar systems and it is possible that a program package exists. A search should therefore be made during the feasibility study for such a package. Useful sources would be:

Aslib's file on software;
manufacturers;
published literature on computers in libraries;
courses run on the topic;
colleagues.

As with hardware, the performance of the package must be checked along with technical factors such as the programming language in which it is written, the operating system under which, and the minimal hardware configuration on which, it will run. The documentation, cost and support available are also factors to be considered when selecting a package.

Again it is at the system design stage that the final decision on packages will be made.

File conversion

When the record format and file structures have been decided in the system design stage, the library, if required, needs to start converting its records to the appropriate form and format. This can happen in one of three ways.

(1) Records are bought in from an external agency

There are several organizations marketing bibliographic information on magnetic tape. One that is of great use to libraries involved in merging catalogues or in retrospective catalogue conversion is the BNB/LASER file. This file, of approximately 700 000 MARC (MAchine-Readable Cataloguing) records from 1950 onwards, was built up by the British National Bibliography (BNB) and the London and South Eastern Library Region (LASER).

(2) A bureau is used to convert manual records to machine-readable form

If no data preparation resources are available within the organization, then the library must pay to have its records converted into some form of input medium as described in Chapter 2. The records must be clear and instructions for conversion unambiguous.

(3) The records are converted within the organization

The manual records must be checked, edited and then converted to machine-readable form. This might be done by library or computer staff.

The costs incurred for file conversion should be estimated at the survey stage.

If a new charging system is being installed, then the bookstock and borrowers' cards will need to be prepared for the new system. The amount of processing depends to some extent on the data collection device to be used. In general, labels need to be inserted into books and special borrower cards need to be prepared. This can constitute a major upheaval in the library to ensure that all is ready in time.

Reorganization of manual procedures

As already stated, the system specification specifies manual as well as computer procedures. Although computer systems, in general, replace routine and perhaps rather boring jobs, they also create some, such as option (3) above.

Some of the questions that must be answered when defining the new manual procedures are:

> how does the data reach the computer?
> what happens when output arrives back in the library?
> what checking of reported errors is to be done?
> what are the stand-by procedures when the system fails?
> how is the new equipment to be operated?
> what data preparation is required?

Education and training of library staff

It is psychologically necessary to keep all the library staff adequately and accurately informed about the introduction of a computer-based system from the beginning. One effective way that Oxford City Libraries adopted was to have representatives from various levels within the library staff structure on the committee responsible for the planning and implementation of the new system. Fear and trepidation may arise in those who find comfort in the routine jobs which will disappear at the advent of the computer system. Library managers should be aware of this and organize appropriate education and training programmes.

The education programme for staff involves intensive and careful planning as the staff are, in many ways, responsible for the success or failure of the new system. The different information requirements of various members of the staff need to be considered. There are several aspects of a general education programme. These might include:

(a) *Newsletters.* These are useful in keeping everyone informed of developments in the planning of the system and also for allowing comments and criticisms to be expressed.

(b) *Seminars.* Internally held seminars are useful to explain the general organization of the new system.

(c) *Discussion sessions.* All members of the library staff could be invited and allowed to comment and advise on the new system.

(d) *Courses.* Externally or internally held courses are useful for giving more insight into computer systems and their applications in libraries.

(e) *Directed readings.*

(f) *Outside speakers.* Suitably experienced people might be invited to talk to the library staff.

(g) *Tours.* These could be organized to visit the computer centre which is to process the library's information or to a neighbouring library already operating a computer-based system.

Staff involved with operating the new system will need more specific training. Some equipment manufacturers provide this when installing the equipment.

If several libraries within a geographical region are implementing computer-based systems then co-operative education and training sessions can be organized.

Education and training of users

Users need to be told about the new system, especially if it directly affects them. Information will be necessary, for example, if the library is installing a COM catalogue or if it has the ability to search large bibliographic files on-line, or if a new charging system is being introduced which will involve readers in re-registering. Information explaining the new system along with detailed instructions, if necessary, should be easily available. This might be in printed form or audio-visual aids can be used. Newcastle University Library produced a tape-slide programme explaining their new charging system to users.

Any new service offered to users should be well advertised. Computer systems are often implemented on the grounds of improved user services and so it is natural that users should know of these. The objectives and cost of implementing the system should also be available to users.

Control

The project leader, who has responsibility for the control of the project, can be either a librarian or a computer person. It is desirable for at least one person from both the library and the computer centre to be seconded full-time to the project.

The first step is to assess the resources required for the project by identifying the tasks to be performed in the analysis and implementation stages. A quantitative assessment must be made of both the work content and the staff-hours available.

Having decided 'who is to do what and when', it is useful to describe this on a chart. Two charting techniques can be used.

(1) Bar chart

A table is drawn listing the tasks down the left-hand side and the timescale for the whole project across the top of the page. The estimated time taken for each task is represented by a horizontal line or bar.

(2) Critical path chart

A network of the tasks is drawn to show the sequence in which the tasks must be performed. The estimated times for the completion of each task are included. These times can be analysed to indicate the path through the network which is most critical to the completion of the project. This is known as the critical path.

For a simple system, this can be done by hand; for complex systems, PERT (Program Evaluation and Review Technique) computer programs are available.

It should be emphasized that these charts should be flexible and will need to be re-drawn as the project proceeds and circumstances alter through strikes, machine failure, and so on.

STAFFING

Vickers[6] reports that the success of a computer-based library system frequently depends on the existence of a key person to provide strength, intelligence and enthusiasm for the project. In some libraries such a person is a senior member of the library staff with little experience of computer systems, whereas in others it is a computer person with little previous knowledge of library systems.

As indicated in Chapter 1, many libraries currently use their parent authority's computer and so the computer staff involved in the project are from the computer department. These would be systems analysts and programmers.

The total number of people involved in the analysis and implementation obviously varies depending on the complexity and the timescale of the project. As indicated earlier in the chapter, there should be a computer person and a member of the library staff working full-time on the project. The committee planning the system will involve others from the computer and library staff who will spend varying amounts of time on the project. Extra staff may be employed by the library to do some of the time-consuming tasks; for example, academic libraries often employ students during vacations to help prepare the bookstock for a new charging system.

In some instances the authority's computer may have spare capacity but there may be no staff resources available in the computer department to develop a computer-based library system. In other instances the computer capacity may not be available but the library management would like to analyse the library with a view to installing a computer-based system. In such situations the management has several alternatives.

Employ computer staff in the library

This has the obvious advantage of having the computer staff under the control of the librarian. However, in the current economic situation it is not always possible to appoint to a vacated librarian's post let alone create a new post. Southampton University Library has some computer people on its staff and operates a successful system.

Train library staff to program

There are instances of librarians who are competent programmers and who can therefore help in the detailed design and programming of the computer system. They are sometimes trained by being seconded to the computer department; this naturally helps personnel communication problems. The main disadvantage of this solution is that the majority of librarians do not wish to be programmers (and who can blame them?). Another problem is that there is a large gap between writing a simple program, as demonstrated in Chapter 3, and a well-documented, easily maintainable and efficient set of programs for a large system.

Use an external organization

During the implementation phase of a large project there may be a peak requirement for experienced programmers. It is often inappropriate to satisfy such a peak by training or recruitment and so an external agency may be used.

There are several software houses offering specialist services to libraries and these will be mentioned where appropriate in the text.

FLOW CHARTS [7]

A flow chart is a device widely used for helping people to understand unfamiliar or complex sequences of operations. It is a graphical method of describing a system using special symbols to indicate the sequence and interaction of decisions and processes. Flow charts might be used at several stages in the analysis and implementation of a system. For example:

(a) at the survey stage to describe the existing system;
(b) at the system specification stage to describe the new system;
(c) at the programming stage as part of the documentation of the system;
(d) in the operating manual to define new jobs or explain the workings of parts of the system.

One of the main purposes of a flow chart is to improve communications between those involved in the various stages of analysis and implementation. So that confusion is kept to a minimum, certain standards should be adopted by flow chart writers. There is an international standard (ISO 1028) which defines the symbols to be used for various tasks and methods of storage. Some of the

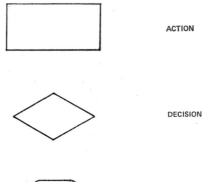

ACTION

DECISION

START/STOP

Fig. 4.2.   Some flow chart symbols.

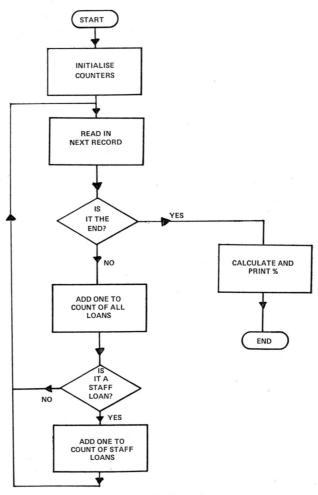

Fig. 4.3.   A flow chart.

symbols most frequently used are shown in Fig. 4.2. The standard also defines conventions, such as the direction of flow should be from top to bottom and from left to right.

Templates or stencils are available to aid in the construction of neat flow charts. These are made of a plastic material with the various symbol shapes cut out so that one can trace around the edge of the shape on to paper.

The solution to the problem discussed in Chapter 3 of finding the percentage of books currently on loan to staff can be described by a flow chart as shown in Fig. 4.3.

A flow chart is given in Ref. 8 to help the new or occasional user of SDC's search system to answer the question 'What do I do now?'.

REFERENCES

1. N. S. M. Cox *et al.*, *The Computer and the Library*, University of Newcastle upon Tyne Library (1966).
*2. F. Robinson *et al.*, *Systems Analysis in Libraries*, Oriel Press, Newcastle upon Tyne (1969). ISBN 0 85362 064 4.
*3. E. A. Chapman *et al.*, *Library Systems Analysis Guidelines*, Wiley, New York (1970). ISBN 0 471 14610 2.
4. P. Brophy *et al.*, *A Library Management Game: a Report on a Research Project*, University of Lancaster Library (1972).
*5. H. H. Bernstein, Some Organization Pre-requisites for the Introduction of Electronic Data Processing in Libraries. *Libri*, **21**, 15–25 (1971).
6. P. H. Vickers, *Automation Guidelines for Public Libraries*, H.M.S.O., London (1975). ISBN 0 11 270269 4.
*7. C. D. Gull, Logical Flow Charts and Other New Techniques for the Administration of Libraries and Information Centres. *Library Resources and Technical Services*, **12**, 47–66 (1968).
8. D. I. Morrow, A Generalized Flow Chart for the Use of ORBIT and Other On-line Interactive Bibliographic Search Systems. *Journal of the American Society for Information Science*, **27**, 57–62 (1976).

* These papers, or parts of them, appear in Lubans and Chapman (1975)—see below.

FURTHER READING

D. Yeates, *An Introduction to Systems Analysis and Design*, Open University Press, Bletchley (1973). ISBN 0 335 01491 7.
F. W. Lancaster (ed.), Systems Design and Analysis for Libraries. *Library Trends*, **21**, 463–612 (1973).
J. Lubans and E. A. Chapman (eds.), *Reader in Library Systems Analysis*, Microcard Edition Books, Englewood, USA (1975). ISBN 0 910972 45 1.
J. J. Eyre and P. Tonks, *Computers and Systems: an Introduction for Librarians*, Bingley, London (1971). ISBN 0 85157 120 4.

CHAPTER 5

MACHINE-READABLE CATALOGUING (MARC)

INTRODUCTION

The arguments for centralized cataloguing have a long history. In 1877, Melvil Dewey pointed out the extravagance of having one of the highest paid employees of a library taking up to half a day to prepare a catalogue entry for an item, when this was also being done by very many other librarians throughout the country. Librarians today are realizing this and are using MARC tapes. MARC stands for Machine-Readable Cataloguing. The acronym is perhaps anachronistic and should now stand for machine-readable bibliographic description. To appreciate the anachronism it is necessary to know a little of the history of the MARC system.

HISTORY

The birth of MARC is frequently ascribed to a report on automation at the Library of Congress in the USA made by G. W. King and others in 1963.[1] The major conclusion of the report was that the bibliographic system within the Library of Congress (LC) could be automated within 10 years. In 1965, a preliminary report on the problems of converting catalogue data to a standard machine-readable record was prepared. This resulted in a grant from the Council of Library Resources for the development of a pilot operation for the distribution of machine-readable catalogue data to a representative segment of the library community.

By the end of 1966, bibliographic records on magnetic tape were being distributed weekly to 16 participating libraries. These represented various types of libraries and included national, public, academic, school and special libraries. Fifty thousand records of English language monographs were distributed to these libraries in the period November 1966 to June 1968 when the pilot project ended.[2] The format of the record at this stage (known as the MARC I format) was closely linked to the structure of the Library of Congress catalogue card and during 1967 it was found that the whole problem was more complicated than originally thought. A reconsideration of the record format was required. Fortunately, this coincided with the decision by the UK Office of Scientific and Technical Information (OSTI) to finance a feasibility study of the requirements of a UK machine-readable bibliographic record. Thus there was close collaboration between the British National Bibliography (BNB) and the Library of Congress in the design of a new record format, known as MARC II or most frequently nowadays simply as MARC. The aim of this format was to communicate a bibliographic description on magnetic tape which would be capable of being reformatted for any conceivable purpose.

During 1968–1974, experimental MARC magnetic tapes were available in the UK and about 20 libraries received them. A report on the ways in which these libraries used the tapes has been produced.[3] The BNB were also using the tapes for various services. In 1969, the catalogue card service was partially computer-produced and from 1971 the production of the BNB weekly list has been by computer. This is achieved by sending the MARC records, on magnetic tape, to a computer typesetting bureau.

The Library of Congress started distribution of records in the new MARC II format in 1969. In 1970, an interesting experiment in microbibliography was carried out. The British and American MARC tapes were merged and the English language records extracted. These were produced on to COM film which was then microfilmed further using a technique known as Photo-Chromic Micro Image (PCMI), which was designed by the National Cash Register Company. The result was a 6 × 4 in. transparency containing 2380 frames which was read with a special viewer. The experiment was successful and since 1972 has been operating as an on-going publication known as *Books in English*. It is now the largest current bibliography of English books with some 80 000 records being added annually. The production of this bibliography is totally automated and currently costs the subscriber a little over £100 per year.

It soon became obvious to libraries using MARC tapes that records in MARC format were required for their whole stock before a complete computer-based catalogue could be produced. Thus, retrospective conversion projects were carried out. In 1970, Project RECON (Retrospective Conversion) was started in the USA. This was based at the Library of Congress but involved the co-operation of a large number of major libraries throughout the USA. In the UK, as was mentioned in Chapter 4, a retrospective file of MARC records since 1950 has been built up by BNB and LASER. Changes in cataloguing and classification practices over the past years have been included in the new records. The purchase cost of the whole file of 700 000 records (from 1950–1974) is £3500, while files of individual years cost £200 each.

CURRENT SITUATION

Since the metamorphosis of the BNB into the British Library Bibliographic

Services Division (BLBSD) in 1974, the MARC service offered in the UK has been formalized and described.[4] These services can be summarized as follows.

Complete tape file service

The current and retrospective UK and LC files are available to subscribers on magnetic tape. Sample yearly costs for the weekly tapes are

UK current file   c. 35 000 records p.a. £400;
LC current file   c. 104 000 records p.a. £650.

Selective record service

A library submits requests for individual records to the BLBSD. These requests are matched against the various MARC files and the appropriate records sent to the library on magnetic tape. The requests are usually in the form of a control number. The ISBN (or International Standard Book Number) is used for UK MARC records and the LC Card Number for the LC MARC records. A charge of 10p is made for each record found.

The various MARC files available at the BLBSD are often referred to collectively as the MARC database. At present this consists of UK and LC current and retrospective records, but as MARC records from other countries become available they will be included.

Full catalogue service

This is subscribed to by libraries not wishing to use their local computer facility. The service is an extension of the selective record service in that libraries specify the records required. However, the records are then produced as a catalogue in whatever physical form the library requires. Specific requirements of the library can be incorporated, such as the form of the entry, addition of local information, and so on. Records of items held by the library but which are not in the MARC database must be catalogued in the MARC format at the library.

Full details of the current costings of these services can be obtained from the BLBSD.

A cataloguing in advance of publication (CIP) scheme has recently been set up jointly by the BLBSD and publishers. About 30 to 40 publishers are currently participating in the scheme. The aim is to include advance information about new titles on the MARC tapes, so that the records can be used by libraries in both ordering and cataloguing operations. It currently takes four and a half weeks for the record of a recently published item to appear on the MARC tape. This is unacceptably long for some librarians.

A similar CIP scheme has been operational at the Library of Congress for several years. The Library of Congress currently has over 600 000 MARC records for English and French language monographs as well as several thousand records for maps, films and serials. A system allowing on-line access to this file has recently been designed. About 250 terminals, which enable on-line inserting, editing and displaying of MARC records, are available in various departments of the Library of Congress. This search service is part of the Multiple Use MARC System (MUMS), a generalized file maintenance and retrieval system that is still under development.

In France, the *Bibliographie de la France*, which contains publications in French from other countries such as Belgium, Switzerland and Canada, is now available in machine-readable form. Some of the cataloguing services of the Bibliotheque Nationale are also being automated. The MARC format used is known as MONOCLE (Mise en Ordinateur d'une Notice Catalographique de Livre). Meanwhile, the Deutsche Bibliothek has been producing magnetic tapes of the West German national bibliography since 1972. Several university libraries in West Germany have been using them experimentally. Universitats- bibliothek, Bochum has also been receiving the UK and LC MARC tapes for several years. A project known as ANNA (Automation in the National) is planned in Italy to produce the *Bibliografia Nazionale Italiana*. Other European countries such as Belgium, Denmark, Holland, Ireland and Sweden receive MARC tapes to cover their English language intake.

Looking further afield, the National Library of Canada established a Canadian MARC Office in the early 1970s. This office is responsible for the implementation and documentation of a Canadian MARC tape distribution service. In 1974, Australia established its MARC service which is used to produce the *Australian National Bibliography* and also to form a MARC database along with British and American MARC tapes. South Africa is also in the process of planning its internal MARC system.

This is obviously a continuously expanding area and current information on nationally available MARC records should be requested from the national bibliographical centre of the country concerned.

As has been shown, the establishment of an international MARC network is theoretically possible. There are several reasons why it has not yet been realized:

(a) some national libraries are very slow in cataloguing and so MARC records for these items are correspondingly slow in appearing;

(b) there is an inadequate technology for the communication of MARC records;

(c) there are problems of international cataloguing standards.

FUTURE OF UK MARC

As was described in the previous section, the BLBSD offers several services based on the MARC database. At present the computer power for these is supplied by bureaux. Recently, the British Library announced that it had ordered an ICL 2970 computer system. A new software system, Machine-Readable Library

Information Service (MERLIN), is being developed for the new computer system.

The twin objectives of MERLIN are:

to provide a national bibliographic database service for on-line access by the library and information community;

to allow for decentralized input of records from the library and information community.

The database will consist of records for UK and LC MARC items, locally input records and records of the holdings of the Department of Printed Books and the Science Reference Library that are not covered by UK MARC.

It is planned that the system will be able to support 400–600 terminals working on-line. These will be installed in libraries around the country and will be used for cataloguing, displaying, ordering records and adding local records to the database. It is hoped that the final system will provide a local, national and international catalogue for general use by anyone.

The internal format of MERLIN records will be an extension of the MARC format which is described later in this chapter and it is intended to be more flexible.

It will take several years to develop and implement the system. The ICL 2970 has not yet been delivered to the British Library and so programs are being developed on another ICL 2970 at W. H. Smith's.

USES MADE OF MARC

Selection

No library receives MARC tapes solely for this application. However, several libraries select records of potential use from the weekly magnetic tapes. Libraries can form a local file which is often referred to as the potential requirements file (PRF). The Aldermaston Mechanical Cataloguing and Ordering System (AMCOS) operated at the Atomic Weapons Research Establishment forms its PRF by matching Dewey Decimal Classification Numbers describing the establishment's interests against the weekly UK and LC MARC records received. A list of potentially useful books, *The Book Selection List*, is produced and circulated.

Aslib investigated the possibility of book selection from MARC records[5] using several search fields. The results showed that the unit cost would be high unless the processing was done by a large number of libraries.

Ordering systems

MARC records are frequently used by libraries running an integrated order and catalogue system. A check of the file of MARC records held by the library is made to see whether the bibliographic details of the item to be ordered are included. If present, these details are used to form the order record for the item.

West Sussex Library has a PRF of six months' records. This file is interrogated on-line at the order stage to see if a MARC record for the item exists.

Southampton University Library uses a locally produced MARC record in its order system. Details of this are given in Chapter 6.

Cataloguing

This is the major use made of MARC records. The method of use obviously varies depending on the source of the record.

(1) Complete tape file service

Many of the libraries involved in experimenting with MARC tapes before 1974 have carried on subscribing to this service and have been joined by others.

The Lancashire Library Service[6] operates an integrated acquisition and catalogue system. MARC tapes are used to extract standard elements in machine-readable form. This reduces both the amount of data preparation to be done and the error rate.

It should be pointed out that such a use of MARC tapes is only cost effective if a comparatively high proportion of the library's stock is covered by the MARC tape service.

(2) Selective record service

Liverpool University Library have used this service for many years. There was a continuous backlog of books in the cataloguing department and not enough cataloguers. A list of ISBNs of items likely to be included in the MARC database is sent to the BLBSD. These are matched against the database each month and the resulting records sent to Liverpool on magnetic tape. Details are processed on to cards which are inserted into the main card catalogue.

(3) Full catalogue service

An experiment to test the feasibility of such a service was carried out with Brighton Public Libraries. The experiment, known as BRIMARC, has been reported.[7] It proved to be cost effective and several libraries are using or planning to use the service. It has been of particular use to the newly formed public library authorities after local government re-organization in 1974.

(4) Local catalogues

Several libraries use the MARC format for records of items in their catalogue. Southampton University Library have been involved with MARC for many years. The catalogue of the monographs in the Wessex Medical Library consists of MARC-based records.

Southampton University Library are also responsible for the conversion of the MARC magnetic tapes to a form suitable for ICL equipment.

Selective Dissemination of Information (SDI)

Several libraries use MARC records for offering an SDI service. Full details on the technique of SDI are given in Chapter 10.

At the New University of Ulster, Dewey Decimal Classification Numbers, describing the interests of staff from various departments in the university, are matched against the weekly tapes. The resulting records are used to keep the staff aware of what is currently being published in their subject. At Trinity College in Dublin, a similar system is in operation for several hundred users. These are from both within and without the university.

The University at Saskatchewan reports running a similar service in the humanities and social sciences.[8] This is one of several such services offered in North America.

Co-operative services

A database of MARC records is at the centre of several co-operative cataloguing services. Details of two such systems, the Birmingham Libraries Co-operative Mechanisation Project (BLCMP) and the Ohio College Library Center (OCLC), are given at the end of the chapter.

The College Bibliocentre in Canada organizes acquisitions and cataloguing services for colleges in Ontario.[9] When the centre was formed in 1967 the MARC project was in its infancy. Now, however, details of items not already in the system, are checked against a file of Canadian, UK and LC MARC records. The subject indexing system PRECIS (Preserved Context Index System) developed at BLBSD is used to meet projected search and print requirements.

In Sweden the Library Information System (LIBRIS) has been set up to make available bibliographic data of non-Swedish titles to Swedish research libraries. The database is being built on a co-operative basis and over the last three years 100 000 records have been included. The records are created by the co-operating libraries and a MARC format is used.[10]

In 1974, the Information Dynamics Corporation introduced the BIBNET service. This offers on-line searching of about four million MARC records. The Library of Congress MARC records are included in the database along with MARC records for non-Library of Congress items which are input by subscribing libraries.[11]

SOFTWARE AND SERVICES

If a library decides to receive MARC tapes it faces the problem of deciding how to process the information on the tapes. In the early days each library 'did its own thing' in that local programs were written. Now there are several program packages and software houses involved with library applications which can be used. Some available in Britain are described below.

British Library software package

This package was written mainly for libraries with access to IBM 360 or 370 series computers.[1 2] The Science Reference Library is currently using this package for catalogue production.

Dataskil

Dataskil, a subsidiary of ICL, has produced the Dataskil Integrated Library System (DILS) in conjunction with several public libraries. The package, which is designed for use on the ICL 1900 series computers, consists of four modules: ordering, cataloguing, charging and short title file maintenance. The cataloguing module allows the use of the full MARC format and accepts input from externally as well as internally produced MARC records.

Lincolnshire Library Service plan to implement the ordering and cataloguing modules. The majority of their records have been extracted from the retrospective file of MARC records at the BLBSD.

ICL MARC package

The third version of this package was issued in late 1975. Although this version includes several enhancements, there are still some limitations. The Department of Library and Information Studies at Liverpool Polytechnic, with ICL co-operation, are re-writing part of the package. Southampton University Library has also been involved in testing the package.

Oriel Computer Services

This firm, based in Oxford, offers a range of computer services to libraries and publishers. A MARC-based cataloguing system written by Oriel has been installed at the Universitaire Instelling Antwerpen in Belgium.

Telecomputing

This too is an Oxford-based company which has developed a series of programs known as Telecomputing's Library Software. One flexible system they offer is TeleMARC. This is an ordering and cataloguing system for ICL 1900 series computers. Telecomputing receive UK MARC tapes and offer a service of converting and editing these for local use. The TeleMARC system can be configured for batch or on-line working and is being used by several different types of library.

Fifteen governmental libraries are developing a union catalogue system which will involve UK MARC tapes being processed by TeleMARC to produce a COM catalogue.

Full details of services and systems offered are obviously best obtained from the organizations directly.

Help for potential users of MARC may be gained from a MARC user group. Such groups have been set up in the UK and the USA to provide a forum for exchange of ideas and problems. The UK MARC user group has formed some special interest groups. Currently, these cover:

system design and automation;
bibliographic standards;
book trade/library interests;
special materials;
management advice.

THE MARC RECORD

The aim of the MARC format, as outlined earlier, was to communicate bibliographic information between libraries which would use the information in widely differing ways. Because of this, much of the detail in the record is not required by libraries and so the record must be reformatted for local use. This has made some librarians critical of the MARC system. The average size of a UK MARC record is 780 characters.

Although the original MARC format was designed to be international, as more countries have tried to use it more variations have been made. To overcome this and allow for international exchange of MARC records a new format known as UNIMARC has been designed. National organizations producing MARC records will produce them to national standards for use within the country, and will reformat these to the UNIMARC format for international exchange. Former names of UNIMARC were SUPERMARC and INTERMARC.

The MARC record structure will be described in broad terms below and will be based on the UK MARC record.[13] The format complies with the international standard of bibliographic information interchange on magnetic tapes (ISO 2709). Cataloguing standards such as the Anglo-American Cataloguing Rules and the International Standard Bibliographic Description for Monographic Publications (ISBD(M)) are also incorporated.

The basic concept of the MARC record is that it is a tagged record. This is similar to the variable field format described in Chapter 3 but a 3-digit number is used for the tag instead of a character; for example, tag 245 always refers to the title field. In fact the MARC record is a mixture of a tagged field and directory structure, as will be seen.

The record consists basically of four parts.

Label

This is a fixed length of 24 characters and contains standard information such as the length of the record, status of the record (new, changed, deleted, CIP), and so on.

Directory

As well as having tags the MARC record includes a directory giving the length and starting character position of each field. For each field in the record an entry appears in the directory. This is of the form:

$$\begin{array}{rl} \text{tag} & \text{3 characters} \\ \text{length of data in field} & \text{4 characters} \\ \text{starting character position} & \text{5 characters} \end{array}$$

Example: 100002600137
Explanation: Field with tag 100 (personal author) is 26 characters long and starts at the 137th character position.
Thus the size of the directory is dependent on the number of fields in the record.

Control fields

Tags 001–009 are defined to be control fields, i.e. they control access to the main record. Tag 001 is the Record Control Number. If an International Standard Book Number (ISBN) exists for the item, then it is used, otherwise the BNB number of the item is used. The ISBN was adopted in 1970 and is a manifestation of co-operation between libraries, central cataloguing agencies and the book trade. It consists of 10 digits which refer to a group identifier, a publisher identifier, a title identifier and a check digit.
Example: 0 14 002648 7
Explanation: This is the 2648th title by publisher number 14 (Penguin) and has group identifier 0 (published in UK, USA, Australia, Canada, Ireland or South Africa). The check digit, 7, is computed from the other digits using the modulus 11 technique. An explanation of this is given in Appendix III.

Variable fields

These fields contain all the bibliographic information in the record. Each field starts with two numeric indicators and ends with a special marker ($\sharp$). The information in the field is divided into sub-fields which are prefaced by sub-field marks. A full definition of the tags, indicators and sub-fields is given in Ref. 13.
Example: Definition of the Imprint Field. Tag 260.
Indicators: First Indicator 0 Publisher not the main entry author heading.
First Indicator 1 Publisher is the main entry author heading.
Second Indicator 0 Imprint relates to work.
Second Indicator 1 Imprint relates to volume or part of work.
Sub-fields: $ a Place of publication.
$ b Publisher's name.
$ c Date.
$ d Full address information.

Thus, this book published in 1977 by Heyden in London and written by Lucy Tedd would have the following entry after tag 260:

00$aLondon$bHeydenc$1977♯.

The information contained in this part of the record includes:

Full bibliographic description.
Subject information. This is covered by several fields:
    050   Library of Congress Classification Number.
    080   Universal Decimal Classification Number (this is only included if available in the publication).
    082   Dewey Decimal Classification Number.
    650   Library of Congress Topical Subject Heading.
    651   Library of Congress Geographical Subject Heading.
    690   PRECIS descriptor string (see Chapter 9 for more details).
Supplementary information.

EXAMPLE 1: BIRMINGHAM LIBRARIES CO-OPERATIVE MECHANIZATION PROJECT[14]

The aim of this project, started in 1969, was to provide a co-operative cataloguing system for the libraries of the universities of Aston and Birmingham and for Birmingham Public Library. A co-operative scheme was investigated in the hope that it would increase the range of possible services and that it would minimize costs by the pooling of resources.

Three very different types of library were involved and therefore much of the early stages was spent on defining cataloguing practices, filing rules, and so on. The decision to make use of MARC records was taken. OSTI, now the British Library Research and Development Division (BLRDD), allocated grants to assist the project during 1969–1975. The remainder of the funding comes from the participating libraries.

BLCMP are currently supplying cataloguing services to nine other libraries with a further five libraries in the process of being included. These include several polytechnic libraries, county libraries and two foreign university libraries: the University of Aarlborg (Denmark) and the European University Institute, Florence (Italy). The system is currently batch processed and can be broadly described by the following stages:

(a) The library fills in a form indicating the control number and local details (accession number, location, etc.) of an item to be included in its catalogue. If the record is not already in the database, another form is filled in giving the bibliographic details.

(b) Forms are sent to the project centre and are converted to machine-readable form.

(c) A weekly batch run on an IBM 370/155 at a bureau is made, updating the database which is held on disc.

(d) A diagnostic listing of all records to be added to a library's catalogue is produced. Using this, checks can be made by the cataloguers at the library of local records input and of the externally produced record.

(e) Catalogues, in varying orders and physical formats, can be produced for individual libraries.

(f) All libraries participating in BLCMP receive a union catalogue of the holdings of all the libraries involved. This is produced on COM microfilm cassette.

Although the MARC tagging structure allows for the inclusion of local information, this would involve very large records if the local information of several co-operating libraries were included. To overcome this, details of local information are held in separate records, known as local records, also in MARC format. In this way the system can deal with any number of libraries adding their local information to the general record.

The MARC tags on the BLCMP form for records not covered by the database include:

001	Control number.
008	Information codes, e.g. data and country of publication, type of document, etc.
040	Library code.
041	Languages code.
082	Dewey Decimal Classification number.
1xx	Author (there are different tags for personal or corporate authors and conference proceedings).
245	Title.
250	Edition.
260	Imprint.
300	Collation.
4xx	Series note.
5xx	Note.
6xx	Subject headings.
7xx	Added entries.
9xx	Cross references.

The cataloguers have to insert the appropriate tag in instances such as 4xx, depending on the type of series note included.

The BLCMP database includes a backfile of UK (to 1950) and LC (to 1972) MARC records and the file of locally produced MARC records. The latter is currently growing at the rate of 115 000 records per year. In addition, MARC records for serials, printed music, music monographs and sound recordings are available.

The cost of participating in the scheme is based on a library's annual intake. For example,

intake of up to   5 000 items—£3300 per year;
intake of up to 20 000 items—£8250 per year.

The project is currently run by a team of full-time staff situated at Birmingham University Library. The team consists of a director and secretary, two assistant directors, two library systems analysts, a computer officer, a data controller, two programmers and eleven data preparation staff.

EXAMPLE 2: OHIO COLLEGE LIBRARY CENTER[15]

In 1965, Frederick Kilgour and Ralph Parker were called in to consult on the setting up of a bibliographic centre for the academic libraries in the US State of Ohio. They suggested that a classic bibliographic system was outdated in the 1960s and that a computer-based system should be developed. In 1967, OCLC, a not-for-profit organization, serving 50 academic libraries in Ohio, was set up with Kilgour as the director.

The two main objectives of the centre are:

(a) to share resources between individual libraries;
(b) to reduce the rate of rise of library costs.

The OCLC system includes plans to integrate the various library procedures of cataloguing, circulation control, inter-library lending and, in the long term, plans to allow library users access to the database.

The catalogue system was the first to be implemented. Again a database of MARC records is at the centre of the system. Details of an item not included in the database are input by the library wishing to catalogue the item. The main differences between BLCMP and the OCLC system are:

(a) OCLC is an on-line system. Cataloguers have almost immediate access to the records. If the record of the item to be catalogued is present in the database it is displayed and edited at once. Access from remote libraries to the centre is by leased telephone line or via a telecommunications network.

(b) At present, output from OCLC consists mainly of catalogue cards. These are produced on line-printers at the centre and then sent through the post to the particular library where they are merged into the library's card catalogue. A few libraries participating in the OCLC system produce their catalogue on COM.

The MARC fields used for inserting local records are similar to those used in the BLCMP system. Classification of items is by Library of Congress Classification numbers.

OCLC is not now limited to academic libraries within the State of Ohio.

Varying types of library from varying geographical locations are currently using the system.

In June 1975, some of the numerical facts about the usage of the OCLC system were:

Number of bibliographic records	1.4M
Number of institutions using OCLC	240
Total number of leased line terminals	728
Rate of cataloguing items	2.5M/year
Rate of adding records to file	3000/day
Access	7.00 a.m.–10.00 p.m.
Average response time	9.4 seconds
Cards printed each day	125 000
Enquiries made by title each day	40 000

Since then the system will have grown. However, there are some problems currently, probably due to the fact that the system was so successful and grew so rapidly that it became overburdened. More hardware is currently being installed to assist the Rank Xerox Sigma 9 and Sigma 5 computers. At the American Library Association's Mid-Winter Conference in 1976 a group of OCLC users met to discuss current problems faced by customers.

The main database is accessed by multiple indexes of keys in a similar way to the Blackwell system described in Chapter 3. TEDD,INTRO is an example of the author/title search key.

The cost of using OCLC is directly dependent on the number of records accessed. It consists of two parts:

(a) first time use of a record not created by the searching
    library $1.81
(b) catalogue cards (arranged in packs and ready to file) $.034 per card

Because OCLC is a not-for-profit organization it is unable to sell shares and so the only method of getting working capital is from earnings. Because of this the costs may have to increase, even though more libraries are becoming involved in the system. One of the reasons for the success of OCLC might be that it appeared at a time when library budgets were being cut and the cheapest solutions were required. It is reckoned that 14 items can be catalogued in an hour using OCLC as compared with one or two items an hour with manual methods.

REFERENCES

1. G. W. King *et al.*, *Automation and the Library of Congress: a Survey Sponsored by the Council of Library Resources*, Library of Congress, Washington (1963).

2. H. D. Avram, *The MARC Pilot Project: Final Report on a Project Sponsored by the Council on Library Resources*, Library of Congress, Washington (1968).

3. J. Wainwright, BNB MARC Users in the UK: a Survey. *Program*, **5**, 271–83 (1972).

4. *British Library MARC Services: a Guide for Intending Users*, British Library Bibliographic Services Division, London (1975).

5. J. Wainwright and J. Hills, Book Selection from MARC Tapes: a Feasibility Study. *Program*, **7**, 123–44 (1973).

6. L. Hodgkinson, Computerisation in the Lancashire Library. *Program*, **9**, 184–98 (1975).

7. R. M. Duchesne and L. Donbroski, BNB/Brighton Public Libraries Catalogue Project—BRIMARC. *Program*, **6**, 205–24 (1973).

8. G. R. Mauerhoff and R. G. Smith, A MARC II Based Program for Retrieval and Dissemination. *Journal of Library Automation*, **4**, 141–57 (1971).

9. G. H. Wright, An Ontario libraries' network or co-operative entanglement, in *Proceedings of the 1973 Clinic on Library Applications of Data Processing* (ed. F. W. Lancaster), University of Illinois Graduate School of Library Science, Urbana (1973). ISBN 0 87845 038 6.

10. M. Sandels, *LIBRIS: a Computerized Library Information System for Sweden*, Swedish Council of Research Libraries, Stockholm (1974). ISBN 91 7000 038 7.

11. D. P. Waite, The minicomputer: its role in a nationwide bibliographic and information network, in *Proceedings of the 1974 Clinic on Library Applications of Data Processing* (ed. F. W. Lancaster), University of Illinois Graduate School of Library Science, Urbana (1974). ISBN 0 87845 041 6.

12. R. M. Duchesne and R. Butcher, BNB/British Library IBM 360/370 Library Software Package. *Program*, **7**, 225–37 (1973).

13. *UK MARC Manual*, First standard edition, British Library Bibliographic Services Division, London (1975). ISBN 0 900220 47 3.

14. A. R. Hall, BLCMP. *Catalogue and Index*, **40**, 7–9 (1976).

15. A. Plotnik *et al.*, A Primer on OCLC for all Librarians. *American Libraries*, **7**, 258–75 (1976).

FURTHER READING

A. E. Jeffreys and T. D. Wilson (eds.), *UK MARC Project. Proceedings of the Seminar of the UK MARC Project*, Oriel Press, Newcastle upon Tyne (1970). ISBN 0 85362 086 5.

R. E. Coward and M. Yelland, *The Interchange of Bibliographic Information in Machine-Readable Form*, Library Association, London (1975). ISBN 0 85365 338 0.

CHAPTER 6

ACQUISITIONS AND CATALOGUING SYSTEMS

INTRODUCTION

Many computer-based acquisitions and cataloguing systems are integrated and so both systems will be covered in this chapter. Since the early 1960s, when computers were first used to aid library housekeeping procedures, the catalogue of a library has been foremost for conversion to a computer-based system. In a recent survey,[1] some US librarians gave their reasons for setting up a computer-based catalogue system. These reasons included:

(a) to provide access to the complete and up-to-date catalogue from many service points;

(b) to provide more and improved access points and search capabilities;

(c) to expand the availability of increased resources through the sharing of resources via regional union catalogues;

(d) to eliminate or reduce some of the inherent problems of manually produced card catalogues;

(e) to satisfy calls for a change of system from staff and users of the library and from external bodies, such as the Library of Congress.

Similar reasons would probably be echoed elsewhere in the world. In all cases though, different emphases would be made by different types of librarian. For instance, the second reason given would be more applicable in academic and special libraries than in public libraries. In North America, academic and special libraries tend to have more computer-based systems than public libraries. This trend is not so prevalent in the UK.

Public libraries were amongst the first to use computers for catalogue production in the UK. This happened around 1964 when local government re-organization of the London boroughs took place. The new, enlarged authorities had to merge differing physical forms of catalogue, classification codes, orders of filing, cataloguing rules, and so on. Many of these new authorities, including Barnet, Camden and Greenwich, adopted a computer-based solution. A similar situation faced the local authority libraries of England and Wales at their re-organization in 1974 and of Scotland in 1975.

Although the logical place to start an integrated computer system might be in the acquisitions department, it frequently happens in practice that the cataloguing system is converted first.

ACQUISITIONS SYSTEMS

The pre-acquisition stage of selection can be computer-assisted as was described in Chapter 5. Some publishers use computers and offer selection services to subscribers. These services are now run totally by Oriel and are known as Oriel Bibliographic Services Ltd. Blackwell Bibliographical Services Ltd. is a recently formed firm involving B. H. Blackwell and Oriel Computer Services. Its main function is to disseminate information about forthcoming publications. This information is collected from co-operating publishers and described using the MARC format. Three main services are offered:

(a) Blackwell Forthcoming Book Service. This is produced monthly on COM microfiche in author, title and class-mark orders for books within 4–12 weeks of publication.

(b) Blackwell Work/MARC Tape Service, which is produced fortnightly.

(c) Blackwell pre-publication SDI Service. This gives subscribers details of items about to be published in their subject field.

Hunt's article[2] describes the basic functions of the acquisitions department of Manchester University Library. These functions, similar for most libraries, can be summarized as:

(a) receive recommendations and establish that the items are not already on order;

(b) order the items and chase the bookseller if no action appears to be being taken;

(c) accession the items on arrival and keep statistics;

(d) maintain a record of items on order or in process;

(e) maintain the accounts.

The basic computer system required to perform these operations will be described in a similar way to the diagram of a system given in Chapter 4, namely, in terms of input, files, processes and output.

Input

The details input to an acquisitions system cover four aspects:

new orders;
amendments to existing orders;
booksellers' reports;
acknowledgements of the receipt of items in the library.

The bibliographic detail for the basic record of the order can come from a variety of sources:

(a) A file of MARC records. Details of this were given in Chapter 5.

(b) The file of items held by the library, if this is held on a computer. Cheshire County Libraries check such a file, as about 60% of their orders are for extra copies of existing titles.

(c) A co-operative file of records held by several libraries.

(d) Local input. If none of the above apply, then the details have to be translated into machine-readable form locally. This would be produced on punched cards, punched paper-tape or magnetic tape for batch-processed systems or entered via a terminal for on-line systems.

Files

A computer-based acquisitions system involves at least two files. The main file contains records of all current orders. The second file contains the names and addresses of the booksellers used by the library. The purpose of the second file is to save having to specify this information with each order, so that a code number can be used on the order record.

Processes and output

The main process of any order system is to deal with new orders and send the appropriate form to the supplier. The forms can be produced in a number of ways.

AMCOS[3] involves loading the line-printer with special pre-printed stationery that can be sent to the bookseller directly. The Ministry of Economic Affairs in Belgium, which has an integrated order, catalogue and charging system, produces the record on ordinary line-printer paper; this is then passed through a reproducing machine with an appropriate mask so that the subsequent form is suitable for sending to the bookseller. In most systems these forms are sorted into bookseller order before being printed.

The date of entering the order record into the file is checked to ascertain whether or not the bookseller needs chasing. If no information regarding the order has been received within a pre-determined time, then an appropriate note is printed and sent to the bookseller. The time allocated for easily available items should be different from the time allocated for an obviously difficult item. Cheshire County Libraries send reminders to booksellers after three months silence and subsequently at intervals of one month.

When the item is received in the library the bibliographic record used for ordering becomes the basis of the catalogue record. In an integrated system this implies that the edited record is added to the catalogue file, otherwise the details are printed on to a processing slip and passed to the cataloguing department.

These are perhaps the three most important processes of an acquisitions system. However, there are several other processes that can be incorporated into the computer system. For example:

(a) production of a list of items currently on order, organized by author, department or subject;

(b) production of a list of recently acquired items;

(c) notification of individuals when an item which they have recommended has been received;

(d) control of accounts so that expenditure can be more easily controlled and the current state of various budgets made easily available;

(e) production of statistics that will aid management decision making. As with most computer-based systems, the collection of data relating to the system is easier, thus aiding the analysis.

CATALOGUING SYSTEMS

Again the basics of a cataloguing system will be described in terms of input, files, processes and output. It should be emphasized that this description, as for other applications, is not aimed at being a 'blue-print' but merely a broad outline giving some of the possible solutions.

Input

The bibliographic details required for the catalogue record can come from any of the sources described under Input for acquisitions systems or of course from the acquisitions system itself. These details would need to be checked, amendments made and local information, such as location, accession number, and so on, added.

Files

There is usually one main file (sometimes referred to as a master file) of catalogue records of the library's holdings. However, because it becomes costly to print this file each time it is updated, there is often another temporary file which is used to cumulate the additional records. The master file will be printed infrequently whereas the cumulative file will be printed more frequently. The periods in both cases will depend on the physical form of the output. This situation implies that the reader searching for an item in the catalogue needs to look in at least two places, and also that the catalogue is never really up-to-date.

This would not be the situation if on-line access to the file of catalogue records were available.

Processes

The first process is normally to check the accuracy of the record. The computer can perform simple tests on the record structure and print out details of records in error. A diagnostic listing is usually produced for all the other records so that the cataloguer can check the details. It must be remembered that the computer cannot alter the quality of the cataloguing; that still depends on the skill of the cataloguer. The corrections to the records are then input.

The next process is to generate added entries for the record. Trinity College, Dublin has been producing its catalogue by computer for several years. At present they have an average of five entries in the catalogue for each item; this compares with one and a half entries per item in their previous manual catalogue.

If the mode of processing is batch, then catalogue records are usually added in a batch. When the added entries have been created the file of additional records is sorted into the order of the master file, and is then merged with the master file. If the catalogue records are added on-line, then these are processed individually, checked, edited and incorporated into the master file.

At some stage the master file or cumulative file will be sorted into the orders required and printed on the physical form specified.

Bath University Library has recently been researching into the orders and forms of catalogues. The Bath University Comparative Catalogue Study (BUCCS) investigated name, title, classified and KWOC (details of this in Chapter 9) orders.[4] Some results of the study are described in the evaluation section later in the chapter.

Output

The decision as to the physical format of the catalogue is an important one for the cataloguing system designer. The three possibilities described under Output in Chapter 2 can be used as well as catalogue cards.

(1) Line-printer paper

The first computer-produced catalogues used this form of output as there was little else available at the time. Although there are obvious disadvantages, such as quality of print, physical size of the catalogue, time taken to print, cost of reproduction, and so on, this solution is suitable for some libraries. Oxford City Libraries produced their catalogue this way and were happy with the product. The continuous stationery is loosely bound and stored in filing racks on movable trolleys. To produce the eight required copies, two print runs are made with four-part stationery in the line-printer. The catalogue is cumulated monthly with a complete print-out every six months. Now that the City Library has been incorporated into Oxford County it is thought likely that the catalogue will be produced on COM microfiche.

(2) Computer photo-typesetting

Some of the problems of line-printer paper are overcome by a typeset catalogue. Such a catalogue is usually produced by a computer typesetting bureau. Computaprint, for instance, is used by many libraries. West Sussex County Library,[5] which has a predominantly elderly readership, chose this method of output. The typographic quality is high, upper and lower case characters are available and there is a reduction in size when compared with a line-printer catalogue. However, some of the disadvantages of line-printer output, such as the cost of reproduction, the cost of production and the need for binding, still remain.

(3) COM

Becker[6] gives some advantages of using COM in the production of library catalogues. These include:

ability to cumulate frequently;
compact storage;
ease of handling;
inexpensive reproduction;
low material and distribution costs.

BLCMP studied forms of output when deciding how to produce their union catalogue. Comparative costs for one year's output for Birmingham University Library indicated COM would be £212, upper-case line-printer would be £900–£1300 and upper and lower-case line-printer would be £3491.

One of the major problems facing a library which decides to produce its catalogue on to COM is whether to use film or fiche. Some comments on this appear later in the chapter in the section on evaluation. Other decisions, of a fairly technical nature, which have to be made include:

Mode of presenting pages on a microfilm. Two methods are used, namely 'cine' mode and 'comic' mode. The difference between these two is illustrated in Fig. 6.1.

Positive or negative film. The choice is between having dark lettering on a light background or light lettering on a dark background.

Reduction ratio. 24×, 42×, 48× are available.

Layout of catalogue entries.

The National Reprographic Centre for Documentation based at Hatfield Polytechnic will give advice to libraries on these aspects and on the general problems of selecting a bureau or selecting a viewer to read the film or fiche.

(4) Catalogue cards

This form of output from a computer-based catalogue system is used more in North America than it is in the UK. It has some advantage in that the computer-produced

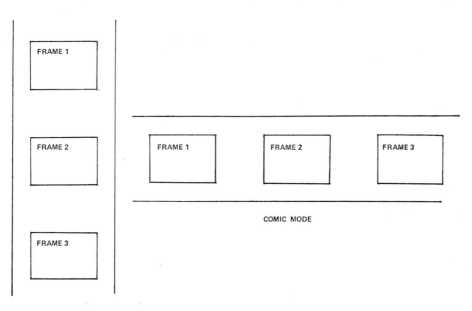

Fig. 6.1. COM: cine and comic mode.

catalogue is easily merged with the manual catalogue and so might save on searching time. The need for a cumulative file disappears. However, cards still have to be filed, which may lead to mis-filing, and no saving of space is achieved. As described in Chapter 5, most of the libraries participating in the OCLC system receive their output on cards.

METHOD OF PROCESSING

The majority of acquisitions and cataloguing systems are batch processed through the parent authority's computer. For the production of order notices, the catalogue and similar lists this is perfectly satisfactory. However, there are shortcomings when using a batch system for creating and editing records. An increasing number of libraries are therefore using on-line systems and in some cases minicomputers are being installed in the library.

Cheshire County Library was one of the first public libraries to introduce an on-line acquisitions and cataloguing system. This was in late 1971 and the system is described in some detail at the end of this chapter. The basic ideas behind Cheshire's system have been used by other local authorities in the UK, mainly Cleveland, Lancashire and Staffordshire. The AMCOS system[3] is an example of an on-line acquisitions and cataloguing system in operation in a special library. In the USA, BALLOTS (Bibliographic Automation of Large Library Operations Using a Time-Sharing System) is a good example of an on-line system in an academic library, namely Stanford University Library.[7]

BALLOTS was implemented in 1972 as a fully integrated system. The main source of bibliographic data is an on-line file of MARC records. The system operates on the university's IBM 360/67 computer, with a powerful mini-computer, a PDP 11/45, controlling the 125 terminals that can be simultaneously connected to the main-frame. Some of these terminals are not ordinary teletype-compatible terminals but can themselves be programmed as they contain a microcomputer. In Ref. 7 some of the reasons for Stanford not developing the total system on a minicomputer are given. These can be summarized as:

Program development. This was much faster, more efficient and less costly on the larger computer because of the available software and the programmers' experience with the computer system. This situation will obviously change in time.

Control of the computer system. Although the library-based minicomputer system gives the library maximum responsibility, Stanford University Library did not want this.

Access to the files. If the system had been implemented on a computer system within the library, then users of the general information retrieval system SPIRES (Stanford Public Information Retrieval System) would have been unable to access the library's files.

Other libraries have decided that minicomputers in the library are useful and these have been installed to aid in the control of acquisitions and cataloguing systems. Camden Public Libraries are perhaps the forerunners of this in the UK and their system is described later in this chapter. Some university libraries, especially East Anglia and Manchester, are already using minicomputers for circulation control and are planning to use them for adding and editing biblio-graphic records to their acquisitions and cataloguing systems. The Bodleian Library in Oxford is using a PDP 11/20 minicomputer to assist in the production of a catalogue of about 1 250 000 books published before 1920.

BIBLIOGRAPHIC RECORD

The bibliographic information required for the acquisitions process and the cataloguing process differs. At the acquisitions stage the information about the book need not be as detailed or as accurate as at the catalogue stage. In either case there are three basic questions to be answered:

should the bibliographic details be extracted from a national MARC, or other centralized, database?

what items should be included in the record?

what form of record structure should be used—fixed, variable, special or MARC-based?

As in many other instances there is no best solution since the circumstances in different libraries vary. Some solutions adopted by libraries are described.

Bath University Library

In 1970, the staff of the library thought that the cost and problems of using MARC tapes in a local situation might be greater than the cost and problems of producing the catalogue locally. It was also suspected that shorter catalogue entries might be more, rather than less, useful. The result, known as Bath's Minicatalogue, consisted of a mixed record structure of fixed and variable fields. Details such as the language, the location and the category of the item formed part of the fixed field format, whereas details of the classification code, author(s) and title(s) formed part of the variable field format. The average length of a record was 123 characters.

In 1974, this format was amended to include more information on analytical entries, edition and volume statements, and so on. The average length of a record is now 266 characters.

Clwyd County Library

In 1967, the county library of Flintshire, which, since local government re-organization in 1974, forms part of Clwyd, decided to use the local authority's computer to aid in the production of the catalogue of the English language and Welsh language stock held by the county.[8] The MARC project had hardly been started and so was not considered; instead, a purely fixed field format was adopted. The record contains about 300 characters; 70 characters are allocated for the title field and 50 characters for the author field.

Loughborough University of Technology Library

It was decided that MARC was too complicated for a local format and so in 1970 work began on defining a simpler structure. This is known as MINICS or Minimal Input Cataloguing System.[9] Some of the aims of this format were:

to use the same record structure for monographs, serials and special informa-tion retrieval systems;

to include fields for cataloguing research reports and for analytical cataloguing;

to allow for the incorporation of local ordering, cataloguing, binding, cost, etc. information;

to use a simpler and more flexible format than MARC but provide for MARC to MINICS conversion.

The resultant format is similar in concept to MARC in that it contains a fixed length label, a directory of the variable length fields and the variable length fields themselves. A tagging structure is used to define the variable length fields. This is simpler than the MARC tagging structure as it consists of only two characters and has no indicators or subfields. Fields can be repeated by using a field divider. The fields at present included in MINICS cover about one-fifth of the available MARC fields.

Newcastle University Library

In 1964, Newcastle University Library started to design its computer-based order system. A record structure was designed that aimed to describe the information in a hierarchical or 'tree' format as opposed to the ordinary linear format. The structure is known as the Newcastle File Handling System (NFHS) and is described in detail in Ref. 10. NFHS has been used at Newcastle for storing MARC records, order records and for catalogue records of special collections held by the library.

Southampton University Library

The acquisitions system operational at Southampton University Library has its records formatted in a MARC-compatible structure[11] (more details on the system are given at the end of this chapter) in order to facilitate matching with centrally produced MARC records. The order is typed onto special stationery using a Friden Flexowriter. This is a tape-typewriter machine which not only produces a punched paper-tape copy of what has been typed, but can also be regulated by 'control' paper-tapes. One control tape supplies the MARC tags to be included in the record of the order.

The tags used include:

    020   for the ISBN;
    100   for the author;
    240   for the title and edition number;
    260   for the publisher and date of publication;
    350   for the price and the fund responsible;
    500   for the bookseller.

SOFTWARE AND SERVICES

All the software systems and services referred to in Chapter 5 are of relevance in this section as many acquisitions and cataloguing systems use MARC or MARC-compatible records.

The London Borough of Islington has been testing the cataloguing module of the DILS package. Their catalogue is produced using the authority's ICL 1903T computer. Once operational it is planned to include the ordering module of the system quickly and in the very long term the charging module.

Kent County Library were operating a MARC-based acquisitions system in 1971. This system has been modified slightly for use by Berkshire County Library. Since local government re-organization the enlarged Kent County Library service are operating an integrated acquisitions and cataloguing system using TeleMARC software.

The acquisitions system developed at Southampton University Library is being used at the New University of Ulster. Some modifications to the programs were made to take advantage of the more powerful computer configuration available at Ulster.

The Cheshire system which is not MARC-based has been used by other authorities. Derbyshire County Library service used the programs directly whilst other authorities have based their design on the system.

Another alternative for the cataloguing system designer is to use an external agency completely. An increasing number of libraries are adopting this approach by using the BLBSD's full catalogue service or by using a co-operative scheme such as BLCMP.

FILING

As described in Chapter 2, the computer's ability to sort depends on 'branching' instructions. Each character (alphabetic, numeric, punctuation or space) is coded for input to the computer and because the code given to A is numerically less than the code given to D they will be compared alphabetically in a branch instruction which compares the values in two computer words. However, the codes allocated vary between computer manufacturers and whilst treatment of alphabetic and numeric characters is similar the treatment of punctuation symbols and spaces differs. This basic letter-by-letter approach which the computer uses might suffice for small files but for large library catalogues it may not be acceptable as the standard library filing rules are not obeyed.

Any solution adds to the cost and complexity of the system and librarians need to study the situation and decide on the most cost-effective approach. There are several solutions:

(a) accept the letter-by-letter approach;

(b) use a system where the filing is achieved by manually assigning a numeric code to each entry and then the computer sorts by number;

(c) change the entry so that the required sequence is achieved with letter-by-letter filing;

(d) write a program to implement the library's filing rules.

It often happens that no one solution is best, but a mixture of all four is needed. In 1966, a working party on computer filing rules was formed and it reported in 1972.[12] BLCMP and the British Library have developed software for the implementation of these rules.

UNION CATALOGUES AND CO-OPERATION

As well as being used to produce catalogues in individual libraries, computers are also used to produce union catalogues.

On a regional basis one of the first schemes in the UK was set up by LASER in 1971. LASER serves about 87 libraries and has about 750 000 additions and amendments to the union catalogue of 1 500 000 entries each year. The union catalogue is used to help inter-library lending within the region. The initial system consisted solely of an ISBN, or other unique identification number, for each title and a list of codes representing libraries in the region holding that title. The union catalogue is produced on cassetted microfilm so that each library in the region can have a copy. Other regional bureaux in Britain have adopted this system. The British Library Lending Division (BLLD) plans to form a master finding list by merging the files produced from the regional bureaux. LASER have recently ordered a minicomputer to provide on-line access to the files for maintenance of the union catalogue and organization of inter-library lending within the region. The minicomputer system will have a disc, magnetic tape and several VDUs for data entry and file access.

The BLLD faced the problem of merging the catalogues of the National Central Library and the National Lending Library when the British Library was formed. Several union catalogues are required in order to run the national inter-library lending scheme. The main catalogues are the Older Books Catalogue, the Foreign Language Union Finding List and the Current English Language Books. MARC records are used where possible to provide the bibliographic detail. The BLLD reckon that it is necessary to produce the catalogues by computer and print them on COM for several reasons:

staffing—the stock grows at a rate of 15% each year;
increase of access points;
flexibility of formats and capability of producing subsets;
ease of duplication;
ease of updating (no more manual filing);
cost decrease.

A preliminary study on co-operation in library automation (COLA) has recently been carried out by LASER.[13] The definition of co-operation used in the report is 'the (reciprocally beneficial) sharing of resources, developed or pre-existing, by two or more bodies'. Several co-operative systems in various parts of the world are described in the report and were referred to in Chapter 5.

An early example of co-operation in the UK was the study that took place after the Brasenose Conference on Library Automation in 1966. This looked at the feasibility of a computer-based catalogue of the pre-1801 books held in London (British Museum), Oxford and Cambridge (LOC).[14] An interesting method of allocating a unique number to each book was used. Known as 'fingerprinting', the technique consisted of picking nine pairs of characters from precise locations in the book. This study estimated that the cost of the whole project would be between £750 000 and £1 000 000 and would take eight years.

A grant has recently been awarded by the British Library Research and Development Department to study the feasibility of a co-operative system in Scotland. The project will be known as SCOLCAP (Scottish Libraries Co-operative Automation Project) and will initially involve the National Library of Scotland, the University Libraries of Dundee, Glasgow and Stirling, Edinburgh City Libraries and the Mitchell Library, Glasgow.

Computer-based systems are often implemented by large library systems. In the USA the INCOLSA (Indiana Co-operative Library Services Authority) was set up in 1974 and one of its aims is to test the feasibility of library automation in small libraries; 44% of libraries in Indiana operate on part-time staff and 62% add less than 1000 books per year.

EVALUATION AND COSTS

The BUCCS project[4] provides one of the most recent evaluative studies on catalogues. The main aims were to:

(a) investigate the performance of four physical forms of catalogue (line-printer, card, COM film and COM fiche);

(b) investigate the performance of four orders of catalogue (name, title, classified and KWOC);

(c) ascertain the effectiveness of short entry catalogues.

The project involved a panel of about 120 people (students, staff and librarians) who carried out specified searches on the various forms and orders.

The average times for searching the forms were:

COM fiche	2 min 50 sec
COM film	2 min 45 sec
Card	3 min 36 sec
Line-printer output	2 min 22 sec

The difference between COM fiche, COM film and line-printer was not statistically significant. The reactions of the panel, however, indicated a marked preference for COM fiche. Further analysis of the comments indicated that many searchers did not like COM film because of the particular hand-wound viewer used in the experiment. A further study was carried out in liaison with the National Reprographic Centre for Documentation. This studied the effect of motorized viewers and indexed COM film on the searchers' attitude to COM film. Quantitatively the performance was not significantly different but the study showed that the searchers preferred motorized viewers and indexed COM film.

As mentioned earlier, the decision between COM film and COM fiche is difficult. Some public libraries are worried about the lack of security of COM fiche. Shropshire County Libraries produce their catalogue on COM fiche and have had no problems from the public with this form of output. They reckon that fiche is cheaper to produce and easier to post than film and they have never regretted their decision to use fiche. Westminster City Libraries were one of the first libraries to use COM. It was in 1971 and they used COM film. Some of the comments made by the public included, 'It was fun to use the catalogue' and 'I see you have a catalogue now'.

The average times for searching the orders of catalogue in BUCCS were:

Classified	4 min 2 sec
KWOC	2 min 57 sec
Name	1 min 51 sec
Title	2 min 39 sec

Panel members preferred using the KWOC catalogue to the classified catalogue for subject searches because it was in 'natural language' and involved only one stage in the search.

Although BUCCS did not set out to cost the various options, some details on costings were included in the report. The costs were based on a seven-year period (1975 was taken as year 1) for the production of Bath's catalogue (Table 6.1). The catalogue consisted of 70 000 items in 1975 and it was estimated that

TABLE 6.1

Form	Order	Copy(ies)	Cost over 7 years in £
Card	Name, classified	1	14 635
Line-printer	Name, classified	1	13 477
COM fiche	Name, classified	10	14 982
COM film	Name, classified	10	16 623
Line-printer	Name, classified, title, KWOC	3	58 766
COM fiche	Name, classified, title, KWOC	10	24 318
COM film	Name, classified, title, KWOC	10	27 611

it would grow at the rate of 10 000 items per year. The costings are based on a complete production of the catalogue on the form specified (apart from card) once a month for ten months of the year (apart from KWOC which would only be produced three times a year) and weekly cumulations on line-printer.

A two-year quantitative study on the use made of card catalogues has recently been undertaken at Yale University. The study aimed to isolate users' requirements in order to design a computer-based catalogue to meet these needs. They wanted to resist the tendency, often prevalent amongst traditional cataloguers, of creating the computer-based catalogue in the image of the card catalogue, thus perpetuating some of the inherent weaknesses.

In 1972, the Standing Conference of National and University Libraries (SCONUL) produced a report on the computer needs for university library operations.[15] Cost details were included in this report, although the rapid rise in the rate of inflation over the past years must be taken into account when looking at these costs.

(a) Surrey University Library have produced a very short entry (a single 80-column card per item) catalogue. The costs were broken down as follows:

		hours	cost (£)	Total (£)
Development	Analysis/design	600	1000	
	Programming	1600	1750	
	Clerical	2600	1500	
	Data preparation	1300	580	4830
Operational/year	Data preparation	350	160	
	Computer time	1200	1200	1360

(b) South Western Academic Libraries Co-operative Automation Project (SWALCAP) identified the costs of the manual acquisitions systems in the libraries co-operating in the project in 1970:

		Unit cost
Bath (not now participating)	£754 for 5 000 vols p.a.	15p
Bristol	£5103 for 27 000 vols p.a.	19p
Cardiff	£2218 for 12 500 vols p.a.	$17\frac{1}{2}$p
Exeter	£2341 for 14 000 vols p.a.	17p

The estimated annual cost of a computer-based acquisitions system which would operate the same basic routines as well as provide regular reminders and management information for all the co-operating libraries was:

£2883 for 20 000 vols p.a. giving a unit cost of $14\frac{1}{2}$p.

The acquisitions module has not yet been implemented.

At a recent seminar,[16] Ashford outlined the software costs and effort required for designing and implementing cataloguing systems. Examples given included:

	Effort	In-house programming costs (£)	Software house costs (£)
Batch system with MARC input	4–6 man-years	20 000–30 000	40 000–60 000
Simple on-line system with many users	6–16 man-years	30 000–80 000	60 000–160 000

As systems become more complex it is often worthwhile to use a software house to aid in the control of technical factors, timeliness, documentation and to make use of the consultants' more specialist skills.

Some approaches to reducing costs were also given in the paper. These included:

(a) Adopting systems from other libraries, e.g.
similar library and same hardware can save up to 90%;
different library and same hardware can save 50–70%;
system design only can save at least 25%.
(b) Checking the value of facilities included in the system, e.g.
is the management information produced really necessary?
could external services be used instead?

Tucker's paper[17] gives details of the cost of producing the catalogue. Two factors attributing to this cost are identified:

(a) processing catalogue entries in the computer system to produce a magnetic tape with entries in the correct sequence and formatted into lines and pages;
(b) conversion of this machine-readable catalogue into a more suitable form.

The paper is a result of a study undertaken for the internal purposes of the British Library and so some of the 10 output media compared are of a very high typographical quality. Tables are included in the paper to indicate approximate costs of producing different numbers of copies of different sizes and with differing frequencies of cumulation.

The decision on how often to produce the total catalogue is difficult. Although catalogue production is cheaper on COM, the following example shows how the costs can increase. In a systems analysis done by BLCMP for a library the costs of producing the COM catalogue over a five-year period were estimated. The catalogue, with 32 500 entries added each year, was to be produced in author and classified order:

		£
(a) A completely updated catalogue printed each month	Year 1	432
	Year 5	3408
(b) One completely updated catalogue printed each year with monthly cumulations of items added	Year 1	300
	Year 5	700

The library opted for option (b).

EXAMPLE 1: CHESHIRE COUNTY LIBRARY[18]

As already mentioned in the text, Cheshire County Library operates an integrated on-line acquisitions and cataloguing system. The system was implemented in late 1971 and is used for all books and also for cataloguing sound recordings. The system can be described by the following steps:

(a) Branch librarians select books to be bought. Appropriate forms are filled in and are sent to the county headquarters weekly in ISBN order.

(b) One of the four VDU operators interrogates the computer files, by ISBN (or 'Cheshire number'), to check whether a bibliographic description for the book exists. If it does, then it is used as the basis for the order record, otherwise the relevant information is keyed in. The number of copies required and the code for the bookseller are also added.

(c) All the orders for one day (80–280) are printed out in a batch run at night and manually checked. This takes someone about three-quarters of an hour and there is about a $2\frac{1}{2}\%$ error rate.

(d) Each week a batch run prints orders to be sent to booksellers and also checks the records to see whether reminders are to be sent. Reminders are sent after three months.

(e) When the book arrives the counterfoil is receipted by keying in the ISBN (or 'Cheshire number'). Cataloguing detail and location information are added to the record. A printed book list of selected new accessions is compiled every three months and a decision is made on whether to include the book.

(f) The catalogue is produced on to COM microfilm cassette, negatively, in COMIC mode. It is cumulated monthly and when the cassette is full (this currently takes about three months) a complete catalogue is produced.

The system is processed, using assembly language programs, on the authority's IBM 370/145 which is situated two miles away. The IBM VDUs are linked to the computer by leased line and operate at 1200 baud. At first, the response time was very good as the library was the first department to use on-line processing. As more departments have changed from batch to on-line processing the response time has deteriorated. However, the library is high in the 'priority list' of being processed by the computer.

The COM microfilm is produced by Lowndes Ajax bureau and costs £8.30 for 1000 frames for an original and £.75 for 1000 frames for a copy. Cheshire produce 70 copies in all. The microfilm is read using Scottish Instruments Planet readers. These cost £84.55 each.

A very simple record structure is used which is not MARC-compatible. It was thought that a county library system needed more of a finding list than a catalogue which gave full bibliographic descriptions. However, since local government re-organization 11 fairly large city boroughs have been incorporated into the new county. Users of catalogues in these libraries have different needs and so the system may change.

The computer expertise for the design and programming came from the local authority's computer centre. One programmer became very interested as it was a new problem for him to solve. Because of this he made especially sure that the system fitted the needs of the library. The programming stage took one person ten months. The organization of the computer centre staff is such that the library has had minimal access to programmers to maintain and make small changes to the system.

EXAMPLE 2: CAMDEN PUBLIC LIBRARIES[20]

As mentioned earlier, Camden Public Libraries were among the first in the UK to set up a computer-based catalogue.

Between 1965–68 a 'rough and ready' system, using two 80-column punched cards for each title, was operated on an ICL computer at a bureau. In 1968, Camden Council acquired its own ICL computer. ICL undertook to do the necessary re-programming with a view to making a general package for the production of library catalogues. This operated for several years but ran into difficulties mainly caused by the size of the catalogue (150 000 items). The catalogue was prepared on line-printer paper, which took an excessively long time, and then needed to be copied and bound, which was expensive. Because of these reasons a new catalogue was only produced once a year. This was not sufficient for a library with as many as 100 000 entries added and withdrawn each year. A new integrated acquisitions and cataloguing system was proposed.

The library decided to invest in its own minicomputer, a Data General Nova 1220, to help organize the new system. One of the main reasons for this decision was to enable the library to have guaranteed access whenever required to the computer.

The system can be described by the following steps:

(a) Orders are input by filling in a 'form' on a VDU linked to the mini-computer. The record is checked and stored on a disc until the weekly transfer to the main-frame. The supplier is indicated by a two-letter code on the order record. Amendments to an order record can be made at any time before the weekly transfer.

(b) Each week the order records are transferred to a magnetic tape which is then transported to Camden Council's ICL computer. This tape is processed and details of orders and reminders are sent to the booksellers.

(c) When a book arrives in the library it is receipted on-line using a VDU. If an ISBN is not available, the minicomputer creates a pseudo ISBN for the book.

(d) Catalogue details are added to the record, again using the VDU. These details are stored on discs and can be edited on-line.

(e) Each month catalogue records are transferred to the main-frame computer to update the master catalogue file.

(f) The updated catalogue is produced on COM film cassette in cine mode each month in various sequences; author, title and classified orders for junior and adult items.

(g) Other products from the system include stock listings (which include the accession numbers used in Camden's computer-based charging system), accessions register, subset catalogues, a subject index, a list of books on order, returns to LASER and stock statistics.

In 1973, Camden awarded the contract for supplying the hardware and writing the software for the new system to Terminal Display Systems Ltd., a software house in Blackburn. Staff from the council's computer centre and staff from the computer liaison unit did the necessary programming for the main-frame. Camden Public Libraries also used an external agency to do the data preparation necessary for recreating the master stock file. As in Cheshire, a non-MARC format was chosen which is simple, flexible and is designed for quick and economical machine-filing where possible.

Camden were worried about the file integrity of a COM fiche catalogue and so decided on COM film. Twenty-five copies of the catalogue are produced by the Microgen bureau. The viewers used are Scottish Instruments Comets (an updated form of the Planets) which were designed to be rugged and safe for public use.

Being one of the first to use a minicomputer in a library, Camden have inevitably experienced teething problems. Some words of warning are given in Ref. 20 and include:

(a) do not underestimate the physical size of the machine;
(b) test the system at the factory;
(c) make no easy assumptions in preparing systems tests;
(d) make response time testing as complicated as possible;
(e) weigh carefully the problems of backfile conversion.

The minicomputer system started to be used for adding catalogue entries in May 1975. The first COM catalogue was not produced until April 1976 due to problems incurred in recreating the backfile.

EXAMPLE 3: SOUTHAMPTON UNIVERSITY LIBRARY'S ACQUISITIONS SYSTEM[11,19]

The development of library automation at Southampton University Library started in 1966 with the development of a computer-based circulation system. In March 1968, the library received a grant from OSTI to develop systems for acquisitions and cataloguing and to help develop the BNB MARC service.

By early 1969, the feasibility study of the acquisitions system had been carried out and the system was designed by late 1969. After discussion with interested librarians the programming for an amended design began in March 1970. A year later the computer-based system started to operate in parallel with the manual system. By August 1972, the computer system was thoroughly tested and totally replaced the old acquisitions system. There were several reasons for this rather slow development. These included:

(a) Lack of testing time on the computer, then an ICL 1901A and now an ICL 1902A.

(b) An administrative error in giving such a complex task to a single programmer.

(c) The fact that it was designed as a complete system. Because of this many special, but rarely used, routines for dealing with second-hand books, government publications, and so on were included. This was the main reason for the slow development.

The system can be described by the following steps:

(a) The collection and checking of suggestions slips and the choosing of the bookseller are the same as for the manual system.

(b) Details of suggestions are typed on to special three-part stationery using the tape-typewriter. The order and delivery note are sent to the bookseller and the bottom copy kept by the library. Southampton put much effort into the design of the stationery used in steps (a) and (b). Bookseller details are entered on the order form by coded numbers.

(c) A paper-tape is produced by the tape-typewriter which includes the MARC tags for the fields in the record. The tags used have been described earlier in this chapter.

(d) When the book is received in the library, another paper-tape including the order number, date, location, accession number and classmark is prepared.

(e) Paper-tapes of new orders, amendments to orders and books received are processed weekly in batch mode. Various processes are carried out:

(i) New orders are validated, re-arranged into a MARC format with a directory, sorted into order number sequence and added to the file of items on order.

(ii) Books on order are checked to see if reminders need to be sent to booksellers. The allocated time is eight weeks for British books and twelve weeks for foreign books.

(iii) A list of books on order and in process is printed out in author order for use in the Acquisitions Section.

(iv) All books newly accessioned are printed out in accession number order to form part of the accessions file, which forms a permanent record of books in the library.

(v) All books with classmarks are sorted into classmark order and the details are punched out on to paper-tape. This paper-tape is used to produce the Arrivals List which contains details of new arrivals before these appear in the catalogue.

(vi) Every item ordered is debited to one of the library's funds. Checks are made on the amount allocated and the amount spent or committed, and details of the fund are printed out when 95% of the allocation is spent or committed.

Other products can be produced on request, or produced at less frequent intervals. These include:

(a) Details of a particular fund.
(b) Register of donations.
(c) Register of major purchases.
(d) A list of the file in order number sequence, produced monthly.
(e) A purge of the order file, made annually. Second-hand orders outstanding for more than a year are transferred to a desiderata file. This file is sorted for distribution to booksellers.

This acquisitions system does not save on staff costs. Its main justification lies in the additional facilities it provides.

The programming, which was in COBOL and PLAN, and the analysis were done by the computer staff who are employed by the library.

REFERENCES

1. K. J. Bierman, Automated Alternatives to Card Catalogs: the Current State of Planning and Implementation. *Journal of Library Automation*, **8**, 277–97 (1975).
2. C. J. Hunt, Evaluating the performance of a computerized library system: the acquisitions system in Manchester University Library, in *The Art of The Librarian* (ed. A. E. Jeffreys), Oriel Press, Newcastle upon Tyne (1973). ISBN 0 85362 151 9.
3. L. Corbett and J. A. German, AMCOS Project Stage 2; a Computer Aided Integrated System Using BNB MARC Literature Tapes. *Program*, **6**, 1–35 (1972).
4. J. H. Lamble, P. Bryant and A. Needham, *Bath University Comparative Catalogue Study: Final Report* (9 parts), Bath University Library (1975). ISBN 0 90084 371 3.
5. R. J. Huse, The West Sussex Libraries Catalogue and Information System. *Library Association Record*, **75**, 127–30 (1973).
6. J. Becker, Computer Output Microform for Libraries. *Unesco Bulletin for Libraries*, **28**, 242–8 (1974).
7. W. Davison, Minicomputers and library automation: the Stanford experience, in *Proceedings of the 1974 Clinic on Library Applications of Data Processing* (ed. F. W. Lancaster), University of Illinois Graduate School of Library Science, Urbana (1974). ISBN 0 87845 041 6.
8. G. Davies, Computer Cataloguing in Flintshire. *Library Association Record*, **72**, 202–3 (1970).
9. R. A. Wall, M. E. Robinson and D. E. Lewis, *MINICS (Minimal-Input Cataloguing System): Development Report*, Loughborough University of Technology Library (1973).
10. M. Cooke and W. A. Gray, A Redesigned Record Structure for the Newcastle File Handling System. *Program*, **7**, 1–23 (1973).
11. R. G. Woods, *Acquisitions and Cataloguing Systems: Preliminary Report*, Southampton University Library (1971). ISBN 0 85432 055 5.

12. Report on the Working Party on Computer Filing Rules. *Catalogue and Index*, **27** 2–16 (1972).
13. J. H. Ashford, R. Bourne and J. Plaister, *Co-operation in Library Automation*, LASER, London (1975). ISBN 0 903764 05 9.
14. J. Jolliffe, *Computers and Early Books*, Mansell Information Publishing, London (1974). ISBN 0 7201 0444 0.
15. N. Higham, *Computer Needs for University Library Operations*, Standing Conference of National and University Libraries, London (1973). ISBN 0 900210 02 8.
16. J. H. Ashford, Software Cost: Making or Buying it. *Program*, **10**, 1–6 (1976).
17. C. J. Tucker, A Comparison of the Production Costs of Different Physical Forms of Catalogue Output. *Program*, **8**, 59–74 (1974).
18. C. G. Berriman and J. Pilliner, Cheshire County Library Acquisitions and Cataloguing System. *Program*, **7**, 38–59 (1973).
19. R. G. Woods, *Library Automation Project: Final Report*, Southampton University Library (1975). ISBN 0 85432 136 5.
20. B. Royan, Minicomputers in cataloguing, in *Minicomputer in Cataloguing and Circulation, Papers Presented at a One-Day Conference on 24 October 1975 at Aslib, London* (ed. J. Ross), privately circulated by John Ross, British Library Bibliographic Services Division, London (1975).

CHAPTER 7

CIRCULATION CONTROL

INTRODUCTION

Although computers were used to control the circulation of library stock in the USA in the 1960s, such systems were not operational in the UK until 1966. In that year both Southampton University Library and the library at AWRE, Aldermaston implemented computer-based circulation systems. Since then the growth of such systems has been rapid. By 1969, there were four, including the county library service at West Sussex. By 1973, there were 33 and in early 1975 it was estimated that there were 59.[1]

One of the basic features of a computer-based charging or circulation system is the recording of details about the item on loan and to whom it is loaned. In the American systems this is frequently achieved by having the book details recorded on an 80-column card and the borrower details recorded on a special badge, which is similar to a credit card. In the UK more sophisticated equipment has been developed to solve this problem. The two major manufacturers involved are Automated Library Systems (ALS) and Plessey. Their equipment, as well as other manufacturers' equipment, will be described in some detail later in the chapter. Both ALS and Plessey equipment is used to collect data for library circulation systems in many other countries, including Australia, Belgium, Canada, Denmark, France, Sweden and the USA.

Buckland and Gallivan[2] have listed the desirable features of a circulation system. In summary, these are to:

(a) link book, borrower and date information rapidly and accurately;
(b) enable rapid and easy consultation of the issue files;
(c) deal with return of reserved books;
(d) prepare overdue notices;
(e) signal overborrowing and prepare lists of books on loan to individual borrowers;

(f) detect problem borrowers at point of issue;
(g) enable rapid updating of the loans file and calculation of fines on return;
(h) facilitate collection of statistics on the system;
(i) undertake (a) to (h) reliably and economically.

These features may not pertain to all libraries and the weights placed on the various factors will need to differ depending upon the environment of the library.

Throughout this chapter the circulation of books will be referred to, but such systems usually operate equally well for slides, records and any other medium. The circulation system will be described in terms of input, files, processes and output in the same way as acquisitions and cataloguing systems were described in Chapter 6.

INPUT

As indicated above, most of the input to a computer-based charging system refers to details of books and borrowers. The books and borrowers need to be defined uniquely to the computer and so a code number is usually allocated for each book and borrower.

Book numbers

There are several ways in which libraries allocate unique numbers to loanable books in their stock.

(1) Accession numbers

These are frequently allocated anyway and so form an existing unique number for a book. Bradford University Library[3] has linked accession numbers for the same title and so the number is of the form accession number, check digit, copy number, e.g. 051648 01 02 (the check digit is formulated using the modulus 11 technique as described in Appendix III).

(2) Alphabetic random code

Most libraries use numeric characters. This is mainly because most data collection devices accept numbers and only a few limited alphabetic characters. Manchester University Library uses a five-character alphabetic code, e.g. ABJNX.

(3) ISBN and copy number

ISBNs can be used for this purpose, but most libraries feel that they are too long. A copy number must be attached as the ISBN is unique for a title, not for a copy. Pseudo ISBNs need to be allocated for books without an ISBN. Dorset County Library use this form of numbering but do not include the first digit of the ISBN, e.g. 112702694 003.

(4) Meaningful number

Brighton Public Libraries use a number of the form C 123456 1, where the first character indicates the type of item (in this case a book), the next six digits are the item number and the last is an area code.

A highly structured number capable of giving detailed management information about the use of the stock was planned for Kingston-upon-Hull City Libraries, but this scheme was dropped after local government re-organization.

(5) Random number

When using a data collection device such as ALS or Plessey it is usually necessary to prepare some form of label, identifying the unique number, which will be inserted into the book. It is usually cheaper to buy these pre-printed labels in long runs than as separate entities and when inserting the labels into the book it is usually easier to pick the next label than to find the book corresponding to the next label. Because of such reasons many libraries use 'the number on the next label' as the unique number. Brunel University use a variation of this in that they order their labels in such a way as to include copy numbers,[4] e.g. 002099 03.

(6) Title number and copy number

Some libraries link the unique numbers for the same titles by forming a title number followed by a copy number. This link is required for dealing with reservations. Oxford City Libraries use this method and the first digit indicates the type of the record, e.g. 1 580672 2.

Borrower numbers

Borrower information is sometimes obtained from other organizations within the parent body, such as the rates department or the college administrative office. In such cases the number already allocated to the person is used.

In some instances coded information is included in the borrower number to allow analysis of the use made of the library or to impose limits on the number of books loaned, period of loan, etc. In academic libraries there are frequently different loan periods for under-graduates, post-graduates and staff and so a code identifying the type of borrower is usually built in to the borrower number.

Camden Public Libraries include an alphabetic code for the branch at which the borrower registered, e.g. C081297. At Bournemouth Public Library the borrower number includes a code for the age (if under 18), a code for the house location and a code defining the borrower's status as resident, non-resident, student or employee. The London Borough of Bromley goes a step further and includes a broad code for the borrower's age, sex and occupation,[5] e.g.

A901 113—the A9 signifies a retired female or housewife;
A214 218—the A2 signifies a boy aged 5–13.

The methods used for collecting book and borrower details are described in the section on data collection units. Some libraries include more information than these codes at the input stage. The extra information is described in the section on records.

FILES

The main file in a charging system is the loans or transactions file which contains records of all books currently on loan from the collection. The interpretation of 'on loan' is usually broad and covers books being bound, in special collections, on loan to other libraries, on display, and so on. The minimal information contained in this file is the book number, borrower number and a date. Variations of this record are described in the section on records later in the chapter.

A file giving more details, such as name and address, of borrowers is necessary since overdue and recall notices should not be of the form 'Dear 2167'. If the borrower number was obtained from another source then the fuller details are often available from the same source, otherwise these details must be extracted from the borrower's registration form and converted to a machine-readable medium.

If author and title information is not included in the details input about the book then it may be necessary to have a book file. The setting up of such a file is time-consuming and costly if the catalogue system is not computer-based. However, if the file is not created, books can only be referred to by their unique number. Borrowers are then likely to come to the issue desk to enquire as to which book the number on the recall or overdue notice refers. This creates costs both in library assistants' time in checking a manual file and in creating and maintaining such a file accurately. When designing a computer-based charging system this aspect must be looked at critically to ascertain if the benefits gained from creating an author/title list justify the cost. Some libraries opt for an interim approach of forming an author/title computer file for the core of their stock that is circulating.

PROCESSES AND OUTPUT

The main processes and output of a charging system were defined in the introduction to this chapter. This section will describe how the processes are carried out in a computer-based system. This varies with the method of processing used.

Linking book, borrower and date information

The cheapest and most error-prone method of recording issues and discharges is to transcribe the details on to pre-printed forms at the issue desk. These are subsequently converted to machine-readable form and input to the computer. Most systems revert to this method in the event of equipment failure. An alternative solution is to type the information straight in to the computer using a teletypewriter or visual display unit. This obviously implies on-line access to the computer system and is feasible only when the number of transactions to be processed is not high. The library at the Ministry of Economic Affairs in Belgium uses such a system as does the Atomic Weapons Research Establishment at Foulness.[6] Most systems use data collection devices such as those described in the next section. They can be used both for on-line or batch systems. If the system is batch processed, the transactions are recorded onto some machine-readable medium. At certain prescribed times this information will be processed by the computer.

Consultation of the issue files

In a system which offers on-line access, files can be consulted by using an appropriate terminal. West Sussex County Library operates a predominantly batch system but has the facility of interrogating files on-line from the library.

Batch-processed systems have to rely on listings of the issue file. Such listings are only accurate as at the time the last batch of transactions was processed. Thus, information about current loans is not up to date and so such a system is not as good as some manual charging systems in this respect. The frequency of printing such lists is usually defined by the library staff; it might be daily, twice weekly, weekly and in some instances lists of current issues are not produced at all.

Reservations

In an on-line system reservations can be dealt with immediately by recording the fact that an item is reserved in the transaction record for the item. When the item is returned the computer notifies the assistant at the library counter that it is a reserved item and the appropriate action can be taken.

With some data collection devices a special piece of equipment known as a 'trapping-store' can be attached. The trapping-store, as its name suggests, consists of some electronic store which is capable of holding book numbers and can 'trap' books when they are returned. This is done electronically by checking the book number of a return transaction against the numbers held in the store. If the number is present then an appropriate lamp lights to inform the assistant at the library counter. Thus, the trapping-store gives some automatic control over reservations, even in a batch-processed system.

If the system is batch processed and there is no trapping-store then a list of reserved items is printed by the computer. This list must be manually checked when books are returned.

If the library possesses several copies of the same title there are several ways of defining which copy should be reserved. Some libraries link book numbers referring to the same title, so that the first copy returned can be reserved. Other libraries search the file of transactions and apply a rule (such as the copy which has been on loan longest) to decide to whom to send a recall notice.

In all situations, when the required title has been returned, a notice indicating this can be automatically produced by the computer.

Overdue notices

One of the frequently claimed advantages of computer-based charging systems is the automatic production of overdue notices, thus saving much clerical staff time. It is important, however, that some human check be made, especially in the first months of operation of a computer-based system, before the overdue notices are sent to users. It is obviously bad practice for readers to obtain overdue notices for books long since returned or, even worse, to obtain an overdue notice for an item not borrowed. The frequency of running the overdue module of the program will depend on the needs of the library. It might be daily in an academic library which has short-loan collections, or weekly or even fortnightly in a public library. Overdue notices are usually produced on a line-printer. This can be loaded with special stationery if required; Camden, for example, use postcards.

Overborrowing and production of lists to individual borrowers

Overborrowing is solved very simply in an on-line system by checking each time a book is issued that the borrower is within the limits allowed. If a borrower tries to take out too many books the computer notifies the assistant at the library counter immediately.

In a batch system this check on overborrowing can only be made after the event. Details of borrowers guilty of overborrowing will be printed out by the computer after processing the latest transaction records. Borrower numbers can also be entered into the trapping-store, and a check is made against these numbers when books are issued. In this way overborrowers are only detected the next time they borrow an item. Again, libraries running a computer-based charging system without on-line access or a trapping-store would have to rely on a list of overborrowers being printed out.

Details of books on loan to individual borrowers are retrieved by interrogation of the transactions file in an on-line system.

In batch systems this facility is usually included and forms one of the modules of the whole program system. The module would probably only be run when specified by the library. In academic libraries the question 'What books are recorded as being on loan to me?' is frequently asked towards the end of terms. It is therefore worth producing the whole transactions file in borrower number sequence at that time so that such questions can be answered immediately.

Lists of books being bound, in the short loan collection, on display, and so on can also be produced if they form part of the transactions file.

Detection of problem borrowers at point of issue

Methods of solving this are similar to those above for detecting overborrowers.

Updating of loans file and calculation of fines

All transaction records should be checked to ensure valid book and borrower numbers. When updating the loans file it may happen that there is a record of a book being returned and no corresponding record of it being issued, or that there are two records for the same book being issued and no intervening record of a return. Checks to guard against this are necessary, and details of faulty transactions should be printed out to be analysed by a member of the library staff.

Only in an on-line system is automatic calculation of fines possible.

Collection of statistics

Simple counts such as number of issues and amount of stock circulating are easily produced. If such counts are stored on the computer then analyses over a period, such as a year, can be made. If any coded information is built into either book number or borrower number then analysis of this can be done; for example, breakdown of books borrowed by category of borrower, breakdown of items borrowed by category of item, breakdown of districts within a borough from which borrowers come.

Bromley Public Library wanted to do some analysis of the use of the library by time of day and so included a 'real-time clock' in their ALS data collection unit.[5] Thus the time of the transaction formed part of the transaction record. Using the subsequent analysis they have been able to allocate staff amongst the branches more effectively.

Recently, some analysis of the archive file of all the transactions processed through the Plessey equipment at Loughborough University Library has been carried out.[7] The system has been operational since 1972, and so the archive file consisted of several hundred thousand records.

If any form of Public Lending Right is established based on a sample of issues, then libraries operating computer-based circulation systems will be able to produce the required statistics fairly easily.

Cost and reliability

The cost of operating computer-based circulation systems is described later in the chapter in the section on evaluation and costs. No equipment is 100% reliable and so suitable back-up measures, for use when the equipment fails, are necessary.

DATA COLLECTION DEVICES

As indicated earlier, several manufacturers have products which are used for collecting details of books issued and returned from libraries. The equipment can, in general, be used in batch or on-line systems. The majority of computer-based charging systems in the UK use either ALS or Plessey equipment for data collection.

ALS [8]

The first ALS system was installed at West Sussex County Library in 1967. Known as the 'card-based' system, details of book numbers and borrower numbers are punched on to cards which are the same size as Browne issue cards. The book card is stored in a pocket in the book. On issue, the book card and the borrower's card are placed in a 'reader' on the library counter. The punched information on the cards is automatically read and then punched on to a reel of paper-tape.

In mid-1971, ALS installed the first trapping-store system in Sussex University Library.[9] By 1974, an alternative to the card-based system had been developed by ALS and installed at the Bolton-le-Sands branch of Lancashire County Library. This is known as the 'label-based' system. A non-magnetic metallic label, as in Fig. 7.1, is mounted in the back of the book. On issue, the closed

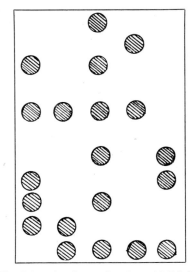

Fig. 7.1.   A schematic of an ALS label.

book is passed over a sensing device on the counter and the number represented by the metallic dots is recorded on to some machine-readable medium. The borrower card consists of a similar label and is 'read' by another sensing device. There is a separate supervisory panel for recording issues when the borrower or book card is not available (e.g. telephone renewals) and for entering and deleting book and borrower numbers to the trapping-store.

For libraries with many branches the ALS equipment can be configured so that there is only one trapping-store which communicates with the issue and return terminals over leased telephone lines. Bolton Libraries operate a sophisticated ALS system in their 22 branches.

ALS have also produced a system which is based on 80-column cards. One such system has been installed at the University of Western Australia.

Plessey [10]

The Plessey Library Pen system was the first light-pen-based system to be used in libraries. In 1972, a Plessey system was installed to collect circulation data at the Kentish Town branch of Camden Public Libraries (Camden also had an ALS data collection device at another branch—St. Pancras).

Book and borrower numbers are encoded on to bar-coded labels as in Fig. 7.2.

Fig. 7.2.   A schematic of a bar-coded label.

This label consists of a series of thick and thin lines so that when a light-sensitive device, or 'pen', is passed over the label the pattern of the lines is detected electrically. Plessey are currently offering two basic services:

(1) The 'hard-wired' system

This is similar in operation to the ALS system. Details of book and borrower numbers are 'read' by the light-pen and recorded, usually onto a magnetic tape cassette. A trapping-store can be included and also a special terminal, the 'composite' terminal, for dealing with telephone renewals and reservations. Many public and academic libraries have installed such a system.

A portable 'data capture' unit is also available which can be used to record issues and returns in mobile libraries, or to record books on the shelves when stocktaking.

(2) The 'stored program control' system (SPC)

This is a more flexible system and is designed for libraries with up to 64 branches. It differs from the 'hard-wired' system because it contains an Interdata 74 minicomputer. The minicomputer acts as an enlarged trapping-store and enhances the system's communication capacity.

The SPC system is really a hybrid system as it offers some on-line facilities but also depends on batch processing on a larger computer. A magnetic tape is usually used to transfer details of the transactions from the minicomputer to the main-frame. The London Borough of Havering was the first to install the SPC system. [11] This was in 1975 and the system controls the loans of the 10 branches. Glasgow Public Libraries are currently implementing an SPC system to control the loans in 45 branches.

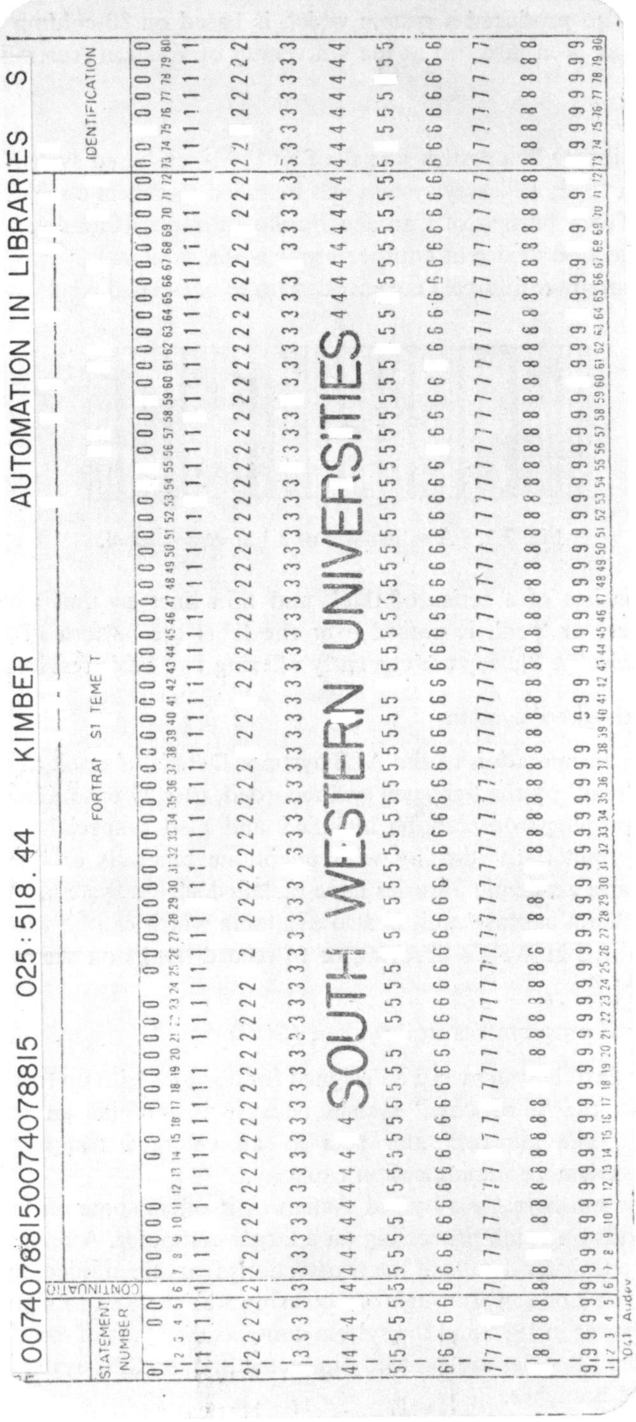

Fig. 7.3. Book card for Bath University Library.

Burroughs

Burroughs TU 100 terminals can be used for reading 80-column punched cards and badges. Bath University Library uses these connected to a Burroughs 1726 computer to operate an on-line system which is described later in the chapter. A Burroughs TU 3500 minicomputer is used as a back-up service to record details onto a magnetic tape cassette.[12] Examples of the card and badge are shown in Figs. 7.3 and 7.4.

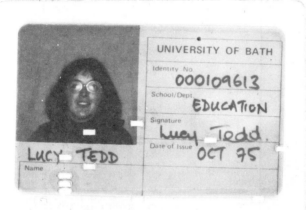

Fig. 7.4.   Borrower badge for Bath University Library.

IBM

Many of the charging systems in America use IBM 357 terminals to read 80-column cards and badges.[13]

Mills Associates

This firm designed the data collection unit in use at Lancaster University Library.[14] The book card includes some bibliographic details but is physically smaller than the 80-column card. An example is given in Fig. 7.5. Mills Associates have also produced a device to read 80-column cards, and one of these has been bought by Southampton University Library to replace their now obsolete Friden Collectadata equipment.

Rontec

This firm designed a data collection device for Bradford University.[3] Forty-column cards are used as book and borrower cards. This system is one of the few designed which allows the operator to define the loan period at the time of issue.

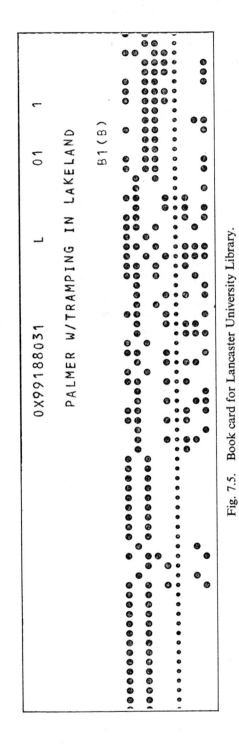

Fig. 7.5.   Book card for Lancaster University Library.

Singer

The University of East Anglia Library has recently installed an on-line charging system which uses Singer 100 Job Input Stations for capturing data to be processed by a Singer System 10 computer.[15] Book and borrower details are recorded on to 80-column cards and badges respectively.

Telepen

Telepen, which stands for teletypewriter and light-pen, was designed by S. B. Electronic Systems Ltd. The pen is of a different technical design to the Plessey pen and allows a more flexible bar-code structure. Alphabetic as well as numeric characters can be 'read' and the labels can be produced at low cost on a wide range of printers. At Cambridge University the bar-code is included, along with a Polaroid photograph, on the students general identification card.

Telepen includes a microcomputer and so the device can be used in many ways. It can be used to transmit details about transactions to a computer. Alternatively, it can be used on its own to record transactions onto a magnetic tape cassette, which can be processed later. A trapping-store function, of trapping reserved books and 'hot' borrowers, can also be included. Another system might include the transaction file itself being stored and processed by the micro-computer within the Telepen. Manchester University Library hopes to install an on-line charging system using Telepens linked to a main-frame computer late in 1976.[16] Cambridge University Library and Sheffield Polytechnic Library are both designing charging systems which use Telepens and minicomputers.

It should be pointed out that the Olivetti RP50 system which is used by some branches in Dorset, Shropshire and Staffordshire County Libraries is no longer marketed.

METHOD OF PROCESSING

Although several on-line systems have already been mentioned, the majority of currently operational computer-based charging systems are batch processed. Details of transactions are cumulated in the library on punched paper-tape or on magnetic tape cassette and processed by the computer at some specified time. The period of processing varies between twice daily, daily, twice weekly and weekly and is dependent on the library's need for up-to-date information. The computer used in most batch-processed systems belongs to the parent authority and some limitation on the frequency of processing is often made by the computer centre. The availability of trapping-stores has greatly enhanced the capability of batch-processed systems to control reserved books and 'hot' borrowers. The batch system in operation at Oxford City Library is described at the end of the chapter.

The advantages of on-line processing can be deduced from the section on processes and output. An on-line system undoubtedly keeps better control over the stock and the borrowers of a library. The charging system designers must decide whether the cost of running such a system is justified by the extra control obtained. In general, academic and special libraries have implemented on-line systems as their need for quick and accurate information on loans is perhaps greater than in public libraries.

The Atomic Weapons Research Establishment's library at Foulness operates an on-line system in a small research library. No data collection device is used as the number of transactions is fairly small. Details of transactions are typed on a teletypewriter terminal connected to an IBM 370/165 computer at Aldermaston. Overdue notices can also be produced on the terminal.[6]

Manchester University Library are in the process of implementing a fairly sophisticated on-line system. Telepen terminals are used to collect and transmit data to the Administration's Computer Unit's ICL 1902T. In case of failure of the ICL 1902T, a back-up system including two Data General Nova mini-computers has been designed.[16]

One of the problems faced by libraries wishing to operate on-line systems is the lack of available on-line facilities on the parent authority's computer. Borrowers are normally allowed to take out and return books during all the opening hours of the library. To provide such a dedicated on-line service is beyond the capabilities of many public authority and academic computer centres. To overcome the problem the hybrid approach, as suggested in Ref. 2, is often adopted. The main feature of such a system is a library-dedicated computer which offers some on-line facilities and a main-frame computer, usually belonging to the parent authority, which offers batch processing facilities.

The library-dedicated computer is often a minicomputer, as this is usually sufficient to validate and cumulate transactions, provide trapping-store capabilities for books and borrowers and provide on-line access to the loans file. The main-frame computer is used to update the bibliographic details of the loans file, do the necessary printing and provide back-up services. The capabilities of the minicomputer vary in different libraries; some merely validate transactions and act as a backing-store, whereas others keep the full loans file up-to-date. In some hybrid systems, such as at Lancaster University Library,[14] the mini-computer completely controls the short loan or reserve collection. The loan period of such a collection may be four or twenty-four hours and often the number of loans from such a collection is a high proportion of the total number of loans from the library.

Several libraries are now adopting this hybrid approach. In the public sector such systems are often based on Plessey's SPC system. Havering, for example, have a stockfile on the minicomputer which gives the current status of all stock held by the library. An example of a stockfile record is given in the next section. Issues, discharges, renewals and reservations are dealt with on-line. Every week a magnetic tape containing the transactions of the week is transferred to the Greater London Council's IBM 370/145 to update the master stockfile, which contains bibliographic information, to print the necessary notices and to produce the required management information. Many university libraries have bought their own minicomputer and data collection equipment and operate a hybrid system by using the university's main computer; Essex has a PDP8A linked to a PDP10, Lancaster a Data General Nova 1220 linked to an ICL 1905F and Newcastle plans to have a PDP 11/10 linked to an IBM 370/168.

Another solution to the lack of available 'on-line time' at the main computer has been adopted by the university libraries of Bristol, Cardiff and Exeter. They have developed a co-operative system in which minicomputers in each library are linked to a main-frame computer which is dedicated to library work. This, the SWALCAP system, is described in the examples at the end of the chapter.

RECORDS

From the descriptions of the various data collection units in a previous section it is apparent that there are basically two levels of information recorded at the input stage.

Bibliographic data contained in the book details

Most of the systems based on 80-column cards include some brief bibliographic details which subsequently form part of the transaction record. This makes the bibliographic information easily accessible when required for overdue or recall notices or when printing the file, but it increases the size of the transaction file.

Southampton University Library use 80-column cards to record details about the book. The information contained on the card includes

accession number	8 characters
author/title	54 characters
classmark	6 characters

The information included on Lancaster University Library's book card can be seen in Fig. 7.5.

Bibliographic data not contained in the book details

The majority of computer-based charging systems in the UK use data collection equipment which is capable of recording a limited number of characters. Because of this, special files containing the bibliographic data are sometimes built and the necessary links made with the book number. There are several ways in which this can be done and these are best described by examples.

(1) Loughborough University Library

Loughborough use Plessey equipment to record book numbers. When the magnetic tape is processed by the computer the bibliographic record relating to each book number is extracted from the book file to form part of the transaction record. Loughborough designed their system this way in order to use some of Southampton's software. The bibliographic details are formed by having one 80-column card, containing the accession number, author/title, location code and class number, for each title.

(2) Oxford City Libraries

Oxford form a 'mini book file' from their main file of computer catalogue records. This file contains the first 12 characters of the author's name, the first 50 characters of the title and the title number, which is the book number used by the Plessey data collection equipment. The 'mini book file' is stored in title number order and is used to extract details for printing overdue and recall notices. Oxford find this file useful for checking that there is no duplication of new title numbers and for checking queries about books referred to by a title number.

(3) West Sussex County Library

Again an integrated system is in operation and the accession number is linked to the bibliographic information by having a special link file. This is in accession number order and gives the corresponding ISBN for each accession number. The ISBN is used to access the 'all titles file' which gives the author and title information needed for printing overdue and recall notices.

It should be reiterated that not all systems, which do not include bibliographic data at the input stage, have a bibliographic file to give author and title details. Such systems are only able to refer to books by number.

As an example of the information stored about a transaction the record structure of the book files at Havering is described. The on-line stockfile stored on the minicomputer's disc contains the following information:

	Length in characters
Item number	8
ISBN or pseudo ISBN	10
Borrower number	9
Date of issue	4
Home branch	2
Away branch	2
Reservation count/marker	2
Medium code	1
Renew count	1
Link to next copy of that title	8

There is an entry in this file for all items held by the library. Immediate information on the status of an item can be retrieved by on-line interrogation of the file. A fuller record, which includes the date acquired, the number of times it has been issued, the number of times it has been bound, the date(s) of sending reminder(s) as well as the information in the on-line file, is held for each item on a magnetic tape at the main computer centre. The fuller record is 93 characters long.

Bradford University Library run a batch-processed charging system. Transaction records are only held for items which are not on the shelves in their normal location. Their record includes the book number, the copy number of reservations and the date(s) of sending the recall(s).

SOFTWARE AND SERVICES

Unlike cataloguing and acquisitions systems there are few packaged programs available for charging systems. This is probably due to the fact that charging systems are more individual and thus it is more difficult to write general programs.

One exception is the DILS package, which includes a charging subsystem. It is divided into three sections:

daily processing of issues, renewals, discharges, book queries and reservations;
weekly production of overdue notices;
stock checking.

This charging part of the DILS package is currently being tested by Sheffield City Libraries with the data being collected on Plessey equipment.

Most of the firms supplying data collection equipment do not supply software. If buying equipment from ALS, libraries are put in touch with similar libraries using ALS equipment. Plessey's SPC system includes the software for the Interdata 74 but not for the main-frame. S. B. Electronics, the firm which markets Telepen, include the programs necessary to operate the microcomputer-based system. Some manufacturers have been involved in the implementation of a system using their equipment with a view to marketing the total system, including the hardware and the software. Burroughs, for instance, did much of the programming and design (with assistance from library staff) of the Bath University Library charging system.[12]

Some operational charging systems have been implemented in other libraries. The Southampton University Library system was used in the design of Loughborough University Library's system and was implemented totally at the University of East Anglia (this was before the on-line system was operational).

EVALUATION AND COSTS

The reasons for installing computer-based charging systems vary and include:

the relief of pressure at the service points;
the ability to deal more effectively with reservations;
the ability to control the short-loan collection more efficiently;
an improvement in accuracy of loans records.

Aslin identified some measures of the existing system which can be made during the feasibility study for a computer-based charging system.[15] These measures included:

> how many loanable items are there in the library?
> how many are loaned each day?
> how does the size of the loans file vary with time?
> how many borrowers are there?
> how many reservations are made each day?
> how does the loading of the service points vary with time?
> how many branches are there?

Evaluating such measures and taking into account external factors such as computer availability and costs, an off-line, hybrid or on-line system can be chosen and designed. Buckland and Gallivan[2] estimated the capital equipment costs for off-line, hybrid and on-line systems and the ratios were 3:5:10 respectively.

Another major decision to be made when designing a computer-based charging system is the choice of equipment to be used for data collection. Some factors to bear in mind when choosing equipment are:

Cost. This must include maintenance cost as well as capital cost. Currently, maintenance cost per year is between 8 and 10% of the capital cost. The capital cost varies greatly depending on the complexity of the equipment and on the manufacturer. Detailed costs should be obtained from the manufacturer.

Facilities offered. Does it have a trapping-store capability? Does it support a full character set? How many characters are allowed for book and borrower numbers? Are variable loans possible?

Reliability. Are the manufacturer's claims borne out by other libraries using the same equipment?

Servicing. Where is the nearest servicing point? Do the maintenance engineers work on Saturdays?

Stationery. Is non-standard stationery required? If so, how is it to be produced and what are the costs?

Support. Is there any support from the manufacturer in training, systems design, programming?

The cost of a computer-based charging system consists of:

(a) Capital equipment cost of the data collection unit and/or the mini-computer for a hybrid system.

(b) Development costs. Ashford[17] estimates the effort required to program a simple batch system which includes reservations to be 5–7 man-years whereas an on-line, multi-site system would take 8–16 man-years. As well as the programming costs, the development costs incurred in the library must be taken into consideration. These include:

the effort taken to build borrower and book files;
the effort required to label books;
the re-registering of borrowers and production of new borrower cards;
the cost of the new stationery.

(c) Running cost. This includes staff, stationery, maintenance, computer and user costs.

Details of the costs involved in implementing the ALS-based system at Sussex University Library are given in Ref. 18:

		£	£ (totals)
Capital equipment		10 158	10 158
Development	Book preparation	10 050	
	Borrower registration	265	
	Systems design	6 300	16 615
Running costs/year	Maintenance	488	
	Stationery	375	
	Computer time	1 800	
	Systems maintenance	1 200	3 863

These costs are based on 1971 values.

The capital equipment cost at the University of East Anglia was £30 000 for the Singer System Ten Data Collection system. The cost of maintaining this equipment is £2160 each year.

Two papers have been published[19,20] as aids in comparing the costs of various circulation systems.

EXAMPLE 1: OXFORD CITY LIBRARIES[21]

In the late 1960s, ICL stopped maintaining the punched card sorting machine which was used by Oxford in conjunction with the photocharging system. The Deputy Librarian studied other methods of charging and decided that a computer-based system would be the best solution, although West Sussex County Library was the only public library using a computer-based charging system at that time.

From the start an integrated charging and cataloguing system was planned to control the 650 000 loans each year from the stock of about 250 000 books (representing about 110 000 titles). After a feasibility study of 6 months it took 18 months to design, analyse and install the system. Throughout this period there was close co-operation between library and computer staff. Committees were set up which included the chief systems analyst and programmers from the city's computer centre and the Deputy Librarian and professional as well as non-professional staff from the library. An interesting sideline is the fact that all meetings were recorded on to audio tape and played back by the Deputy Librarian to check on the steps that led to the acceptance or rejection of a particular plan of action. The charging system went live in May 1973 when the new Central Library opened.

There were few data collection devices being marketed at the time of the feasibility study. Oxford were against any system which depended on loose stationery after their experiences with lost transaction cards in their photo-charging system. Plessey had recently installed their light-pen system in a super-market for stocktaking purposes and it was thought that it could also be used in libraries. The public libraries of Camden, Luton, Oxford and Sutton all experi-mented with the new equipment. The simplicity of the light-pen appealed to Oxford who have been happy with their decision even though there were several 'teething' problems with the equipment.

Four issue, four discharge and two composite terminals (capable of issuing, discharging and renewing) were bought as well as a trapping-store which can currently hold about 4000 numbers. Each day's transactions are recorded on to magnetic tape cassette. If the library is particularly busy the cassette may fill up and, since it takes three minutes to change cassettes, queues can build up. Every week the cassettes are converted to $\frac{1}{2}$-in magnetic tape which is processed by the computer, currently an ICL 1902A. The loans file is updated and overdue notices produced. As explained earlier, a 'mini book file' is used to extract the author and title information for the overdue notices. A list of books currently on loan is not produced as it is not required. Some statistical analyses have been built into the system. These include analysis of readers by place of residence, analysis of issues by department, branches, fiction and non-fiction and analysis of reservations and renewals.

The form of the book number, as explained earlier, is a title number and copy number. This form was chosen for several reasons:

(a) To enable linking of copies of reserved books. When a borrower reserves a book the title number only is entered into the trapping-store. At each discharge the book number is checked against the title numbers in the trapping-store and so the first copy of the reserved book to be returned will be trapped. The title number will then be deleted from the store.

(b) To enable precise identification of records in the catalogue files.

(c) To enable amendment and deletion of stock records by title number.

There were inevitable problems at first on the software and hardware side but now everything is working smoothly and the system is being extended to Oxfordshire County. The programs are written in COBOL and PLAN.

EXAMPLE 2: BATH UNIVERSITY LIBRARY[12]

As referred to in the last chapter, Bath University Library staff were involved in the initial stages of the SWALCAP project. However, they decided to leave the co-operative system for several reasons.

In January 1973, the library and the administrative unit started negotiations with computer manufacturers. In July 1973, a Burroughs 1726 computer was ordered and Burroughs undertook to write all the software necessary for the library's charging system. The software has been designed for general use by any library.

The system went live in October 1975. Although it was not fully tested it was thought to be better than the previous slip system for controlling the 77 000 issues per year.

The book information, giving author, title, classmark and loan period, is punched on to 80-column cards which are stored in a pocket in the book. These cards were produced from the library's computer catalogue, which is processed on the main university computer, an ICL System 4-50. The cards were produced in classified order thus minimizing the time taken to prepare the stock. It took eight students ten days to process the 70 000 volumes. Some librarians are afraid of borrowers punching extra holes in cards, but Bath have not experienced this.

The borrower information is recorded onto a badge as in Fig. 7.4. Student information and numbers were gathered from the administrative unit's records to form the borrower file whereas staff information had to be converted into machine-readable form. One problem encountered with borrowers' badges involved a student who had punched a hole in his badge to keep it on his keyring!

The on-line system operates from 9.00 a.m. to 7.00 p.m. on weekdays and consists of the following features:

(a) *Loans*. The borrower's badge and book cards are entered through the Burroughs TU 100 terminals. Each transaction is checked by the 1726. If everything is all right the appropriate message is received on a strip printer, if the transaction is not all right a coded message is received on the strip printer.

(b) *Returns*. Book cards only are entered through the TU 100. Again the transaction is checked by the 1726. If the book is overdue the amount of the fine is printed, if the book is reserved a coded message is printed, otherwise an appropriate message is printed.

(c) *Reservations*. These are communicated to the 1726 via a Burroughs TD 700 VDU.

(d) *Enquiries*. These are also made via the VDU. Four types of enquiry are possible:

what books has a particular borrower on loan?
who has a particular book on loan?
what reservations are there on a particular copy, or a particular title?
when is a particular book due for return?

A back-up system is in operation from 7.00 p.m. to 9.00 p.m. on weekends and when the 1726 is not available. Loans and returns are made in the same way, but the transactions are not checked, only recorded onto a magnetic tape cassette attached to a Burroughs TC 3500 minicomputer in the library. When the 1726 is available the cassette can be read through directly in about 10 minutes. Obviously no enquiries and reservations can be handled directly when in back-up mode.

The 1726 produces various outputs including:

overdue and recall letters;
availability letters for reserved items awaiting collection;
a list of reserved books;
a list of blacklisted borrowers;
the borrower file in name order—this is used at the counter when borrowers have mislaid their card and forgotten their number;
statistical reports;
list of books being bound.

The senior library management are generally satisfied with the system's operation. The students accepted the new system readily but there have been reservations amongst the staff. Several enhancements are planned; for example, to include the short-loan (four-hour) collection, to program the TC 3500 to do some checking of transactions and to replace the charging terminals as the TU 100s are very slow.

EXAMPLE 3: SOUTH WEST ACADEMIC LIBRARIES CO-OPERATIVE AUTOMATION PROJECT (SWALCAP)[22]

SWALCAP came into being in late 1969 and currently consists of the university libraries of Bristol, Cardiff and Exeter. Between 1969 and 1972 a feasibility study was undertaken which concluded that a co-operative approach to library automation would cost half as much as individual approaches.

In 1974, the hardware was ordered. This consists of a Rank Xerox 530 computer, which is the central computer and is based at Bristol University, and terminal equipment at each of the libraries. The terminal equipment consists of a minicomputer, an Alpha LSI, a VDU and teletypewriter, and ALS data collection units. The total order was over £100 000 and some support came from the British Library Research and Development Department.

The first part of the totally integrated system to be implemented is the charging system. The book and borrower numbers are both 10 characters long and each include a check digit computed using the modulus 11 technique as explained in Appendix III. The book number contains codes for the university, the library within the university and the type of material (at present monographs and serials are included). There is no linking of book numbers referring to the same title. Both book and borrower numbers are coded onto the labels necessary for the ALS 'label-based' charging terminals. The system has the following features:

(a) *Loans*. The borrower label and book labels are read by the ALS equipment and the numbers validated by the minicomputer. The borrower number is also checked against an interception list of borrowers which is held in the minicomputer and the book number is checked by the central computer. The ALS terminal has been modified slightly; for example, a lamp lights if the book is from the short loan collection, thus aiding in correct date stamping.

(b) *Returns*. The book labels are read by the ALS equipment and a lamp lights if the book is overdue or reserved.

(c) *Reservations*. An author/title enquiry is made at the VDU and details of all copies of the title held by the library are displayed. The assistant chooses which copy to reserve and uses the VDU to make the reservation.

(d) *Other transactions*. The VDU is used for making enquiries and for other transactions. Author/title or number enquiries can be made to ascertain the current state of an item; and author/title enquiry can also be made on the union file of items held by all the participating libraries. Renewals, issuing of serials, entering borrower numbers into the interception list are some of the available transactions.

It is envisaged that the system will be on-line for the majority of the time. However, a back-up system has been devised in case of failure. If the central computer or the leased line linking the library to the central computer fails, the transactions will be recorded onto a paper-tape attached to the teletypewriter. If the ALS equipment fails then the VDU can be used to issue and discharge books. The most serious case of failure would involve the minicomputer failing and so a very reliable minicomputer was chosen.

The system is due to go live in 1976 and at present libraries are busy processing the book stock. Labels are being inserted into books and author/title details are being extracted from catalogue cards and punched onto 80-column cards to form the book file. Listings of cards punched are produced and circulated to participating libraries. Senior staff are being kept aware of progress by receiving minutes of all meetings. Junior staff have had some practical demonstrations of the equipment and more intensive training is planned. It is hoped that the staff manual will be produced co-operatively.

The system is designed in a general way so that libraries can specify their parameters to the system. These parameters include loan periods, categories of borrowers, information on overdues and fining rates.

The project is run by a central staff consisting of about five people. Two programmers have written the software for the circulation part of the system. COBOL and FORTRAN were used on the Rank Xerox 530 and assembly language on the Alpha LSI. A systems analyst has recently been appointed to do the initial design work for a shared cataloguing system.

As mentioned in Chapter 2, Rank Xerox are no longer marketing computer equipment. This decision was made after SWALCAP, in consultation with the government's Central Computer Agency, placed their order.

REFERENCES

1. R. C. Young, United Kingdom Computer-Based Loans Systems: a Review. *Program*, **9**, 102–14 (1975).
2. M. K. Buckland and B. Gallivan, Circulation Control: On-line, Off-line or Hybrid. *Journal of Library Automation*, **5**, 30–8 (1972).
3. P. Ford and G. J. Cole, The University of Bradford Library Issue System. *Program*, **6**, 295–305 (1972).
4. C. B. Beale and M. Carter, Brunel University Circulation System. *Program*, **7**, 238–48 (1973).
5. R. G. Surridge, *Management Information in the Bromley Computerised Book Charging System*, privately published by R. G. Surridge, Wallington (1974). ISBN 0 9503838 0 5.
6. B. G. Eunson, UPDATE—an On-line Loans Control System in Use in a Small Research Library. *Program*, **8**, 88–101 (1974).
7. C. G. Senior and M. E. Robinson, Management Information from an Automated Issue System: Design of an Archive File of Transactions. *Program*, **9**, 146–57 (1975).
8. Automated Library Systems. *A very informal newsletter on library automation*, **12**, 34–6 (1975).
9. R. C. Young, P. T. Stone and G. J. Clark, University of Sussex Library Automated Circulation Control System. *Program*, **6**, 228–47 (1972).
10. Plessey Library Systems. *A very informal newsletter on library automation*, **12**, 25–30 (1975).
11. D. A. Partridge, On-line Circulation Control in Havering Public Libraries. *Program*, **9**, 113–16 (1975).
12. Bath University Library. *A very informal newsletter on library automation*, **12**, 18–20 (1975).
13. *Library Circulation Control at Bowling Green State University*, International Business Machines, New York (1970).
14. B. Gallivan, University of Lancaster Hybrid Issue System. *Program*, **9**, 117–32 (1975).
15. C. Aslin, Minis in circulation, in *Minicomputers in Cataloguing and Circulation, Papers Presented at a One-Day Conference on 24 October 1975 at Aslib, London* (ed. J. Ross), privately circulated by John Ross, British Library Bibliographic Services Division, London (1975).
16. Manchester University Library. *A very informal newsletter on library automation*, **13**, 26–8 (1975).
17. J. H. Ashford, Software Costs: Making or Buying it. *Program*, **10**, 1–6 (1976).
18. N. Higham, *Computer Needs for University Library Operations*, Standing Conference of National and University Libraries, London (1973). ISBN 0 900210 02 8.
19. J. Ross and J. Brooks, Costing Manual and Computerised Library Circulation Systems. *Program*, **6**, 217–27 (1972).
20. T. K. Burgess, A Cost Effectiveness Model for Comparing Various Circulation Systems. *Journal of Library Automation*, **6**, 75–86 (1973).
21. L. White, Oxford City Libraries Computer System. *Catalogue and Index*, **32**, 8–9 (1973).
22. R. F. B. Hudson, SWALCAP On-line Circulation System: Plans and Progress. *Program*, **9**, 133–42 (1975).

CHAPTER 8

SERIALS CONTROL

INTRODUCTION

The definition of a serial which is used by the International Serials Data System (ISDS) is:

> 'A serial is a publication issued in successive parts and intended to be continued indefinitely. Serials include periodicals, newspapers, annuals (such as reports, yearbooks, directories, etc.), journals, memoirs, proceedings, transactions, etc. . . . of societies and monographic series. A serial can be in print or near print form and its parts usually have numerical or chronological designations'.[1]

The question of controlling serials by computer produces mixed reactions from librarians. Some believe that it is one of the most difficult housekeeping operations to perform by computer because of the unpredictable nature of serials, whilst others claim that it is this volatility which makes serials a good subject for control by computer. One of the reasons for such different reactions is that computers are used to control several functions of the serials system.

(a) *Bibliographic*. Lists of serials holdings are produced. This is a fairly simple system to design and implement and many libraries have experimented with the use of computers to control this function because it can be implemented independently of other housekeeping procedures.

(b) *Accessions*. This includes the selection, ordering, checking-in, renewal of subscriptions and sending of claims notices when issues are not received. Most systems use the computer to assist rather than control this function.

(c) *Inventory*. This includes the binding and circulation control of the issues of a serial.

Because of the wide variety of possible applications of computers to serials control each application will be described separately.

It should be pointed out that the majority of libraries using computers for serials control are either special libraries or academic libraries.

CATALOGUING AND LISTING

One of the main differences between cataloguing monographs and cataloguing serial publications is that the former is static whilst the latter is dynamic. Changes of name frequently occur, as do changes in period of publication and all this must be reflected in the catalogue.

Titles of serials are subject to change and so attempts have been made to allocate a unique code for each serial title. One system is known as CODEN and consists of a six-character alphanumeric code which is assigned to serials on a world-wide basis, e.g. AISJB6 is the CODEN for the *Journal of the American Society for Information Science*.

More recently, International Standard Serial Numbers (ISSNs) have been introduced. These are eight-digit numbers and, as with ISBNs, the last digit is a check digit formed using the modulus 11 technique as described in Appendix III. Unlike an ISBN, an ISSN does not contain any information. ISSNs are being allocated as part of the ISDS. ISSNs are closely linked to the 'key-title', or most commonly accepted form of the title, and when this changes so does the ISSN.

The cataloguing system obviously depends on a bibliographic record for the serial being available in machine-readable form. Examples of typical serials records are given later in the chapter. From the master file of serials records, lists in various orders, such as title, subject, location and supplier, can be produced. Selective listings by subject or location can also be produced when required. The physical form varies, as with catalogues of monographs, with COM and typesetting being used more frequently for large numbers of titles. The period between the production of complete lists varies between one month and a year, with supplementary lists of additions and deletions sometimes being produced. Several copies of serials lists are normally produced for use in branches of the library and sometimes for sale to external organizations.

Union lists of serials holdings by libraries within a geographic region are obviously useful and can be easily done by computer. Essex County Library service has been producing a union list of serials by computer since 1971. This is produced in book form and covers over 8000 titles. A similar system operates from Kingston-upon-Hull City Libraries where a union list of 4000 titles in the participating libraries is produced by computer. The region can be country-wide; for instance, the *Irish Union List of Current Periodicals* is computer produced. The region may cover several countries, and the Scandinavian countries of Denmark, Finland, Norway and Sweden plan to produce a union catalogue of serials by computer.[2]

Union lists can also be produced by subject. The DISISS (Design of Information Services in the Social Sciences) project recently completed at Bath University produced a machine-readable file of 5500 titles of serials in the social science field.[3] This was seen as being a temporary file for use until a comprehensive database of serials in all subjects and from all countries is established. The 23 libraries of the Institutes and Schools of Education in Britain have recently produced the third edition of their union list, which covers 3800 titles, of serials holdings. An interesting form of production is used which was originally devised at Southampton University Library. The machine-readable catalogue file is output on to COM and then on to hard copy. This method allows the final catalogue to be produced in upper and lower case and to have diacritics. It is also cheaper to produce the catalogue using this method than to use a line-printer or computer typesetting. In the USA the Periodical Holdings in Library School of Medicine (PHILSOM) system covers 8300 serials titles held by seven medical libraries.[4]

As with the cataloguing of books, the conversion of the bibliographic records of serials into machine-readable form can be costly and time-consuming. The BLCMP includes serials as well as monographs in its co-operative database and currently has machine-readable records of about 20 000 serials. Copies of this file have been bought by the university libraries of London, Newcastle and Utrecht and also by the UK National Serials Data Centre. In North America it was decided to build an on-line national serials data base in 1974. The project, known as CONSER (Conversion of Serials Records), will involve the three national libraries of the USA, namely the Library of Congress, the National Agricultural Library and the National Library of Medicine, as well as the National Library of Canada.[5] The goal is to convert 200 000 serials titles in the first two years. On-line access to the database will be available through the OCLC network.

ACCESSIONING

As with accessioning of monographs, the serials control system must be able to record receipt of issues, to generate claims to suppliers for items not received and to update the holdings file.

Predicting when issues are due in the library is inherently problematic with serials because of their method of publication and distribution. The July and August issues of a monthly periodical may be merged into one issue due to organizational problems in the summer months in the Northern Hemisphere. A dock strike or postal strike might cause one issue of a quarterly to arrive before another. However, if a library subscribes to, say, 5000 serials then it might expect about 100 issues to arrive daily, thus involving a fair amount of clerical processing time. Computers are usually used to assist the accessioning system and to leave the decision-making of when to send claim notices and so on to the serials librarian.

The method of recording receipt varies. Several systems are based on the following method:

(a) 80-column punched cards for all the expected issues within a period are punched by the computer and contain details of the serial title, volume, issue number, and so on—the period might be a month, three months or a year;

(b) when an issue arrives the file of punched cards is manually searched and the appropriate card extracted;

(c) if no punched card exists for the issue one is made;

(d) the punched cards, which are records of issues received by the library, are batched together and processed by the computer at intervals of perhaps a day or a week;

(e) punched cards for issues expected but which have not been received remain and appropriate action can be taken by the serials librarian.

This method is obviously economical on data preparation. The University of Gottingen in West Germany operates such a system.

A more sophisticated version splits the serials into 'regular' and 'irregular' items. Cards for regular items expected within the next period are produced with the expected volume and issue numbers, whereas incomplete cards are produced for the irregular items. The serials accessioning system at the Technical Information Department of Pfizer Inc. operates in this way.[6]

This method was devised originally at the University of California at San Diego, which was one of the first libraries to implement an automated serials system. When their collection grew to 12 000 active titles the system proved to be inefficient as there were too many cards for 'irregular' items in the file of pre-punched cards. They have modified the system so that a list of expected issues is printed by the computer each month. When an issue is received, it is checked against the printed list which gives the number in the file of the pre-punched card. The card can then be extracted quickly from the file.[7]

The methods described all depend on the computer producing an 80-column punched card. There are other systems where the information concerning an issue is translated into machine-readable form when the issue arrives. At the Bibliothèque de l'Université Laval in Quebec, Canada, an on-line method of data entry is used. When an issue arrives an assistant manually finds the unique seven-digit number for the serial title. The number is typed in on a VDU and the full details and holdings of that title are displayed. The number of the new issue is added to the master file.[8]

Loughborough University Library has been experimenting with using a Plessey light-pen for inputting data of new accessions. On issue, a bar-code representing the serial title was 'read' and, along with details of the date, was recorded on to a magnetic tape cassette. This information was processed daily by the computer and lists of arrivals were printed. The system was designed to automatically produce claims to be sent to suppliers. These claims had to be checked manually which was not satisfactory without access to an up-to-date record of past issues. The experiment ended in 1974.

A useful by-product of any automated accessioning system is the production of a list of recent accessions. This list can be circulated to users and thus forms an embryo current awareness service.

A general model to aid designers of accessioning systems in their prediction of arrivals has been formulated.[9]

SUBSCRIPTIONS CONTROL

Again computers are often used in this area to assist the serials librarian rather than control the whole system. Details of when a subscription is to be renewed are included in the master record for the serial. Every week, or month, a list of subscriptions due for renewal is produced by the computer so that the serials librarian can decide which should be renewed.

More sophisticated systems include the production by computer of the renewal notices which are sent to the supplier. The accounting function can also be included by subtracting the subscription rate from the appropriate fund when the subscription is renewed. The serials accounting is sometimes linked with the accounting for monographs. Details of the current state of the funds can be produced at any time and also historical analyses showing variation in costs, suppliers used and funds. Such analyses are useful for the serials librarian when budgeting, especially during the current inflationary period.

A computer-based serials accounting system has been operational at Stirling University Library since 1971. Selective lists by fund, supplier and country of origin are produced as well as analyses of the number of titles bought and their total and mean costs.

Loughborough University Library also operates an automated subscriptions control system. Two lists are produced each month, one showing subscriptions due in the following month and the other showing subscriptions already due but not yet paid. These have proved valuable since some publishers cease supplying periodicals when subscriptions lapse, rather than sending reminder notices. The system is also producing a guide to the rate of inflation in serial subscriptions.

The situation at the Shell Research Laboratories at Sittingbourne, Kent is probably typical of many industrial libraries. The expenditure on serials is the largest single item in the cost of the library service. A computer-based system was introduced to keep journal subscription under review and provide accurate figures of money spent during the year.[10]

BINDING

The main purpose of computer assistance in this function is to include the necessary binding decisions in the master record of each serial so that the note to be sent to the binders can be automatically produced when necessary. These decisions include the style and colour of the binding, whether the index is to be included or not and how many issues should be bound in a volume.

If the library operates an automated accessioning system, the computer can alert the serials librarian and produce the bindery notice when all the issues of a volume have been received. If the accessioning system is not automated, the expected date when all issues of a volume should have been received can be included in the master record and again the computer can alert the serials librarian and produce a bindery notice. On going to the shelves all the issues and the index can be found, hopefully, and sent to the binders.

Other functions that can be carried out include the production of a list of all volumes being bound, updating the master record when the bound volume returns (if bound and unbound volumes are differentiated) and producing a list of missing issues.

Dundee University Library has operated a serials control system since 1970. The master record includes the approximate date for binding and the file is listed by that field to assist the serials librarian in checking whether all the issues have been received.

The Kent Automated Serials System (KASS) in operation at Kent University Library also produces lists of serials that should be ready for binding.

CIRCULATION

There are two aspects of circulation control which relate to serials: first, 'routing', or sending an issue of a serial to a prescribed set of people in turn, and, second, charging and discharging serials from the library collection.

In a small special library which may serve users on different sites and which may not have enough physical space for users to come and browse in the library, the routing of serial issues is an important function. To operate such a system a list of the serials to which the library subscribes and a list of users, their location, department and details of the serials they would like to see are input to the computer. Lists of readers for each issue of a serial are produced. Ideally the list should be produced in an order which minimizes the movement of an issue between different departments and locations and also reflects the priorities which existed in the manual routing system.

The routing system forms a rudimentary selective dissemination of information (SDI) service as users are given selected information about new arrivals. The service could be extended to provide bulletins of recently received serials in various subject areas and still further to provide a full SDI service where users are sent details of articles that are specific to their needs.

Routing systems can be installed independently of any other serials control system. Libraries which have done this include the Alcan Technical Information Centre in Jamaica and the library of Pressed Steel Fisher Ltd. in Oxford. At Pressed Steel Fisher Ltd., 364 serials are circulated to 239 individuals. The system is based on a file of 80-column punched cards which contains a card for each person on each list. The file is processed by the computer to produce circulation labels, the circulation list for each circulated copy and a list of serials seen by each person.[11]

A system has been developed at Goodyear Aerospace Corporation in Akron, Ohio which controls the subscriptions and routing of serials.[12]

As already mentioned, the circulation of serials might imply charging and discharging, in which case the method employed for monographs would be used. Newcastle University Library has operated an ALS card-based system since 1973, with the accession numbers of monographs being used. Serial publications did not have accession numbers and so a unique number for each volume needed to be allocated. ISSNs were thought to be too big with copy, volume and check digits added, and so a special form of number was designed.[13] The number is of the form:

title number for the serial —5 digits
year code (76 for 1976) —2 digits
a running number to differentiate
between different volumes in a year —1 digit
modulus 11 check digit —1 digit
(see Appendix III for details)

METHOD OF PROCESSING

The majority of computer-based serials control systems operate in batch mode. This is usually perfectly adequate for the production of lists at fairly infrequent intervals. There are instances of on-line processing being used for some functions.

Updating the master serials file

In cases where records have to be amended frequently, on-line access is used to update the master file. The Biomedical Library of the University of California at Los Angeles operates an integrated serials control system for its 6500 current titles. The system includes the production of lists of holdings, claims letters for issues not received and bindery notices. Until 1971 the system was batch processed, which involved weekly processing of the 80-column punched cards for each amendment. This system was not efficient when 15% of the records needed to be amended each week and so an on-line system was designed. Records are now updated and verified using VDUs connected on-line to the computer. Significant savings in cost and time have been achieved with the on-line system (despite a doubling in computer costs) as well as an improvement in the accuracy of records. A comparison and cost analysis of the batch and on-line systems has been reported.[14]

As already mentioned, the Bibliothèque de l'Université Laval in Quebec operates an on-line serials control system. The system is known as CAPSUL,

Computerized Access to Periodicals and Serials or Controle Automatise des Periodiques et Publications en Serie. Five VDUs, three of which are in the main library and two in major faculty libraries, are used to update the master records of some 19 000 serial titles.

Searching the serials file

Several serials files which are available on an on-line system can be searched.

The CONSER file which will be available through the OCLC system is one example. Another is the SERLINE file available on the MEDLINE system operated at the National Library of Medicine in the USA (more details on MEDLINE are given in Chapters 9 and 11). SERLINE is a union list of some 6500 titles of medical serials held by over 100 libraries.[15]

A union catalogue of serials is planned for 45 libraries of London University. It is hoped that access to this file will be available on-line.

Circulating serials

The AWRE system referred to in Chapter 7 is an on-line system used for the charging and discharging of serials.

BIBLIOGRAPHIC RECORD

The details included in the bibliographic record vary depending on the part of the serials system being controlled or assisted. Many systems use a fairly simple fixed field format, although libraries producing large union catalogues of serials often use a MARC-based record. As in Chapter 6, solutions adopted by different libraries are described.

Sunderland Polytechnic [16]

The library at Sunderland Polytechnic produces a list of the 1200 journals taken. Up to nine 80-column punched cards are used to describe each title (in practice not more than four cards have ever been used). The cards contain the following information:

> title, class number and location information (1 card);
> details of holdings (up to 6 cards);
> references, such as SEE references, and changes of title (up to 2 cards).

Moraine Valley County Community College, Illinois [17]

The library at this college operates an integrated system to control its 715 serials. The system generates subscriptions, sends claims, records subscription histories as well as producing a list of holdings. The details are recorded on to twelve 80-column punched cards using a fixed field format.

Loughborough University of Technology Library

After experimenting with a fixed field structure in their Periodicals Data System, Loughborough have now developed the MINICS format. This was described briefly in Chapter 6. It is a MARC-type structure which is more suited for local processing than the more general MARC format. MINICS is suitable for describing monographs as well as serials.

Loughborough have also been involved with BLCMP in designing a MARC-based system for serials. The result is MASS (MARC-based Automated Serials System) which is used to describe all the serials in the BLCMP database.[18]

University of California at Los Angeles (UCLA)

As was mentioned in the previous section, the Biomedical Library at UCLA operates a serials control system of its 6500 titles. The record format used is a mixture of fixed and variable fields. There are two fixed fields and an average of eight tagged variable length fields. The average length of records is 400 characters.

University of California at Berkeley (UCB)

The library at UCB has built up a serials database of some 200 000 records. These are structured using the MARC format. Up to 150 separate fields of variable length are allowed, within an overall maximum of 7200 characters, in one record. Details of the MARC fields used are given in Ref. 19. A MARC format is also being used to build the Minnesota Union List of Serials (MULS).[20] Both the MULS and the UCB databases are being used to form the CONSER file which will also be in a MARC format.

ISDS record

Records of serials included in the ISDS are fairly simple, but conform to MARC standards. The simplicity is due to the fact that the record is aimed at uniquely defining the serial (in cases where the ISSN is unavailable) and not at providing a full catalogue record. The elements included in the record are ISSN, key-title, variant titles, abbreviated title, imprint, start and finish dates of publication, frequency, country of origin and a field which links with records of associated serials, such as former and successor titles and supplements.

SOFTWARE AND SERVICES

Since many systems are based on individually designed fixed field record structures, interchange of programs to control serials systems has been limited. One exception is the Periodicals Data System (PDS) which was developed at Loughborough University Library. This produces lists of holdings, a subject index, a corporate body index and a shelf number list.[21]

The programs are written in COBOL. The libraries at the New University of

Ulster and Wolverhampton Polytechnic make use of the package in their serials control systems.

Another package designed specifically for periodicals control is PERDEX, Periodicals Index. This was designed at the Organics Division of ICI and is now used by many libraries within ICI.

A PERDEX record contains standard information on each title as well as local information such as holdings, location and circulation details. Each title is identified by a unique number which appears in ICI's *Combined List of Periodicals*. Using this number, libraries building their own PERDEX files can extract the standard information from a master file. The package is fairly comprehensive and is of particular use in special libraries. PERDEX can be used to:

> produce lists in title, subject, sponsoring body and CODEN sequence;
> order and renew subscriptions;
> produce a list of items to be bound;
> control circulation (or routing) of serials;
> produce disposal instructions.

A subscription accounting system is also being developed.

PERDEX programs are mainly written in PL/I and run on IBM 360 or 370 computers.

The union catalogue of the serials holdings of the libraries of London University is being developed using the TeleMARC software designed by Telecomputing Ltd.

In the UK, the National Serials Data Centre (NSDC) has been formed as part of the ISDS.[1] It is foreseen that this will offer services such as:

> giving aid to libraries involved in the conversion of serials catalogues by providing machine-readable records;
> being an access point to an international network of serials publications and the ISDS;
> providing a computer-based information service on the holdings of serials throughout the country (this would be an extension of the *British Union Catalogue of Periodicals*).

In North America on-line access to serials records will be available via the CONSER data base on OCLC.

INTERNATIONAL SERIALS DATA SYSTEM

In 1967, the world science information system, known as UNISIST, was set up. It was realized by the working group on bibliographic descriptions that an internationally accepted coding system for serials was necessary. An effective system for compiling and disseminating information on serials was also needed. Thus, at the sixteenth general conference of UNESCO it was resolved to set up an International Serials Data System (ISDS) within the UNISIST Programme.[22] An international centre was set up in Paris and UNESCO member states were expected to set up national or regional centres to be responsible for serials published in their respective countries. The aims of the ISDS are six-fold:

(a) to develop and maintain an international register of serial publications;
(b) to define and promote the use of international standard serial numbers;
(c) to facilitate the retrieval of scientific and technical information in serials;
(d) to make this information currently available to all countries, organizations or individual users;
(e) to establish a communications network between libraries, secondary information services, publishers of serial literature and international organizations;
(f) to promote international standards for bibliographic descriptions, communications formats and information exchange in the area of serials publications.

Over 20 national centres have been set up including those in Argentina, Australia, Canada, France, Japan, the USA, the USSR, West Germany and the National Serials Data Centre in the UK. These national centres are responsible for the registration of serials published in their countries. At present most are concentrating on the registration of newly published serials. It is at the time of registration that the ISSN is allocated to the key-title of the serial.

An initial large-scale assignment of ISSNs was made by authorizing the Bowker Publishing Company to allocate ISSNs to entries in the *Ulrich's International Periodicals Directory* which it publishes.

The International Centre in Paris is compiling a master file of information on serials which is known as the ISDS Register. The initial records in this file came from merging records of the machine-readable files of some abstracting and indexing services. Details of the registration of new and changed titles are sent from the national centres to the International Centre where they are added in to the ISDS Register. Details are also published in the *ISDS Bulletin*.

There are the inevitable communication problems of a large network within the ISDS. Guidelines, standards and procedures are continuously being developed.

EXAMPLE 1: THE BELGIAN UNION CATALOGUE OF PERIODICALS[23]

In 1965, a union catalogue of the foreign periodicals available in libraries in Belgium and Luxembourg was produced by the Royal Library in Brussels. This covered 46 000 periodicals in 250 libraries. After the publication of the catalogue it was decided that as the number of periodicals and libraries was increasing, subsequent editions of the catalogue would be computer-produced. In 1975, the first supplement appeared and this covered 28 000 periodicals in 300 libraries.

Details of the libraries' holdings are punched on to 80-column cards. The information on the cards includes

title;
sub-title;
series;
references to the bibliographic evolution of the serial, i.e. previous titles;
references to parallel titles, translations and editions in different languages;
holdings of the library;
place and date of edition.

The information is stored internally in the computer using a special record structure which was developed at the Royal Library of Belgium for the production of catalogues in the Quetelet Fonds Library. The structure is known as FBR (Forma Bibliothecae Regiae). The cataloguer inserts the necessary codes to indicate parts of the record on which special action is taken. Such action might be specifying which characters are not to be included in the printing or filing of the record or specifying which characters should be entries in a keyword index. A description of the record structure is given by Goossens.[24] The format is economical in storage space and allows for fast processing.

The programs are written in assembly language for a Siemens 4004/135 computer. There are four main steps in the programming system:

(a) inputting and validating the records;
(b) creating the internal format for each record;
(c) sorting records into alphabetic order;
(d) preparing the file for output.

At present the output is produced on to COM fiche by a bureau. 42x reduction is used and the supplement covers nine microfiche. The cost is $4 for a master microfiche and $0.25 for a copy. An enriched character set is used which includes upper and lower case and diacritics. If users of the supplement react unfavourably to COM the form of output may be changed for the production of the next cumulated edition.

Apart from the production of the catalogue in title order, several other products are possible:

(a) the catalogue in corporate author sequence;
(b) subset catalogues by language or library;
(c) A KWIC (Keyword In Context) index to the titles (the KWIC method of indexing is described in Chapter 9).

It is hoped that the whole catalogue will be computer-produced in time. To aid more rapid amendment of records, on-line access is being investigated. The bibliographic description might be upgraded to include ISSNs or CODENs and also some subject approach, either by UDC or keyword indexing. This would enable the production of subset catalogues by subject.

The Royal Library currently operates a selective dissemination of information service and the possibility of linking the periodicals file to this is being studied. Then, participants would be told not only of relevant articles but also of libraries where those articles might be found.

EXAMPLE 2: UNITED KINGDOM ATOMIC ENERGY RESEARCH ESTABLISHMENT AT HARWELL[25]

In the early 1960s, a periodicals listing system was in operation in the library using 80-column punched cards. The cards were sorted, collated and printed by a tabulator machine. By 1968 a computer was being used and the system has been described.[26]

The input medium is still 80-column cards and the records are formatted using fixed fields. The entry for a periodical title consists of:

Title card(s). This gives the serial number, title and CODEN. A continuation card can be used which allows up to 132 characters for the title. This field may include references to translations or later titles.

Holdings and subscription information card. Details on this card include holdings (first year and volume for current subscriptions, first and last years for closed subscriptions), UDC classification number, subscription rate, country of origin and binding code.

Locations card(s). The number of copies of the title held by each location is specified.

The output is produced on line-printer paper and various listings are possible. These include:

A complete print-out in title order, including cross-references and closed entries, of periodicals held (there are about 2000). This list is updated every two months.

A list of titles which are bound.

A list of the holdings of the divisional libraries.

A holdings list which is produced for publication. A subject index by UDC is also produced.

Listings by several fields, e.g.

a list of the periodicals subscribed to and standing orders sent to the main supplier (this is produced twice a year);

a list of standing orders sent to Her Majesty's Stationery Office (this is produced three times a year);

a list of holdings by country of origin.

The programs are written in PL/I and run on an IBM 370/165.

A computer-based loans system (COBLOS), which covers periodicals and other types of document, is also run by the library.[27] COBLOS is a batch-processed system and details of the loan are recorded on to a teletypewriter (off-line) which has a paper-tape attachment. The paper-tape of transactions is then processed by the computer which produces a list of current loans and reservations every two days.

Periodicals are identified by the CODEN, volume number, part number and date of publication. As this is insufficient information to include on recall notices a periodicals file linking the CODEN to the title is necessary. This file was generated by and is updated by the computer-based periodicals system. Various statistical analyses, including the number of periodicals loans each month and the number of loans of each periodical title by division every six months, are made.

REFERENCES

1. P. M. Woodward, The National Serials Data Centre. *Program*, **9**, 158–65 (1975).
2. B. Bernhadt, A Union Catalogue of Serials in Scandinavian Libraries. *Libri*, **25**, 1–12 (1975).
3. R. G. Bradshaw *et al.*, CLOSS (Check List of Social Science Serials): a Machine-Readable Data Base of Social Science Serials. *Program*, **8**, 29–39 (1974).
4. P. Mayden, The PHILSOM network: the co-ordinator's viewpoint, in *Proceedings of the LARC Institute on Automated Serials Systems* (ed. H. W. Axford), The LARC Association, Tempe, Arizona (1973). ISBN 0 88257 097 8.
5. L. G. Livingston, The CONSER Project: Current Status and Plans. *Network*, **2**, 16–17 (1975).
6. M. E. D. Koenig *et al.*, SCOPE: a Cost Analysis of an Automated Serials Record System. *Journal of Library Automation*, **4**, 129–40 (1971).
7. D. Bosseau, Case study of the computer assisted serials system at the University of California, San Diego, in *Proceedings of the LARC Institute on Automated Serials Systems* (ed. H. W. Axford), The LARC Association, Tempe, Arizona (1973). ISBN 0 88257 097 8.
8. R. Varennes, On-line Serials System at Laval University Library. *Journal of Library Automation*, **3**, 128–41 (1970).
9. A. N. Grosch, Serial Arrival Predicting Coding. *Information Processing and Management*, **12**, 141–6 (1976).
10. G. Griffin, Computer Handling of Periodical Subscriptions and Holdings at Shell Research, Sittingbourne. *Program*, **3**, 120–6 (1969).
11. D. J. Campbell and M. Morton, Computerising the Recording and Control of Periodical Circulation in an Industrial Information Service. *Program*, **5**, 19–25 (1971).
12. A. N. Yerkey, Computer-Assisted Periodical Routing and Renewal Audit. *Special Libraries*, **64**, 126–9 (1973).
13. R. Fern, Periodical Volume Identification for an Automated Issue System. *Program*, **7**, 147–51 (1973).
14. J. Fayollat, On-line Serials Control in a Large Biomedical Library. Part III: Comparison of On-line and Batch Operations and Cost Analysis. *Journal of the American Society for Information Science*, **6**, 80–6 (1973).
15. C. C. Quintal, SERLINE: on-line serials bibliographic and locator system, in *Proceedings of the LARC Institute on Automated Serials Systems* (ed. H. W. Axford), The LARC Association, Tempe, Arizona (1973). ISBN 0 88257 097 8.

16. J. R. Haylock, Library Automation at Sunderland Polytechnic. *Program*, **8**, 209–14 (1974).
17. V. Harp and G. Heard, Automated Periodicals System at a Community College Library. *Journal of Library Automation*, **7**, 83–96 (1974).
18. *BLCMP MASS Manual. Input Procedures for Serials Cataloguing*, Birmingham Libraries Co-operative Mechanisation Project (1973). ISBN 0 903154 04 8.
19. S. M. Silberstein, Computerized Serial Processing System at the University of California, Berkeley. *Journal of Library Automation*, **8**, 299–311 (1975).
20. A. N. Grosch, The Minnesota Union List of Serials. *Journal of Library Automation*, **6**, 167–81 (1973).
21. A. J. Evans, R. A. Wall and J. C. Mackay, *Periodicals Data Automation Project*, Loughborough University of Technology Library (1969).
22. C. J. Koster, ISDS and the Functions and Activities of National Centres. *UNESCO Bulletin for Libraries*, **27**, 199–204 (1973).
23. G. Goudeme *et al.*, The Belgian Union Catalogue of Periodicals. *Information Processing and Management*, **12**, 161–4 (1976).
24. P. Goossens, Techniques for Special Processing of Data Within Bibliographic Text. *Journal of Library Automation*, **7**, 168–82 (1974).
25. K. R. Greenhalgh and S. M. Bishop, Revision of the Periodical Records System at AERE Library, Harwell. *Program*, **6**, 248–57 (1972).
26. S. M. Bishop, Periodical Records on Punched Cards at AERE Library, Harwell. *Program*, **3**, 11–18 (1969).
27. C. W. J. Wilson and K. R. Greenhalgh, AERE Library Computer Based Loans System—COBLOS. *Program*, **5**, 89–118 (1971).

CHAPTER 9

COMPUTER-PRODUCED INDEXES

INTRODUCTION

Computers began to be used to aid information retrieval systems in the 1960s and the first applications were in the production of indexes. Applications in other areas of information retrieval are covered in the following two chapters. The term information retrieval will refer to the retrieval of information about documents as this is of primary interest to librarians.

An index to a document collection normally consists of the following:

A lead term. This is the entry point to the index. The index is usually arranged in alphabetic or numeric sequence of lead terms.
The context. This describes the way in which the lead term is considered.
Link. This might be the bibliographic details or a key to another index.

If the link contains the bibliographic or other necessary details, the index is referred to as a 'one-stage' index. The index at the back of this book is an example of a one-stage index. On the other hand, an index which provides a link to another index or list is known as a 'two-stage' index. The subject index to the classified catalogue in a library is an example of a two-stage index. The searcher uses the subject index to find the classification number used by the library to describe the books on a particular subject. The classified catalogue must then be used to find details of the books themselves. There are many organizations which produce indexing and abstracting journals to the literature of a particular subject. These are obviously of immense help to researchers and anyone needing information on recently published material.

Librarians, therefore, come across indexes of several types; for example, published indexes to broad collections, in-house produced indexes of fairly narrow collections and indexes to books themselves.

Computers can be used to format the entries in a printed index and also to generate the entries for an index. The latter is done by either deriving keywords from the bibliographic description or assigning keywords to describe the document. Experiments into fully automatic indexing and classification systems have and are being carried out.

Attempts at automatic indexing usually depend on the original text being available in machine-readable form. The indexing is then achieved by carrying out statistical analyses on the text. Such analyses are often based on word frequencies. Weights (or numbers) are then allocated to the words in accordance with the result of the analyses. These weights are used when searching for relevant documents. At Cornell University, the SMART system is an example of an experimental system which uses automatic indexing techniques to generate a set of content identifiers which are subsequently used in the retrieval process. [1]

This chapter will be limited to the use of computers in the generation and production of indexes which are manually searched.

MACHINE-FORMATTED INDEXES

In such systems the decision as to which terms or codes are to be used to describe the document is taken by the indexer or cataloguer and the computer is used to sort, reformat, update, cumulate and print the index.

A computer-produced library catalogue, as described in Chapter 6, is one example of a machine-formatted index. The cataloguing process of defining the author, title, imprint and classification number is carried out by the cataloguer and the computer is used to produce the catalogue in the required orders. In most library catalogues one number, the classification number, is used to describe the subject of the document. Thus, it is necessary for a library to produce a subject index to the classification numbers which it has used. Several libraries have a computer-produced subject index to their classification scheme. Aston University Library, for instance, has been producing its subject index by computer since 1967. One 80-column punched card is used for each subject entry. The index is produced once a term and gives an alphabetic list by subject which is used by readers and staff. A list in classification number order is also produced for the cataloguing staff to see the subjects described by a particular classification number.

Some alphabetical subject indexes consist of a list of subject headings and a link which refers to the number of a document (or documents) which is (or are) described by the subject heading. This sort of index is known as a co-ordinate index.

An extension of such an index is the dual dictionary. This consists of a co-ordinate index which has been duplicated and the two copies mounted side-by-side. With this format, searches on two terms can easily be made. The subject index to the *Catalog of Selected Documents on the Disadvantaged* produced by the Educational Resources Information Center (ERIC) is in this form.

The terms or subject headings used to describe the documents may be drawn from a controlled vocabulary (a thesaurus) or be the free choice of the indexer.

The work of the producers of indexing and abstracting journals has rapidly increased with the exponential rise of journal articles since the 1940s. In order to minimize the searcher's time such indexing journals need to be cumulated quarterly, annually and five-yearly. Consequently, many of these journals are produced using computer-driven photo-composition equipment.

It was soon realized that the bibliographic information about the articles, once in machine-readable form, could also be used for computer-searched systems. Therefore, many organizations which produce printed indexing and abstracting journals also sell their collection, or database, of bibliographic records. Some examples of printed indexes and their related databases are given in Table 9.1.

TABLE 9.1

Printed source	Database name*	Producer
Bibliography and Index of Geology	GEOREF	American Geological Society
Biological Abstracts	BIOSIS Previews	Biosciences Information Services
BNB Weekly List	MARC	BLBSD
Bulletin Signalétique	Bulletin Signalétique	Centre National de la Recherche Scientifique, France
Chemical Abstracts	Chemical Abstracts Condensates (CACON)	Chemical Abstracts Service
Drug Literature Index	DRUGDOC	Excerpta Medica Foundation
Engineering Index	COMPENDEX	Engineering Index Inc.
Index Medicus	MEDLARS	National Library of Medicine
INIS Atomindex	INIS	International Atomic Energy Agency
Psychological Abstracts	PAIS	American Psychological Society
Resources in Education	ERIC	US National Institute of Education
Science Abstracts	INSPEC	Institution of Electrical Engineers, London

* See acronym list (p. 198) for full details of name.

Another type of index that falls into the machine-formatted category is the citation index. The items referred to in an article are included in the index and arranged so that searches can be made on them. Thus, by searching an early document, which then becomes an indexing term, all later papers citing that document can be retrieved, thus giving more current articles on that subject. The two major citation indexes are the *Science Citation Index* and the *Social Sciences Citation Index*. Both are produced by the Institute for Scientific Information in the USA and again databases are available for computer searching.

As can be seen, most of these indexing and abstracting services cover the scientific or social scientific fields.

KWIC-TYPE INDEXES

The most widely used form of machine-generated index is the KWIC-type index. KWIC is an acronym for Key Word In Context. H. P. Luhn, of IBM, was the first to produce such an index by computer when he produced an index to the titles of articles appearing in *Chemical Abstracts* in 1961. The index was seen primarily as a current-awareness tool. In a KWIC-type index an entry for a document is made under each keyword in the title of the document. A book entitled *An Introduction to Computer-Based Library Systems* might be referred to under the lead terms *computer* and *library* in the index. Obviously the computer must be told how to derive the keywords, these being the words which characterize the subject. There are three ways in which this might be done.

Stop-list

A list of words, which are not required as keywords, is given to the computer. A program compares each word in the title with each word in the stop-list and if no match occurs then that word is assumed to be a keyword. For example, if *an, introduction, to, systems* are included in the stop-list, then *computer-based, library* would be keywords of the title of this book.

Go-list

This is the opposite of a stop-list in that the computer is given a list of words which will be required as keywords. A program compares each word in the title with each word in the go-list and if there is a match then it is a keyword.

Manual tagging

The words that are required as keywords, or key phrases, are tagged in some manner at the input stage. This involves more human processing but usually creates a better index. A technique known as nested tagging can also be used. For example,

if * were inserted in the input record to delimit a keyword or phrase then: *An introduction to * computer-based ** library * systems* would produce entries under *computer-based* and *library*.

Or if £ were used to indicate a nested key phrase then:

An introduction to £ computer-based library systems £ would produce entries under *computer-based library systems, library systems* and *systems*.

Having worked out the lead terms the computer must then sort the keywords into alphabetic order and format and print the index.

The format of KWIC-type indexes varies. The original format consisted of the keyword being printed in context, i.e. the preceding and succeeding words, as many as the allotted space would permit, were also printed. A reference number to another list giving full bibliographic details of the document is also included.
Example
Given a width of 40 characters for the entry, the entries for 'library' for the following three books:

1. An introduction to computer-based library systems
2. Computer needs for university library operations
3. Clinic on library applications of data processing

would be as follows.

Index 1—KWIC

CLINIC ON	LIBRARY APPLICATIONS.	3
EDS FOR UNIVERSITY	LIBRARY OPERATIONS.	2
TO COMPUTER-BASED	LIBRARY SYSTEMS.	1

To make maximum use of the space available the title is sometimes 'wrapped around' to give:

Index 2—KWIC

OCESSING. CLINIC ON	LIBRARY APPLICATIONS	3
EDS FOR UNIVERSITY	LIBRARY OPERATIONS . C	2
TO COMPUTER-BASED	LIBRARY SYSTEMS . AN I	1

Usually the space available is more than 40 characters and so the entries become a little more meaningful. Line-printer paper is often 132 characters wide and this is used to determine the width of the KWIC index entry. With this format each entry takes up only one line, and the title appears once under each keyword. Each entry therefore consists of the index word, the context and a reference number. In an alternative format the lead term appears at the left-hand side of the page, instead of in the middle.

Index 3—KWIC

LIBRARY APPLICATIONS OF DATA PROCESSING	3
LIBRARY OPERATIONS . COMPUTER NEEDS FOR UN	2
LIBRARY SYSTEMS . AN INTRODUCTION TO COMPU	1

A variation on this is to bring the keyword out of context and replace it by a symbol, say *, in the title. The original idea of using a replacement symbol instead of the index term was to save space.

Index 4—KWOC

LIBRARY

AN INTRODUCTION TO COMPUTER-BASED*SYST	1
CLINIC ON*APPLICATIONS OF DATA PROCESS	3
COMPUTER NEEDS FOR UNIVERSITY*OPERATIO	2

This format is known as KWOC or Key Word Out of Context.

There is another variation, which is similar to KWOC, called KWAC or Key Word And Context. In this index the keyword remains in the title. It should be pointed out that KWACs are sometimes referred to as KWOCs.

Index 5—KWAC

LIBRARY

AN INTRODUCTION TO COMPUTER-BASED LIBR	1
CLINIC ON LIBRARY APPLICATIONS OF DATA	3
COMPUTER NEEDS FOR UNIVERSITY LIBRARY	2

There are many variations on this method of index production.[2] One of these is the Double-KWIC format.[3] This is basically a KWAC index with a left-handed KWIC (!). Given the key-phrases for each title to be

computer-based, library, systems
computer, university, library
data processing, applications, library

there is an entry for all other key-phrases under the lead term for one key-phrase.

Index 6—Double-KWIC

LIBRARY

APPLICATIONS OF DATA PROCESSING.CLIN	3
COMPUTER NEEDS FOR UNIVERSITY LIBRAR	2
COMPUTER-BASED LIBRARY SYSTEMS.AN IN	1
DATA PROCESSING.CLINIC ON LIBRARY AP	3
SYSTEMS.AN INTRODUCTION TO COMPUTER-	1
UNIVERSITY LIBRARY OPERATIONS.COMPUT	2

This method greatly increases the size of the index. But, if there are many entries under one lead term, it sub-divides the entries and so would cut down the search time. Brooke Bond Liebig Services Ltd. produce such an index to periodical articles, books and reports.

The KWIC-type method of indexing is used by many special libraries for indexing reports, technical literature, patents, journals and books. Some academic libraries also make use of the technique.

Bath University Library produce a KWOC index to the titles in their catalogue. (Note: This index is really a KWAC but will be referred to here as a KWOC because that is the terminology used at Bath.) Keywords are derived by using a stop-list with the stop-words being automatically derived by computer program. Any word of more than two characters is included in the stop-list if it appears more than 30 times in the titles of the catalogue. Words of one or two characters are automatically stop-words and words of more than 14 characters are automatically keywords. The stop-list consists of about 500 words. The index for 70 000 titles has about 250 000 entries. Liverpool Polytechnic Library's KWAC index is described in the examples at the end of the chapter.

This method of indexing can be used for personnel files, marketing data and in many other instances. An index to the *Proceedings of the Public Inquiry on the Greater London Development Plan* was produced using this technique. Limited time, a need for multiple copies and the large volume of material were factors which led to the decision to use a KWIC-type index. The index is produced on COM and accompanies the transcripts of the proceedings which are on microfiche.[4]

The Building Research Establishment uses this technique for producing lists of the journals held in the library. The lists are produced in title, subject, country of origin, frequency of publication and supplier sequence by using a program for producing KWIC-type indexes.[5]

There are disadvantages in using this method of indexing. The main disadvantage is the heavy reliance made on words in the title, which can be misleading and uninformative. KWIC-type indexes are usually used for scientific and technical literature which, in general, does have informative titles. The problem can be overcome by enriching the title with extra keywords at the input stage.

The Technical Information Systems department of the Strip Mills Division of the British Steel Corporation uses a modified KWIC-type system.[6] A string of keyword identifiers are added after each title. Two symbols can be used to link keywords so that both indexing time and the number of entries in the index are reduced. For example:

(a) INDEX £ PRODUCTION
 gives an entry for *index* with *production* as a sub-heading.
(b) COMPUTER & CATALOGUE
 gives two entries. Firstly *computer* with a sub-heading *catalogue* and secondly *catalogue* with a sub-heading *computer*.

INDEXES GENERATED BY STRING MANIPULATION

There are several techniques for manipulating strings of document descriptors, which are prepared by indexers, to produce indexes. Three examples of indexes produced by string manipulation will be described in this section.

Articulated subject indexes

A subject description of the document is written in a sentence-like manner, perhaps using words chosen from a controlled vocabulary. The words or phrases which are to be lead terms in the index are indicated in some manner by the indexer.

Example: Teaching of computers in Welsh schools   1.

This sentence-like structure describes the subject of the document. The sign < > is used by the indexer to delimit keywords and so the input record looks like

<teaching> of <computers> in <Welsh <schools>>

The structure of the phrases is analysed, particularly in regard to the positions of the prepositions and the connectives, and the following entries are generated:

Teaching
   of computers in Welsh schools   1
Computers
   teaching of, in Welsh schools   1
Welsh schools
   teaching of computers in   1
Schools, Welsh
   teaching of computers in   1

The indexes to the *World Textile Abstracts* and the *Safety in Mines Research Establishment Bibliography* are produced using this method.[7]

British Technology Index (BTI)

This alphabetic subject index is a one-stage index which contains subject headings as well as bibliographic details of technological articles. The input details for a document include a string of subject headings and punctuation marks which symbolize the relationships between the subject headings. 'See' and 'see also' references are generated from the input details by using a machine-readable thesaurus.

The production of the BTI has been computer-assisted since 1968. It is produced monthly and is computer typeset.[8]

PRECIS

PRECIS stands for *Pre*served *C*ontext *I*ndex *S*ystem.[9] It is a two-stage index (usually), with structured entries. The input details include a string of concepts written in a pre-determined order and linked by special operators, which are known as role operators.

PRECIS was developed at the British National Bibliography in the late 1960s to meet demands for a new indexing system for the UK MARC team. From the beginning it was decided that the computer and not the indexer should generate all the index entries. The development work was carried out under a grant from OSTI.

A typical PRECIS entry might look like:

Libraries . Europe
        Information services. Applications of digital computer systems—
                         Conference proceedings   13590

Other entries in the index for the same document would include:

Digital computer systems
        Application in information services. Libraries. Europe—
                         Conference proceedings   13590
Information services. Libraries. Europe
        Application of digital computer systems—
                         Conference proceedings   13590

In general terms a PRECIS entry consists of the items shown in (**I**)

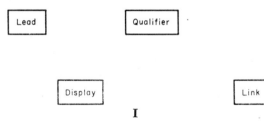

I

The computer also generates the 'see' and 'see also' references.

PRECIS strings are now included in the UK MARC record and are used to produce the subject index to the *British National Bibliography*.

Several public and academic libraries which subscribe to the BLBSD Full Catalogue Service have established PRECIS indexes to the more recent part of their collection. East Sussex Libraries and the libraries of the City of London Polytechnic and the Polytechnic of Central London are examples of such libraries.

PRECIS indexes to various bibliographies of non-book materials have been produced. In 1976, the citations in the *British Education Index* will be arranged under PRECIS-derived subject headings. In the British Library's Department of Printed Books the catalogue of the current European intake also has its entries arranged under PRECIS-derived subject headings.

PRECIS has aroused international interest. Subject indexes to the *Australian National Bibliography* and the film catalogue of the College Bibliocentre in Canada are produced using PRECIS. PRECIS training courses have also been held in Denmark, France, India and Malaysia.

OTHER MACHINE-GENERATED INDEXES

Some further types of machine-generated indexes exist and are described in this section.

Back-of-the-book indexes

To generate such an index by computer it is usually necessary for the full text of the book to be in machine-readable form. In fact, with the gradual increase in the number of books being computer typeset the availability of machine-readable texts is becoming more common. As with the production of KWIC indexes, the keywords, or lead terms, in the index can be generated using a stop-list technique or alternatively by tagging keywords at the input stage.

Most operational book indexing systems are computer-assisted rather than fully computer-generated. Human intervention is necessary either at the input stage (with a tagged system) or at the output stage (with a stop-list system).

An alternative use of computers in book indexing is described by Kuch.[10] The index (and not the book) is prepared in machine-readable form so that each computer record corresponds to a card in the traditional indexing process. The computer can help the indexer to:

associate words and word roots;
produce proof or draft copies of the index;
roughly sort the entries into the required sequence;
replace strings (the indexer can use shorthand expressions which can be amplified by the computer).

Recently, work has been undertaken in the USA on cumulating back-of-the-book indexes. The aim of this is to fill an information gap between the library catalogue and the book itself. It has been shown that there is a constant factor of 30 relating to the number of characters at each level of information access in a book. Tables of contents are about 30 times as long as book titles; indexes are about 30 times as long as the table of contents and the text is about 30 times as long as the index. An amalgamated index to 113 books on statistics has been produced to fill the information gap in statistics.[11] It is known as *The Statistics CumIndex* and was generated by computer. Information from the individual back-of-the-book indexes was typed using an OCR font. The text was then processed by an OCR bureau (at Wells Fargo Bank) and converted onto a magnetic tape. There are obvious problems in dealing with proper names, singular and plural forms and in the standardization of spelling. The computer assists in this but there is much hand editing necessary.

Literary and linguistic indexes

A concordance, which is an index to the words or passages of a literary work, is one example of such an index. It is obviously a tedious task to accomplish by hand and so many literary scholars are now using computers to generate their concordances. The full text of the work is required in machine-readable form. Common words are often eliminated by using a stop-list.

One mammoth linguistic index which is being computer-produced is the *Index Thomisticus*. This is an index to the 118 works of St. Thomas Aquinas and to 61 works of authors in the period from the ninth to the fifteenth century. The production of the index started in 1949 and was the first example of a computer being used to process non-numerical information. Since then over 1 000 000 lines of text, some 15 000 000 words, in four alphabets (Latin, Greek, Cyrillic and Hebrew), have been processed. It has been estimated that 1 000 000 man-hours were used and less than 5000 computer-hours. The result will be a 50-volume work of about 58 000 encyclopedia-size pages. This is being photo-composed by computer. The work has been directed by Father Roberta Busa.[12]

In the UK the Association for Literary and Linguistic Computing has been formed to bring together all those involved in processing literary and linguistic information by computer.

SLIC indexes

SLIC stands for selective listing in combination. A set of terms describing a document are assigned by an indexer and input in alphabetical order to the computer.[13] Some entries are selected from the total number of combinations to ensure that the minimum number of combinations necessary for search purposes are produced.

Example: The following terms have been assigned to a document:

computer, library, system.

Total number of possible combinations $(2^n - 1)$	Entries in a SLIC index $(2^{(n-1)})$
computer	*computer, library, system*
computer, library	*computer, system*
computer, library, system	*library, system*
computer, system	*system*
library	
library, system	
system	

Thus with three terms the saving of index entries is $(2^3 - 1) - 2^2$, or $7 - 4$ which is 3. The saving becomes more dramatic with more terms. If eight terms were used to describe the document the saving of index entries would be $(2^8 - 1) - 2^7$ or $255 - 128$ which is 127.

The index to the 1974 volume of the *Journal of the American Society for*

Information Science was produced using this technique by students of library science at McGill University, Montreal.

SOFTWARE AND SERVICES

Several program packages for generating and printing indexes are available and have been reported.[14,15] (*Note:* Some of the packages referred to in Refs. 14, 15 are no longer available. These include the INDACS package which was supplied by London University Computer Services and the NIC package supplied by ICL for the 1900 series computers.) Brief details of some of the packages currently available in the UK are given in Table 9.2.

TABLE 9.2

Name of package	Supplier	Language	Comments
ASSASSIN	ICI Agricultural Division	COBOL	A general information retrieval package which includes the ability to produce KWIC-type indexes. It is used by several libraries within ICI.
AUTOLIST	National Research Development Council	PLAN	Produces articulated subject indexes and is used for the index to World Textiles Abstracts.
Burroughs KWIC/ ICLKWIC	Fraser Williams, Liverpool	COBOL and Assembly Language	These programs were written in conjunction with ICI Pharmaceuticals Division.
COCOA	Atlas Computer Laboratory	FORTRAN	A text-processing package which produces concordances and can be used for general index production.
COIN	National Computing Centre	COBOL	A package which can generate KWIC-type indexes and produce various lists. It is used by the Building Research Establishment.[5]
FILETAB	National Computing Centre	Assembly Language	A general package which can be used to produce indexes.
KWAC	Unilever Computer Services Ltd	Assembly Language	This versatile package produces KWIC-type indexes and various lists. Nested keyword tags can be used.
KWIC	IBM	Various	Several packages are available from IBM for producing KWIC-type indexes.
PRECIS	BLBSD	Assembly Language	These programs are currently written for IBM 360 and 370 series computers but are being re-written for the ICL 2900 range.
SLIC	ICI Fibres Ltd	COBOL	
Univac KWOC	Shell, Sittingbourne Research Centre	Assembly Language	A package to produce KWIC-type and author indexes for UNIVAC 9300 computers.

Some of the packages listed in Table 9.2 are available for sale whilst others are available via a computer bureau. Information on availability and costs should be obtained from the supplier.

If no package exists to satisfy the requirements of both the library and the computer system, either a specific program must be written or a total system, including a computer, purchased.

The library at the Aircraft Research Association adopted the former approach. A suite of programs in ALGOL 60 have been written to suit the particular needs of the library.[16]

The library at the Leatherhead Food Research Association has adopted the latter approach. They have bought a system known as CAIRS (Computer Assisted Information Retrieval System) which is marketed by Libra Information Systems Ltd. A minicomputer, a Texas Instruments 980, with two magnetic tape drives, two disc drives, a VDU, a line-printer and a teletype, is used in the library. The software produces listings in various orders and a subject index as well as offering other information retrieval functions such as searching files of retrospective material and providing a current-awareness service.

GENERAL COMPUTER SYSTEM

Input

Most index production and generation systems depend on the input details being converted to machine-readable form off-line and then processed by the computer. In some cases the indexers have to prepare details on special forms to be punched by data preparation staff whereas in other cases editing of the original record is possible.

The CAIRS system allows for on-line input of bibliographic details and subject information. All the details are validated and the keywords checked against a thesaurus and where necessary the computer informs the indexer of the preferred keyword. The system at the British Steel Corporation at Port Talbot also allows for on-line input of bibliographic and subject information via 'intelligent' VDUs.[6]

Files

The main file is obviously the file of records to which the index is to be produced or generated. In some instances other files such as a thesaurus, stop-list or go-list are necessary.

Processes and output

The main process is to generate the index entries, if required, sort the file into the specified sequences and prepare for the output medium. Batch processing is ideal for this.

As with the production of catalogues, indexes can be produced on line-printer paper, COM or can be computer typeset. Similar arguments for and against the various methods, as outlined in Chapter 6, apply.

At the British Steel Corporation at Port Talbot the indexes to the library's collection are produced on line-printer paper. A double column layout has been adopted which saves on space and is more presentable. The indexes are cumulated monthly, quarterly, six-monthly and nine-monthly with a complete reprint each year.[6]

Several of the PRECIS indexes referred to earlier in the chapter are produced on COM microfilm or microfiche.

The majority of the large-scale indexes which are computer produced are at present typeset. The *British National Bibliography*, the indexes to *The Times* and *The Times Atlas* are a few examples of the indexes produced by the Computaprint typesetting bureau. Since 1970, this bureau has used an RCA 70/800 phototypesetter which enables several thousand characters to be set in a few seconds. The indexes to the INSPEC abstracting journals are produced using a Linotron 505 photo-composing machine. Each issue of an abstracting journal contains up to five indexes. The author and subject indexes are cumulated twice-yearly and in addition cumulative indexes over periods of three to five years are available.

EVALUATION AND COSTS

When evaluating printed subject indexes some of the performance criteria and measurements which should be considered are:

(a) *Coverage of the material indexed.*

(b) *Currency.* This is the delay between the appearance of the document and its inclusion in the index.

(c) *Recall.* This is now a standard measure of an information retrieval system and is defined as

$$\frac{\text{number of relevant references retrieved in a search}}{\text{total number of relevant references in the system}} \times 100$$

Thus, if a given search retrieved 20 relevant references and there were 32 relevant references in the system then the recall would be $(20/32) \times 100$ or 62.5%.

(d) *Precision.* This is another standard measure of an information retrieval system and is defined as

$$\frac{\text{number of relevant references retrieved in a search}}{\text{total number of references retrieved in a search}} \times 100$$

Thus, using the above example, with 50 references being retrieved, the precision would be $(20/50) \times 100$ or 40%. The recall and precision measurements are inversely related to each other. This means that as one increases in value the other decreases.

(e) *Time.* The two timing factors involved are the time taken to index the document and the time taken to search the index for relevant documents.

(f) *Effort.* This refers to the effort involved in producing and using the index.

(g) *Presentation.* This depends on the layout and typography used in the production of the index which in turn depends on the physical form of the index.

(h) *Cost.*

(i) *Usability.* An experiment which studied users' reactions to published, printed indexes has been carried out by INSPEC.[17] Librarians and scientists were asked questions about their use of the indexes to *Science Abstracts*.

Research into the Evaluation of Printed Subject Indexes by Laboratory InvestigatiON (EPSILON) is currently in progress at Aberystwyth under Keen.[18] The different types of index entry which are being tested include:

> rotated term (with no structure words in between);
> term only (analogous to the dual dictionary);
> rotated string (analogous to a KWAC index of assigned terms);
> articulated prepositional (analogous to an articulated subject index);
> chain procedure (analogous to BTI);
> broad heading;
> shunted relational (analogous to PRECIS).

The results of the BUCCS project indicated that searchers tended to prefer using the KWOC catalogue to the classified catalogue.[19] Moreover, if searching for a precise document, searchers would be more likely to find its reference in the KWOC catalogue than in the classified catalogue. The BUCCS team concluded that more work in the area of keyword catalogues, and in particular in the KWUC technique, should be undertaken.

KWUC is an acronym for *KeyWord* and *UDC*. A KWUC catalogue has been produced at the Universitaire Instelling Antwerpen.[20] The catalogue is arranged using broad UDC classes with each class being sub-divided by means of alphabetically arranged keywords from the titles. The keywords are specified by manual tagging. Homonymous keywords are taken care of by combining the keyword with a UDC class number.

An extension of Aslib's study on the availability of packages covered the costs of producing KWIC-type indexes.[21] The study consisted of:

> (a) Varying the input types between
>   original title;
>   enriched title;
>   enriched, edited title;

a list of terms selected from a thesaurus;

an ordered list of terms selected from a thesaurus with weights and connectives added;

a PRECIS-like string of terms.

(b) Varying the methods of selecting keywords between

stop-list;

go-list;

manual tagging.

(c) Varying the output format between

KWIC;

KWOC (really KWAC);

Double-KWIC.

The various options were processed using the INDACS package on London University Computer Services computer. Unfortunately this package is no longer available.

Three components of the costs were identified:

indexer costs;

data preparation costs;

computer costs.

The study concluded that indexing costs generally formed a substantial part of the total cost and were a significant factor in variations of cost.

In general, computer costs vary greatly between using a bureau, doing-it-yourself completely and using a package on a local machine.

EXAMPLE 1: LIVERPOOL POLYTECHNIC LIBRARY

This library serves 7000 students and about 670 members of staff.

In 1974, the decision was made to install a computer-based catalogue system which would eventually be part of a fully integrated computer system in the library. Various program packages, both MARC-based and otherwise, were examined but none proved suitable.

The system, known as AMY, was designed and programmed in the polytechnic. The record format is not compatible with MARC and consists of fixed fields (e.g. 200 characters for title, 60 characters for author). The format is flexible and is used to describe all types of catalogue record. The catalogue is produced on to COM microfiche by the EUROCOM bureau. The programs are written in COBOL and PLAN and run on the polytechnic's ICL 1903A computer.

After discussions during the design stage with members of the BUCCS team it was decided that keywords would be included in the catalogue. It is this aspect of the system which will be described here.

The decision was made to use the manual tagging method of assigning keywords in order to produce more meaningful lead terms in the catalogue. Words in the title are tagged on input and there is also space in the record format for extra keywords to be added. The methods of defining keywords or key phrases are:

(a) Preceding the keyword with a ↑. Thus
     ↑UNDERDEVELOPMENT AND ↑CLASS
would produce
     Underdevelopment
     Class
as lead terms.

(b) Including an * to specify a key phrase. Thus
     ↑CLASS * CONFLICT
     ↑PEOPLE * AND * PLANNING
would produce
     Class conflict
     People and planning
as lead terms.

(c) Allowing for nested key phrases by using =. Thus
     ↑ROGETS = THESAURUS
     ↑SOCIALLY * DEPRIVED = FAMILIES
would produce
     Rogets Thesaurus
     Thesaurus
     Socially deprived families
     Families
as lead terms.

The catalogue is produced in classified and author/keyword orders and is fully updated each month. If the title for this book was input as

AN ↑INTRODUCTION TO ↑COMPUTER-BASED = LIBRARY * SYSTEMS

a reference to this book would appear under

Computer-based library systems
Introduction
Library systems

EXAMPLE 2: *INDEX MEDICUS* **AND MEDLARS**[22]

Index Medicus, which is an index to the biomedical literature, was first published in 1879 and since 1964 has been produced by computer; 2800 journals in several languages, giving an additional 200 000 articles each year, are covered by the system. *Index Medicus* is now part of MEDLARS (Medical Literature Analysis and Retrieval System) which is based at the US National Library of Medicine in Washington.

Trained indexers fill in prescribed forms giving the bibliographic details of an article and also allocate terms to describe the article. These descriptor terms are chosen from a controlled vocabulary of about 10 000 MESH (MEdical Subject Headings) terms. MESH is a structured thesaurus with several categories and up to seven levels within each category.

The indexers always use the most specific MESH term available to describe a document and this fact must be remembered when searching.

The indexer can use one of 68 subheadings to enable subdivision of a heading. For example, the term SODIUM/*METABOLISM would make an entry in *Index Medicus* under *Sodium* subheaded by *Metabolism*. The asterisk is assigned by the indexer if an entry is to appear in *Index Medicus*. MESH terms that are allocated without an asterisk are used in computer-searched systems. On average, 12 MESH terms, of which 3 are asterisked, are allocated to each article. Check-tags can also be used by the indexer to signify general species (humans, dogs, frogs, etc.), age (child (2–5), adolescent (13–18), mid-age (45–64) etc.) and type of article (proceedings, monograph, symposium, etc.). Since 1975, the abstract to the article has been included if it is published with the article and if the permission of the publisher is given.

Indexing takes place in eight centres scattered throughout the world. The British Library Lending Division is responsible for indexing most of the medical journals published in the UK. One hundred and thirty journals are covered, which amounts to about 150 000 articles each year to be indexed. It takes 15 minutes on average to index an article and fill in the required form. It takes a further 5 minutes for the information to be checked by an experienced indexer.

The forms which have been filled in by indexers are sent to the National Library of Medicine and the information is added to the database.

Broadly speaking, there are three services produced from this input.

(1) *Index Medicus*

A magnetic tape is produced which forms the input to the Graphic Arts Composing Equipment (GRACE). This is a high-speed phototypesetting machine which is used to produce the monthly issues of *Index Medicus*.

(2) MEDLARS magnetic tapes

The details of the month's input are produced on a MEDLARS magnetic tape. Copies of the tape are sent to the eight centres throughout the world, where they are used for running retrospective searches in response to specific requests. Searches which are on subjects of wide interest are published.

Recurring bibliographies in specialized subject areas of medicine are also prepared from the MEDLARS database.

(3) MEDLINE

This is the on-line information retrieval service operated by the National

Library of Medicine on the MEDLARS database. All the retrospective and current-awareness searches run by the UK MEDLARS centre are currently produced via MEDLINE at Washington. MEDLINE is used by over 300 institutions in the USA, Canada, Europe and Australia. It is described more fully in Chapter 11.

REFERENCES

1. G. Salton, *Dynamic Information and Library Processing*, Prentice-Hall Inc., Englewood Cliffs, New Jersey (1975). ISBN 0 13 221325 7.
2. F. W. Matthews and A. D. Shillingford, Variations on KWIC. *Aslib Proceedings*, **25**, 140–52 (1973).
3. G. Thomas and T. Whitehall, A KWIC–KWOC Double Index with Manual Keyword Selection. *Program*, **5**, 211–19 (1971).
4. P. A. Thomas, A KWIC Index to the GLDP Inquiry Transcripts. *GLC Intelligence Unit Quarterly Bulletin*, **22**, 5–11 (1973).
5. P. J. Elvin, Adapting the KWOC Indexing Technique to Produce Journal Listings. *Program*, **8**, 196–201 (1974).
6. M. J. Patten, Experiences with an In-house Mechanized Information System. *Aslib Proceedings*, **26**, 189–209 (1974).
7. J. E. Armitage *et al.*, Experimental Use of a Program for Computer-aided Subject Index Production. *Information Storage and Retrieval*, **6**, 79–87 (1970).
8. E. J. Coates, Computerized Data Processing for British Technology Index. *The Indexer*, **6**, 97–101 (1968).
9. D. Austin, PRECIS in a Multi-lingual Context. Part 1. PRECIS: an Overview. *Libri*, **26**, 1–37 (1976).
10. T. D. C. Kuch, Computer-Supported Indexing. *The Indexer*, **9**, 16–17 (1974).
11. J. L. Dolby and J. W. Tukey, *The Statistics CumIndex*, The R & D Press, Los Altos, California (1973). ISBN 0 88274 000 8.
12. R. Busa, Guest Editorial: Why Can Computers do so Little? *Association for Literary and Linguistic Computing Bulletin*, **4**, 1–3 (1976).
13. J. R. Sharp, The SLIC Index. *American Documentation*, **17**, 41–4 (1966).
14. L. H. Campey, *Generating and Printing Indexes by Computer*, Aslib, London (1972). ISBN 0 85142 047 8.
15. L. H. Campey, Generating and Printing Indexes by Computer—a Supplement. *Program*, **8**, 149–65 (1974).
16. C. C. Barnett, Reports Cataloguing in the Aircraft Research Association Library. *Program*, **6**, 60–73 (1972).
17. A. M. Gould, User Preference in Published Indexes. *Journal of the American Society for Information Science*, **7**, 279–86 (1974).
18. E. M. Keen, Research on the design and evaluation of printed subject indexes, a paper presented at the 2nd European Conference on Research into the Management of Information Services and Libraries, Amsterdam, March 1976.
19. J. H. Lamble, P. Bryant and A. Needham, *The BUCCS Project: Conclusions and Recommendations*, Bath University Library (1975). ISBN 0 90084378 0.
20. H. D. L. Vervliet, The Machine-Readable Catalogues of the UIA Library, Antwerp: an Experiment with an Interim MARC-Compatible Cataloguing System. *Program*, **8**, 117–33 (1974).
21. L. H. Campey, Costs of Producing KWIC/KWOC Indexes. *Information Storage and Retrieval*, **10**, 293–307 (1974).
22. J. G. B. Frankland, *UK MEDLARS: a Handbook for Users*, British Library Lending Division, Boston Spa (1975). ISBN 0 85350 158 0.

CHAPTER 10

SELECTIVE DISSEMINATION OF INFORMATION

INTRODUCTION

H. P. Luhn, writing in 1961, defined the Selective Dissemination of Information (SDI) concept as 'that service within an organization which concerns itself with the channeling of new items of information, from whatever source, to those points within the organization where the probability of usefulness in connection with current work or interests is high.'[1]

SDI developed outside the library although individual libraries and librarians had been running rather less formal SDI systems for many years. Librarians would keep account of users' interests and when an item of potential interest to a user was received the librarian would inform the user.

In the early 1960s there was much experimentation of programming SDI systems. This work was undertaken mainly by the IBM Corporation in which Luhn worked. In 1962 the producers of *Chemical Abstracts* decided to provide details of the titles of documents contained in the journal which were available on magnetic tapes. This was done to enable individual libraries to use the magnetic tape and run their own SDI service. By 1963 the Ames Laboratory of the US Atomic Energy Commission had designed an SDI system which could receive machine-readable data from any source. In 1965 the first commercial SDI service started to operate. This was the Automatic Subject Citation Alert (ASCA) and was run by the Institute for Scientific Information. The bibliographic details used for ASCA are those used to produce the printed *Science Citation Index*.

Since the mid-1960s the growth of SDI services has been rapid and many organizations now offer such a service.

The concept behind SDI is that of an individualized information service. It is one example of a current-awareness service which a library can offer. Other current-awareness services might include the production of a list of the serials held by the library, a bulletin detailing the serials, or contents of the serials, which have recently been received or a bulletin, arranged by subject, of recently received articles. An SDI service does not have to be computer-based, although only such systems will be described in this chapter.

AN SDI SYSTEM

An SDI system comprises the following four features:

(a) descriptions of the information requirements of a user are compared with descriptions of the contents of recently received documents;

(b) documents that match are selected;

(c) information about these documents is sent to the user;

(d) the user is asked to assess the details of the documents received so that a better description of requirements can be obtained.

This can be shown in diagrammatic form as in Fig. 10.1.

The 'feedback' loop, also Luhn's idea, is important in obtaining a 'better' system and also in involving the users actively in the system. Users are asked to fill in a slip giving the number of documents they received and how many they

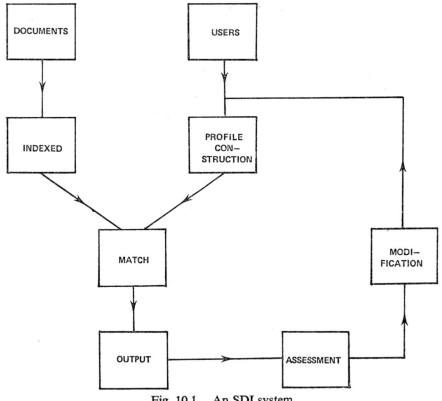

Fig. 10.1.   An SDI system.

thought to be relevant. As can be seen in the diagram the input to the SDI system is two-fold:

(a) *Profiles of users' interests.* These are usually produced by information scientists from within the organization.

(b) *Document descriptions.* These can be externally or internally produced.

It is necessary for the 'language' of these descriptions to be the same. If a controlled vocabulary has been used to index the documents then terms from that vocabulary must be used in constructing the users' profile.

The output of the system can vary, from the documents themselves to a reference number in an indexing and abstracting journal. A common format is one which includes the basic bibliographic detail and the descriptor terms for the document so that the user can see how the document was selected. The output can be produced on line-printer or on cards which are suitable for filing in a personal index.

SDI programs are usually batch processed and are run at regular intervals of perhaps a week, a fortnight or a month. In an SDI system which uses externally produced information the frequency of running the program is often the same as the frequency of receiving the information. In a recent questionnaire which was sent to subscribers of the INSPEC database it was found that:

(a) the majority of the subscribers used the database to offer an SDI service;

(b) the SDI programs were most frequently run twice a month when the new references arrived on magnetic tape.

One example of an on-line SDI system is SDILINE. The most recent month's batch of input to the MEDLARS database is available on this file and can be searched in the same manner as MEDLINE on the National Library of Medicine's computer at Washington. The file consists of 17 000–20 000 records and is completely replaced each month. The software includes a command to save a search profile on the computer and so the user does not have to construct the search profile each month. With an on-line system such as this the user must take a positive role and carry out the search each month whereas with a batch system the user can take a passive role and just receive the output.

Before describing how to construct user profiles it is necessary to know how to formulate computer searches.

SEARCH METHODS

Keen[2] refers to six steps necessary in formulating search strategies. These are:

(a) translate the user's request into the language of the system;

(b) add other related terms to extend the search to cover all possibly useful topics;

(c) state search terms in their required logical combinations;

(d) decide on the order of trying various searches (e.g. whether to try a broad or narrow search first);

(e) decide on when to end the search (e.g. what is the maximum number of references required by the user?);

(f) alter the original strategy as a result of studying some relevant documents which have been retrieved.

There are basically two methods used in computer searched systems for combining terms.

Boolean logic

This method was named after a logician, George Boole, who formulated the logical operators AND, OR, NOT.

> AND   This operator is used to link different concepts of a search, e.g. COMPUTER AND LIBRARY.
> Articles that include both *computer* and *library* in the description will be retrieved.
>
> OR   This operator is used to link synonymous concepts, e.g. COMPUTER OR AUTOMATION OR MECHANIZATION.
> Articles that include any of the terms *computer, automation, mechanization* will be retrieved.
>
> NOT   This operator is used to exclude concepts from the search, e.g. COMPUTER AND CATALOGUE NOT MARC.
> Articles that include both *computer* and *catalogue* but do not include *MARC* will be retrieved.

Brackets can normally be used to build more complicated search strategies, e.g. (COMPUTER OR AUTOMATION OR MECHANIZATION) AND LIBRARY NOT MARC.

Weighted term logic

Weights (or numbers) are assigned to each term and a threshold set. Articles are retrieved if the addition of weights of terms in that article reaches or exceeds the threshold. Take as an example a threshold of 5:

MARC (5), COMPUTER (4), CATALOGUE (1), ORDER (1), ACQUISITION (1)

Articles including the following terms, at least, will be retrieved:

	Sum of weights
MARC	5
computer, catalogue	4 + 1
computer, order	4 + 1
computer, acquisition	4 + 1
whereas articles including:	
computer	4
order, acquisition	1 + 1
catalogue, order, acquisition	1 + 1 + 1

will not be retrieved.

The equivalent Boolean search would be:

MARC OR (COMPUTER AND (CATALOGUE OR ORDER OR ACQUISITION))

With this form of searching, articles can be ranked on output so that the article with the highest total of weights is printed first and so on.

In either method an article which included the term *catalog* would not have been retrieved. To overcome this most systems allow terms to be truncated, e.g.

CATALOG*   would match with *catalog, catalogue, cataloguing, cataloguers*, etc.

This is referred to as right truncation. Some systems also allow left truncation as well as left and right truncation, e.g.

*OXIDE   would match on *monoxide, dioxide, oxide, peroxide*, etc.
COGNIT   would match on *cognition, recognition, cognitive*, etc.

In a similar manner an article which included the term *mechanisation* would not have been retrieved from the second search strategy. To overcome this a 'universal character' is often allowed, e.g.

MECHANI£ATION   would match on *mechanisation, mechanization*
ON£LINE   would match on *on-line, online, on line*

To aid the searcher in the use of truncation, KLIC (Key Letter In Context) indexes to the database can be produced. The United Kingdom Chemical Information Service (UKCIS) have produced such an index to all words that occurred more than five times in a six-month sample of the Chemical Titles database. The index also includes the frequency with which each word occurred in the sample.

As an example, suppose the following title was in the database: 'The use of ALS equipment in charging and also in periodicals or serials systems'. The KLIC index would contain:

ALS

PERIODIC ALS

SERI ALS

ALSO

(*Note: Also* would probably have appeared in a stop-list but has been included here to aid explanation.)

The fields of a record which are capable of being searched vary between systems and databases. It is usually possible to search on the author field. Thus, if a relevant reference is known it can be retrieved by an author search and a check made of the descriptor terms used. It is also usual to be able to search on a date which is either the year of publication or the year of inclusion of the record into the database. This field can be used to limit the search to documents published after a certain date.

PROFILE CONSTRUCTION

This is the job of describing the user's interests to the SDI system and, as already mentioned, this must be done in the 'language' used for the document descriptions.

To illustrate this an example of constructing an ASSASSIN profile to be run against a subset of ICI's Techno-Commercial Unit database is given.

(a) *Decide on area of interest*
How the Equal Pay Act affects women's earnings.
(b) *Divide the search into concepts*
Equal pay.
Women.
Earnings.
(c) *Use the thesaurus to formulate terms for the concepts*
Code numbers, known as term codes, are given in the thesaurus for each term and these are also needed:

Term	Term code	Concept
EQUAL PAY	0318462	1
EQUAL PAY ACT	0318473	1
WOMEN	0150331	2
FEMALE	0115840	2
EARNINGS	0012724	3
SALARY	0146469	3
WAGES	0039538	3

(d) *Allocate weights to each term and a pass weight or threshold*

All terms in concept 1 weight   +10.

All terms in concept 2 weight   + 5.

All terms in concept 3 weight   + 5.

Pass weight = 15.

This is not a simple weighted term system since only the weight of one term from within each concept can be added in to the total weight.

The Boolean equivalent of this search would be (EQUAL PAY OR EQUAL PAY ACT) AND (WOMEN OR FEMALE OR SALARY OR EARNINGS OR WAGES).

(e) *Fill in appropriate profile form for the profile to be converted to machine-readable form.*

Documents entering the system are matched against the profile. Two references are shown in Fig. 10.2:

(a) Matched on equal pay (10) and women (5), thus reaching the threshold of 15.

(b) Matched on sex discrimination (10) and women (5). The term code for sex discrimination was 0318462 which is the same as the term code for equal pay.

```
PROFILE NUMBER 01.00015                          DATE 10.12.74
         ABSTRACT NUMBER 01.33025..7410              CARD 1 CF 1
                                                     SECURITY Z


     EQUAL PAY ACT.  THE ARTICLE LCCKS AT PRCBLEMS LIKELY TO BE
ENCOUNTERED AT THE END OF 1975 WHEN THE ACT COMES IN FORCE.  THE
PROBLEMS OF DEFINING 'EQUAL VALUE' OR 'BROADLY SIMILAR' JOBS AND
          INDUSTRIAL MANAGEMENT, JULY/AUG 74, V.4, P.24-6
  THE IMPORTANCE OF JOB EVALUATICN ARE STUDIED.  TRACE UNION
ATTITUDES AND THE DEMANDS BY MALE EMPLOYEES FOR RESTORATION OF
DIFFERENTIALS ARE DISCUSSED.
<00>SEX DISCRIMINATION;PAY;ECUAL PAY;WOMEN;LEGISLATION;PERSCNNEL;
```

(a)

```
PROFILE NUMBER C1.00015                          DATE 10.12.74
         ABSTRACT NUMBER 01.33019..7410              CARD 1 CF 1
                                                     SECURITY Z


   U.S.  LARGE COMPANIES ARE UPGRADING WCMEN EMPLOYEES IN A
BROADER SEARCH FOR EXECUTIVE TALENT.  SENIOR MANAGEMENT SAY IT
IS SOUND BUSINESS POLICY.  THE CCNCEPT IS NCW BACKED BY LAW.
          CHEM WEEK, 7.8.74, V.115, P.15-16
   ARTICLE.
<00>SEX DISCRIMINATICN; DCW CHEMICAL COMFANY ;
```

(b)

Fig. 10.2. Output from an ASSASSIN SDI profile (reproduced by kind permission of Imperial Chemical Industries Ltd.).

Synonyms are linked by having the same term code; however, two extra digits, not shown in the example, are used to define uniquely the individual terms within a synonymous group. Thus, by quoting the term code as well as the term in the profile the computer matches with all the synonyms of the term. This is done to increase the recall of the system. Thus, in this particular database sex discrimination and equal pay are defined as synonymous terms.

The profile is usually constructed by a librarian or information scientist who is well trained in the language of the system.

The Information and Documentation Centre at the Royal Institute of Technology (RIT) in Sweden offers an SDI service from 18 databases. Each query is matched against all databases that are considered relevant and therefore each query generates four or five profiles. At present about 6500 profiles are processed each year. An example of a profile is given in Ref. 3. RIT's experience has shown that users who are engaged in applied research and technical processes in an industrial environment require high precision whereas users involved in basic research require high recall. Such information as to the nature of the output is just one of the factors to be ascertained from the user by the profile constructor. As with any reference process in a library, there is need for good communication between searcher and requestor so that the searcher can find references which are relevant to the requestor.

INSPEC have carried out an experiment in which the degree of user participation in profile construction was varied.[4] It was found that users who were completely responsible for constructing and modifying their profiles obtained higher precision and therefore lower recall than when the profiles were compiled by INSPEC staff. The report concluded that users should be encouraged in the compilation of their own profiles and be given the appropriate training and documentation.

EXTERNALLY PRODUCED DATABASES

One of the main problems to be solved by anyone designing an SDI system is whether or not to use an external database. A database simply refers to a collection of bibliographic references. Magnetic tapes containing numerical or textual information exist but these will not be covered in this section.

The growth of SDI systems was, to some extent, dependent on the growth in availability of machine-readable databases. As indicated in Chapter 9, these are often by-products of a computer-produced index. The number of databases currently available is growing rapidly and there are a number of directories to guide the user.[5-7] However, it has been estimated that only about 12 of these are widely used for SDI systems.

Most of the databases cover scientific or social science material. However, with databases such as Sciences Religieuses, Bundesinstitut fur Sportswissenschaft and America: History and Life available it can be seen that some aspects of religion, sport and history are now covered.

Most databases cater for a single subject although there are exceptions such as those formed from the *Social Sciences Citation Index* which is multi-disciplinary and *Pollution Abstracts* which is problem-oriented.

Table 10.1 indicates the types of organization which produce databases:

TABLE 10.1

Type	Example	Database
Academic institution	University of Tulsa	Petroleum Abstracts
Commercial organization	Derwent Publications Ltd	Central Patents Index (CPI)
Individual	Dr W. J. Hayes, Jnr.	Hayes File
International organization	Food and Agriculture Organisation	Agricultural Information System (AGRIS)
Learned society	American Institute of Physics	Searchable Physics Information Notices (SPIN)
National library	National Agricultural Library	Catalogue and Index (CAIN)
National organization	National Aeronautical Space Administration	Scientific and Technical Aerospace Reports (STAR)
Research institution	Rubber and Plastics Research Association	RAPRA

In 1968, the Association of Scientific Information and Dissemination Centers (ASIDIC) was formed in North America by people using externally produced databases for their information services. It is interesting to note that in 1975 the acronym changed to Association of Information and Dissemination Centers, which recognized the growth of non-scientific databases. In 1973, the equivalent European organization, European Association of Scientific Information Dissemination Centres (EUSIDIC), was set up. These two organizations are trying jointly to standardize on the type of information contained in the databases. Their current thoughts are that the basic record should contain ISSN, full journal title, volume and issue identification, date of issue, title, personal author(s), corporate author(s), corporate identification, country of origin, pagination, language of text and the type of publication.

The potential subscriber to an external database needs to consider several factors.

(a) *Coverage.* What type and range of material does the database cover? Are journal articles, conference proceedings, books, theses, government reports, etc. covered?

(b) *Currency.* How long does it take for a reference to appear in the database?

(c) *Cost.*

(d) *Format.* There are many ways of formatting bibliographic information on the magnetic tapes that are the communication medium.

(e) *Frequency with which the database is updated.*

(f) *Indexing policy.* What subject approach is available? Has a thesaurus been used in the indexing? Is the indexing consistent?

(g) *Overall quality.* Is the information accurate? Are there many input or spelling errors?

(h) *Physical features of the magnetic tape:*

> Recording density (556 or 800 bpi?);
> Parity (odd or even?);
> Number of tracks (7 or 9?);
> Coding (ASCII or EBCDIC?).

To obtain the necessary coverage many libraries or information centres subscribe to more than one external database in the same way as they might subscribe to more than one indexing or abstracting publication.

The library at the Colworth/Welwyn Research Laboratory of Unilever subscribes to three external databases in order to run its information service. These are Chemical Abstracts Condensates, the Science Citation Index and the Food Science and Technology Abstracts database which is supplied by the International Food Information Service. The records on the tapes are converted to a common MARC-type format and processed in-house. A package known as MANDARIN (Machine Aided Notification Dissemination and Retrieval of Information) is being developed.

The information section at ICI Pharmaceuticals Division subscribes to four external databases. These are Chemical Abstracts Condensates, the Science Citation Index, the Central Patents Index and the Rubber and Plastics Research Association databases. Records from each database are 'sieved' before merging into one file in order to minimize storing multiple copies of the same references. All records are then converted to the format necessary for using ASSASSIN.

The library at the Wellcome Research Laboratories subscribes to Excerpta Medica's DRUGDOC database. Profiles are written using the Master List of Medical Terms (MALIMET) and are processed weekly using a special-purpose program written in PLAN for their ICL 1903A. The profiles can be amended on-line.[8]

SOFTWARE AND SERVICES

Software

Another problem to be solved by anyone designing an SDI system is whether or not to use a program package. Some of the packages which can be used for offering SDI services are described.

(1) ASSASSIN—Agricultural System for the Storage and Subsequent Selection of Information [9]

This package, although designed and used at ICI's Agricultural Division, is not limited to processing agricultural information. Input to the package can be from a variety of sources such as published serials, patents, internal reports, external databases or library accessions. Each input record is formatted into fields such as the bibliographic source, author, title, text (or abstract) and added terms (used for extra indexing terms). The package matches each word in the record against a stop-list and a thesaurus. Words that don't match are printed out for intellectual consideration. Synonymous words are dealt with as described in the previous section on profile construction. The various outputs from the package include an SDI service, KWOC (really KWAC) indexes, the ability to perform retrospective searches (currently in batch) and a list of the structured thesaurus.

The package, which consists of 120 COBOL programs, can be bought or used at ICI's computer bureau. Many divisions within ICI use the package and it is also used by external organizations.

The Greater London Council use ASSASSIN to run their information service ACOMPLIS (A Computerised London Information Service). The database used is *Urban Abstracts* which is produced by the GLC. The SDI service has over 100 profiles and is run every four weeks.[10] The information system run at RAPRA, which also uses ASSASSIN, is described in the examples at the end of the chapter. There is now an ASSASSIN Users Group.

(2) CAIRS—Computer Assisted Information Retrieval System

This total information retrieval system, which includes a minicomputer, is used at the Leatherhead Food Research Association. The system is capable of producing current-awareness lists of recently acquired items and is capable of running an SDI service.

(3) CAN/SDI—Canadian SDI

CAN/SDI is the name of the current-awareness service operated by the Canadian Institute for Scientific and Technical Information.[11] The programs used for running the service have been made available. Currently organizations in Australia, South Africa, the Netherlands, India, Mexico and Argentina are receiving assistance with CAN/SDI programs. The input record for the package needs to be in a MARC-type format.

(4) FIND-2

This is a general information retrieval package which is written in PLAN and marketed by ICL for their 1900 series computers. Loughborough University Library use this package to offer an SDI service on the COMPENDEX database. The COMPENDEX magnetic tapes are available in two formats: the American National Standard for Bibliographic Interchange on Magnetic Tape and the TEXTPAC format. Loughborough receive the latter and reformat the information for use by FIND-2 on their ICL 1904A computer.[12]

(5) STAIRS—Storage and Information Retrieval System

STAIRS is an on-line information retrieval system written in assembly language and marketed by IBM for use on their 360 and 370 series computers. This package is used to run the Current Information Selection service at the IBM Technical Information Retrieval Center (ITIRC). The profiles are matched against internal databases as well as the external databases such as Chemical Abstracts Condensates, COMPENDEX and SPIN. About 4000 IBM personnel from all over the world use the service.[13]

(6) TEXTPAC

This is a general text processing package which is written in assembly language and marketed by IBM for use on their 360 and 370 series computers. It can be used for several information retrieval functions.

Services

The third problem to be solved by anyone designing an SDI system is whether or not to subscribe to an external service and therefore not be involved in compiling or buying databases and designing or buying-in packages. One obvious factor in this decision is the number of potential subscribers to the service. A sample of some of the services offered are described in Table 10.2

TABLE 10.2

Name	Type*	Database	Supplier
ASCA	I	Science Citation	Institute for Scientific Information,
ASCATOPICS	S	Index and Social Sciences Citation Index	USA
BIS	I	BIOSIS Previews	United Kingdom Chemical Information Service
CAN/SDI	I	14	Canadian Institute for Scientific and Technical Information
CARD-A-LERT	S	COMPENDEX	Engineering Index Inc., USA
CHEMINFORM	I	Chemical Abstracts Condensates	Chemie Information und Dokumentation, West Germany
CLASS	I&S	BIOSIS Previews	BIOSIS, USA
COMPENDEX	I	COMPENDEX	Loughborough University, UK
DRUGDOC	I	DRUGDOC	Excerpta Medica, Netherlands
GEODE	I&S	Part of Bulletin Signalétique	Bureau de Recherches Geologiques et Minieres, France
INSPEC (SDI)	I	INSPEC	Institution of Electrical Engineers, UK
MACROPROFILES	S	Chemical Abstracts Condensates	United Kingdom Chemical Information Service
RIT (SDI)	I	About 18	Royal Institute of Technology, Sweden
TOPICS	S	INSPEC	Institution of Electrical Engineers, UK
UKCIS (SDI)	I	Chemical Abstracts Condensates	United Kingdom Chemical Information Service
WELDASEARCH	I	Welding Abstracts	The Welding Institute, UK

* I = Individual Profile. S = Standard Profile.

Many services offer group or standard profiles on general areas of interest.

It can be seen that the organizations which offer SDI services are either the database producers or are special centres which in some cases have been set up to offer information services.

UKCIS is an example of such a special centre. It was set up in 1969 and offers a variety of computer-based information retrieval services in chemistry and biology. Databases are received from the Chemical Abstracts Service and the Biosciences Information Service of Biological Abstracts (BIOSIS). UKCIS are also responsible for indexing about 11 000 documents annually for the Chemical Abstracts Service. The UK MEDLARS centre at the British Library Lending Division runs an SDI service on the MEDLARS database. At present the on-line search system MEDLINE at the National Library of Medicine in Washington is used for this service.

In some countries the national library is responsible for offering an SDI service. The CAN/SDI system has been operating since 1969 and currently serves about 6000 people.[11] Australia, Belgium and Denmark also run SDI services on external databases from the national library.

In some instances academic institutions have become information processing centres. The Royal Institute of Technology offers SDI and retrospective search services to local industry in Stockholm. This has been operational since 1967.[3] The University of Georgia in the USA is another example of an academic institution as an information processing centre. Their system has grown from 10 profiles and 1 database in 1968 to 3500 profiles and 10 databases in 1973.[14]

EVALUATION AND COSTS

Evaluation and monitoring of SDI systems is necessary for obtaining information on the performance of the system and in assessing users' reactions to the service. Running an SDI system can be costly and in the current economic climate it is necessary to ensure that a cost-effective service is being offered. When setting up an SDI service the various alternatives outlined above need to be investigated to find the optimum solution. Services, databases and program packages can sometimes be used for a trial period so that their suitability to the system can be evaluated. Some criteria for assessing the effectiveness of SDI systems are:

(a) *Coverage of the database(s) used.*
(b) *Currency of the database(s) used.*
(c) *Ease of use.* This should be studied from the user's viewpoint, the information scientist's viewpoint for profile construction and the administrator's viewpoint for the reliability of the tapes, constancy of format, etc. if an external database is used.
(d) *Output.* There are various factors to be considered:
    content of reference;
    form—line-printer or card, and if card what size?
    order of references—can it be specified?

(e) *Retrieval performance*. Recall and precision measures are usually used.

(f) *Search keys available*. The number of access points in the record affects the recall and precision measurements. The method by which search keys are combined should also be considered, and whether or not truncation of terms is allowed.

A comparison of two commercial services, ASCA and UKCIS, was recently undertaken by the Central Electricity Generating Board.[15] The number of relevant references retrieved from ASCA was higher than those retrieved from the UKCIS search. However, the UKCIS search retrieved relevant references which had been missed by the ASCA search. It was decided, therefore, to continue both subscriptions. Some general conclusions made were:

(a) some manual searching and following up of references is required to be reasonably sure of good coverage;

(b) it is necessary to keep assessing the output and modifying the profile appropriately;

(c) it is necessary to take considerable care when writing new profiles.

Another type of evaluation study was undertaken by the Wellcome Group of Companies.[8] They wished to compare the performance (in terms of selectivity, timeliness and quality of indexing) of an externally produced database (DRUGDOC) with their own indexing. Thirty-nine journals which are regularly scanned by Excerpta Medica and Wellcome were used in the experiment. The results of the evaluation showed that DRUGDOC would be useful as a supplement to the literature covered by Wellcome and so they have continued their subscription.

Some of the criteria for the evaluation and selection of databases and database services are described in Williams' paper.[16]

As well as measuring the system, it is necessary to measure users' requirements and reactions. Suggestions from users can sometimes be used to improve the service. Costs of running SDI services usually decrease with an increase in the number of users. Education in the possibilities of SDI is therefore necessary, although this in itself involves a cost to the organization. The system should be oriented towards the user and be quick to amend profiles, changes of address, and so on.

At the University of Calgary the information service was designed after users' requirements had been analysed.[17] The draft design which was prepared during the feasibility study was also discussed with potential users. The system is now operational and a monthly analysis of costs is made. The cost per relevant hit and the cost per profile are used to measure the cost-effectiveness of the system.

The effect which an SDI service has on the library also needs to be monitored and included in the costs. If external databases are used, users may well want the library to acquire the relevant documents retrieved from the search which are not already in the library. An increase in inter-library loans is therefore likely.

As with most computer-based systems in the library, the cost of setting up an SDI service splits into three parts:

    development;
    running;
    staff.

The differences between these costs are obviously dependent on the type of SDI service offered.

Costs of services obviously change but some are included here:

(a) Database costs

Name	Cost/ year	Frequency of update	References/ month	Cost/year of printed product
COMPENDEX	$6500	Monthly	7000	about $600
ERIC (JOURNALS)	$280	Quarterly	2500	$50
SCI (SOURCE + CITATION)	$20 000	Weekly	16 000	$2850

(b) SDI services

Name	Type	Database	Frequency	Cost/year/ profile
ASCATOPICS	S	SCI + SSCI	Weekly	$100
CARD-A-LERT	S	COMPENDEX	Weekly	$65
CLASS	I	BIOSIS	3 × month	$175
CLASS	S	BIOSIS	3 × month	$50
COMPENDEX	I	COMPENDEX	Monthly	£50
MACROPROFILES	S	CACON	Fortnightly	£38
MEDLARS (UK)	I	MEDLARS	Monthly	£15

The cost of running an SDI system in-house is made up of the fairly fixed cost of maintaining the database and the variable cost of profile construction, computer processing and distribution of output.

In a recent survey commissioned by the Organization for Economic Co-operation and Development,[18] 18 operational computer-based SDI systems in the USA and Europe were analysed using a structured cost analysis scheme. There was a wide variation from 5 cents to 111 cents (all costing was done in US dollars) for the total cost per item output.

The three main conclusions were:

(a) organizational management, salary variations and staff productivity have more influence on costs than technical factors;
(b) staff costs constitute a much higher proportion of total costs than computer processing costs;

(c) however accurately processing costs can be estimated, individual factors such as marketing, overheads and development are peculiar to each organization.

Dammers reports that several surveys have indicated that the composite annual cost per profile term of processing a database such as Chemical Abstracts Condensates is around £1.[19] He also reports that users are prepared to accept lower precision and recall measures than the information system designers had assumed.

EXAMPLE 1: RUBBER AND PLASTICS RESEARCH ASSOCIATION (RAPRA)[20]

RAPRA is one of the many research associations in the UK offering services to a particular industry. One of these services is information and 25% of RAPRA's staff is employed in the information department.

Since its establishment in 1919 the association has collected information and recorded this in the form of classified abstracts on cards. A current-awareness periodical, *RAPRA Abstracts*, is produced for the 500 or so members of the association. 25 000 abstracts are produced and about 13 000 queries answered each year. In the 1960s, there was an increase in publications covered, as well as an increase in demand from the industry. Additional services such as SDI, selected bibliographies and abstracts in machine-readable form were required and so it was therefore necessary to convert to a computer-based system.

After an investigation of available packages, ASSASSIN was chosen in late 1971. At this time RAPRA was the only non-ICI user of the package.

Documents to be input to the system are studied and a short indicative abstract of about 10 lines is written. The bibliographic details and the abstract are written on to specially prepared ASSASSIN input sheets. The information is punched on to paper-tape at RAPRA. As well as being used as input to ASSASSIN, the punched paper-tape is used in the production of the printed *RAPRA Abstracts* journal. The information, on punched paper-tape, is sent to ICI's bureau where it is processed on an IBM 360/65 computer. The ASSASSIN package is used to produce:

a weekly SDI service;
author indexes to *RAPRA Abstracts*;
magnetic tapes of *RAPRA Abstracts* which are sold to other organizations;
retrospective searches of the file back until 1971.

The SDI system was run experimentally on amenable in-house staff before being released to members of the association. The members were apprehensive about losing the personal touch and so the SDI service was introduced gradually. So far, experience has shown that the computer-based SDI system costs much less than the manual SDI system.

RAPRA also make use of ASSASSIN for producing author and title lists of books held by the library.

EXAMPLE 2: SHELL RESEARCH LTD., SITTINGBOURNE RESEARCH LABORATORIES

The RAPRA system is an example of an organization running an SDI system with an in-house database on an external package. Shell is an example of the opposite, in that it uses external databases on an in-house program.

The laboratories at Sittingbourne house 650 people who are involved in biological, chemical and biochemical research.

In 1956, the Technical Information Services group was set up. This group is responsible for the computer services as well as the library and information services. In the early 1960s, no current-awareness service was offered although specific groups were provided with bibliographies. By the mid-1960s, the staff of the group became aware of a need for a current-awareness service. The announcement by the Chemical Abstracts Service of the availability of the Chemical Titles magnetic tape service initiated thoughts of a computer-based information service.

In 1966/67, a pilot computer-based SDI service ran for 18 months. The system was based on the Chemical Titles database and was run on an IBM 1401 computer at the Shell Centre in London. One hundred users received notifications from the service and despite technical problems with the tapes and the programs the users responded enthusiastically to the designers.

In 1968, the decision to implement a full in-house information service was taken. The designers were faced with three problems:

(a) *Whose hardware to use?* The choice was between the local Univac 9300 and the remote IBM 360 series at the Shell Centre in London.

(b) *What software to use?* Packages such as ASSASSIN, CAN/SDI and TEXTPAC were available on the IBM computer but not on the Univac computer.

(c) *What database(s) to use?*

They decided to write their own programs for the Univac computer and to use the Chemical Abstracts Condensates database, which became available late in 1968. This database offered the best coverage for the laboratories, keywords are included in the record and the group had experience of the Chemical Abstracts Service products. The system began operation in 1969 and in 1970 the BIOSIS Previews database was added.

Some of the features of the SDI system at Shell are:

(a) the profiles are created using Boolean logic;

(b) left- and right-hand truncation of terms is possible;

(c) searches can be made on text (title or keyword), author, CODEN or Biological Abstracts codes;

(d) output is on 6 × 4 in cards;

(e) all records are stored using a format defined by EUSIDIC.

Currently about 1000 profiles, consisting of an average of 10 terms, are being processed. These profiles come from on-site users and from other Shell organizations. The running costs break down into:

database (currently £3300 per year for CACON, £2500 per year for BIOSIS Previews);
computer time (£17 per hour);
special stationery (cost of cards was £750 per year in 1973/74);
customer liaison.

The average cost is about £1.50 per term per year per database. Thus, an average profile of 10 terms costs the organization £15 per year to be run against one database. These figures suggest that a computer-based SDI system is justified if there are more than 100 profiles or 1000 search terms.

Since the system at Sittingbourne is so popular some studies of the users and the benefits to them have been made.[21]

Some of the factors that contributed to the growth of the SDI system were:

it is relatively cheap;
it is strongly user oriented;
profile formulation is simple;
there is no alternative current-awareness service;
the two databases give good coverage of the relevant subject interests.

A full cost benefit analysis of the SDI service was undertaken at the end of 1971. The users were asked to assess the value of the service in terms of time saved in literature searching over the year. The results showed that the users assessed the cost benefits of the service at three times more than the actual cost of running the service.

The database is also used for retrospective searching and for the production of lists and KWAC indexes.

EXAMPLE 3: INSPEC—INFORMATION SERVICES IN PHYSICS, ELECTROTECHNOLOGY, COMPUTERS AND CONTROL[22]

This example is aimed at showing some of the services offered by a database producer.

In 1898, The Physical Society and The Institution of Electrical Engineers started a joint publication of abstracts of all appropriate papers on physical and electrical engineering subjects. This was known as *Science Abstracts*. Currently there are three abstracts journals published by INSPEC: *Physics Abstracts*, *Electrical and Electronics Abstracts* and *Computer and Control Abstracts*. In 1965, preliminary studies, under a grant from OSTI, were made into the feasibility of using computer techniques in the publication of these journals. Early in 1967 it was decided to go ahead and the computer-based system went into operation in 1969 on a self-supporting basis.

(1) *Input*

Forty-five full-time information scientists (and several hundred part-time abstractors) index and abstract items to be included in the database. Items are selected on their subject coverage although some journals are abstracted 'from cover to cover'. About 140 000 (1975/76 figures) items are processed each year from journals, theses, reports, patents, books and conference proceedings. Items are described by controlled index terms from the INSPEC thesaurus (2–3 terms per item) and by free index terms (7–8 terms per item). This is done to ensure that optimum search strategies can be employed.

(2) *Database*

This exists as a single database covering three sections, namely physics, electro-technology, and computers and control. During 1975, 87 000, 45 000 and 27 000 items respectively were added in to the three sections. As can be seen from the figures some records appear in more than one section.

(3) *Output*

Apart from the printed and the microform journals, the two main services offered are the magnetic tape service and the SDI service.

(a) *Magnetic tape service.* All combinations of the three sections are available. Some sample current (1976) costs for the base subscription are:

Computer and Control Abstracts	£1450 per year;
All three sections with abstracts	£2700 per year;
All three sections without abstracts	£2000 per year.

The tapes are produced twice monthly. Back issues of the tapes with abstracts are also available.

When the tape service started in 1970 there were three subscribers, in 1973 there were 23 and in 1975 there were 40. The majority subscribe to all three sections with abstracts. Subscribers use the tapes for:

Offering in-house SDI and retrospective search services. The average number of SDI profiles per subscriber (according to a partial survey carried out in early 1975) was 160.

Offering on-line search services to large communities. The INSPEC tapes are currently licensed to the following information processing centres:

Lockheed in California,
Canadian Institute for Scientific and Technical Information for the CAN/OLE system;
European Space Agency in Frascati, Rome.

The magnetic tapes have been processed on a wide range of computers.

(b) *SDI service.* As shown in Table 2, INSPEC offer an individual and a topic-based SDI service. The subscriber receives output weekly on 105 × 100 mm cards. The information on a card consists of:

title;
author name(s);
organization where the work reported was carried out;
full bibliographic reference of source document;
language (if it is not English);
classification codes and free index terms;
abstract—as much as space will allow (this was added in mid-1976).

The individual profile costs from £80 per year. The TOPICS profile costs £30 per year. There are currently about 80 topics which include:

information science (mechanized systems);
adaptive and learning systems including artificial intelligence;
holography.

REFERENCES

1. H. P. Luhn, Selective Dissemination of New Scientific Information with the Aid of Electronic Processing Equipment. *American Documentation*, **12**, 131–8 (1961).
2. E. M. Keen, Search Strategy Evaluation in Manual and Automated Systems. *Aslib Proceedings*, **20**, 65–74 (1968).
3. Z. Gluchowicz, User interface in an information dissemination network mode, in *The Interactive Library: Computerized Processes in Library and Information Networks* (ed. S. Schwarz), Swedish Society for Technical Documentation, Stockholm (1975). ISBN 91 7390 000 1.
4. L. Evans, *Optimum Degree of User Participation in SDI Profile Generation*, Institution of Electrical Engineers, London (1973). ISBN 0 85296 4137.
5. R. Finer, *A Guide to Selected Computer-Based Information Services*, Aslib, London (1972). ISBN 0 85142 045 1.
6. A. T. Kruzas, *Encyclopedia of Information Systems and Services*, 2nd edition, A. T. Kruzas, Ann Arbor, Michigan (1973).
7. G. Pratt, *Databases in Europe*, Aslib, London (1975). ISBN 0 85142 076 1.
8. E. J. Scott, H. M. Townley and B. T. Stern, A Technique for the Evaluation of a Commercial Information Service and Some Preliminary Results from the Drugdoc Service of the Excerpta Medica Foundation. *Information Storage and Retrieval*, **7**, 149–65 (1971).
9. C. R. Clough and K. M. Bramwell, A Single Computer-Based System for Both Current-Awareness and Retrospective Search: Operating Experience with ASSASSIN. *Journal of Documentation*, **27**, 243–53 (1974).
10. W. Thom, ACOMPLIS: a Computerised Information Service. *Greater London Intelligence Quarterly*, **30**, 15–17 (1975).
11. G. R. Mauerhoff, CAN/SDI: a National SDI System in Canada. *Libri*, **24**, 19–29 (1974).
12. P. M. Linn, The Engineering Information Service at Loughborough University: Practical Experience in Providing an SDI Service from COMPENDEX Tapes. *Program*, **9**, 64–77 (1975).
13. D. L. Hines, Computerized Literature Searches in an Engineering Library. *Special Libraries*, **66**, 197–204 (1975).
14. J. L. Carmon, A Campus-Based Information Center. *Special Libraries*, **64**, 65–9, (1973).

15. A. A. Parry, R. G. Linford and J. I. Rich, Computer Literature Searches—a Comparison of the Performance on Two Commercial Systems in an Interdisciplinary Subject. *Information Scientist*, **8**, 179–87 (1974).
16. M. E. Williams, Criteria for Evaluation and Selection of Data Bases and Data Base Services. *Special Libraries*, **66**, 561–9 (1975).
17. O. R. Standera, Costs and Effectiveness in the Evolution of an Information System. A Case Study. *Journal of the American Society for Information Science*, **7**, 203–7 (1974).
18. P. H. Vickers, A Cost Survey of Mechanized Information Systems. *Journal of Documentation*, **29**, 258–80 (1973).
19. H. F. Dammers, The Economics of Computer-Based Information Systems: a Review. *Journal of Documentation*, **31**, 38–45 (1975).
20. D. R. Dawson, RAPRA—Looking to the 80s. *Aslib Proceedings*, **26**, 396–402 (1974).
21. H. F. Dammers, Economic evaluation of current-awareness systems, in *EURIM— A European Conference on Research into the Management of Information Services and Libraries*, Aslib, London (1973). ISBN 0 85142 059 1.
22. D. H. Barlow, Serving six user areas from the INSPEC database: some of the collection and indexing problems involved, in *First European Congress on Documentation Systems and Networks*, Office for Official Publications of the European Communities, Luxembourg (1973).

FURTHER READING

P. Leggate, Computer-Based Current-Awareness Services. *Journal of Documentation* **31**, 93–115 (1975).
M. L. Mathies and P. G. Watson, *Computer-Based Reference Service*, American Library Association, Chicago (1973). ISBN 0 8389 0156 5.

CHAPTER 11

RETROSPECTIVE SEARCH SYSTEMS

INTRODUCTION

A retrospective search system can be described as the reverse of an SDI system. In an SDI system a document initiates a search of a user file whereas with a retrospective search system a user initiates a search of a document file.

Computers were first used for this application during the late 1950s and early 1960s. The majority of these first systems were extensions of punched card systems and were batch processed.

One of the first computer-based retrospective search systems was the MEDLARS search service. Typically, the user would fill in a query form and send it to the nearest MEDLARS centre where trained information scientists would translate the query into a search strategy using MESH terms. The searches for a number of users would be batched up and processed at periodic intervals against the MEDLARS database. The matching references would be sent to each user. The MEDLARS search service started to operate in the USA in 1964 and in the UK in 1966. More details on the MEDLARS database are given in Chapter 9.

One factor in the growth of these systems in the 1960s was the increased availability of machine-readable databases. Other factors were the advances in computer technology and the realization of the high labour costs of running an information service using manual techniques.

By 1965 there were several projects in progress concerned with on-line searching of bibliographic databases. These included:

(a) The work at the Massachusetts Institute of Technology on the Technical Information Project.[1] The aim of this project was to provide a test-bed for evaluating search strategies and learning how modern technology could aid scientific information interchange. This system formed a basis for several subsequent on-line systems.

(b) The System Development Corporation (SDC) of Santa Monica, California was operating a service which provided on-line access for four hours a day to 200 000 documents for 13 government and private organizations. The work was sponsored by the Advanced Research Projects Agency (ARPA) of the US Department of Defense.[2]

(c) The Lockheed Missiles Corporation of Palo Alto, California started to develop an on-line search package for the National Aeronautics and Space Administration. The package is known as RECON (Remote Console) and was based on their own package called DIALOG®.[3]

By 1968 SDC had also written a software package for on-line searching. This is known as ORBIT (On-Line Retrieval of Bibliographic Information Time-Shared). A modified version of this package, AIM-TWX (Abridged Index Medicus by Teletypewriter Exchange Network), was run experimentally, for two and a half years, with the MEDLARS database at the National Library of Medicine.

SDC and Lockheed are the two largest commercial organizations currently offering information services. They buy in databases and use purpose-built software and, through international telecommunications networks, offer on-line search services to very many countries. There are other organizations also offering both batch and on-line searching of retrospective files.

As with SDI systems, many organizations run their own retrospective search systems and sometimes buy in databases or software.

A RETROSPECTIVE SEARCH SYSTEM

A retrospective search system has the following features:

(a) translation of the user's request into the language of the system;
(b) comparison of the request with the descriptions of the documents in the database;
(c) selection of documents that match;
(d) receipt of information about these documents by the user.

In the 1960s, most retrospective search systems were batch processed. However, in the 1970s, there has been a rapid increase in the number of on-line systems.

On-line searching of retrospective files does have several advantages over batch searching:

(a) it gives immediate access to the database and so time delays are overcome;
(b) it allows the searcher to browse through the database;
(c) it allows the search strategy to be quickly refined and altered after the inspection of some retrieved references.

In the early days of on-line searching it was thought that this method would overcome the need for an intermediary person. However, current thinking points to the need for such a person as knowledge of the system commands, the telecommunications, the database and their interactions is required. An optimum situation exists when the requestor sits beside the intermediary and assists with the subject content of the search. An analogous situation exists with on-line ticket booking systems for air travel. In answer to a request for a ticket an operator locates available flights on a VDU. The system works best when the future traveller is present and can indicate which flight is most convenient.

The document descriptions that form the database of the retrospective search system can be internally or externally produced. The machine-readable databases which were described in Chapter 10 are frequently used for retrospective search systems.

When formulating search strategies for retrospective systems it is necessary to know the answers to the following questions:

what fields are in the record?
which fields are capable of being searched?
what records are in the database?

Some retrospective search systems have several databases available for searching and so the coverage and features of each needs to be ascertained.

In a batch-processed system the references are normally produced on a line-printer. In an on-line system some references can be viewed at the terminal. However, if many references are required these are normally produced on a line-printer and then sent to the requestor.

Retrospective search systems typically have very large files of document descriptions. These are frequently organized in an inverted file structure.[2,3]

Because of the advantages of on-line-processed systems, it seems likely that this will be the method of processing retrospective search systems in the future. Therefore, this chapter will place more emphasis on on-line systems.

ACCESS

With batch-processed systems the user's query is usually communicated to the information scientist by telephone, telex, letter or personal visit. The resulting references are then communicated to the user in a similar way. Thus, the normal channels of communication are sufficient for batch-processed retrospective searches. This is not so for on-line systems and there are several aspects to the access problem.

Equipment

As outlined in Chapter 2, teletypewriters and visual display terminals are used for on-line processing.

Teletypewriters are in general slow but do have the advantage of producing hard copy, or a printed record of the search, which can be taken away by the searcher.

Visual display units can operate much faster but typically do not have an integral printing unit. Hard copy output must be printed either on a line-printer or on a printer attached to the VDU. The latter increases the cost of the VDU and decreases the speed of operation.

Form of output

Most retrieval systems are based on a bibliographic description, some descriptor terms and sometimes an abstract for each document being stored in the computer. This information forms the output of the search and is used in deciding the relevancy of the document. The document itself must be accessed in the normal manner.

Some retrospective search systems, however, are making use of microfiche or ultrafiche to store the original document.

In the UK an experimental terminal for information retrieval work has been developed by GEC Marconi Systems.[4] The terminal is based on a system whereby only the searchable terms and their reference number are stored on the computer. When the user's request is compared with the searchable terms the matching reference number(s) are used to automatically locate a frame (or frames) on a set of ultrafiche. The frame which contains the original document is then displayed to the searcher. A prototype of this terminal is currently being used at the Wellcome Laboratories in their hybrid computer/microform information storage and retrieval system.

The Swiss Department of Defence also operates a hybrid computer and microform information system. A PDP 11/40 computer is used to store information on books, abstracts from serials, laws and legal texts. The database is searched on-line and the output is a frame number which is used to select automatically a frame from a cartridge of microfiche. This system has been operational since early 1975.

Supplier communication

When using an on-line retrospective search service supplied by an external organization, communication with the supplier may be difficult. Some of the questions to be answered include:

    (a) are all the databases available all the time?

    (b) are there any general newsletters about the service?

    (c) how does one find out how long the system will be down if informed that it is inaccessible?

    (d) how does one obtain the necessary passwords to use the system?

    (e) how long will it take for the references which have been printed off-line to be received?

(f) is special equipment required?
(g) is the daily NEWS printed at 'log-on'?
(h) is there any documentation about the system?
(i) is there any training provided?
(j) when is the system available?
(k) when will the bills arrive?

Telecommunications

This aspect of the access problem is dependent on the communications authority in individual countries. The situation in the UK is described.

If the distance is not too great and public land is not crossed, the terminal can be hard-wired to the computer to provide an on-line search service. An organization on a geographically compact site that runs an on-line search service from the local computer would use this method of connection.

In other instances the telephone network is used. This can either be via public lines or from a special line leased from the Post Office. The decision as to which of these is most cost-effective is dependent on the frequency and the time of day of use.

To access some of the international telecommunications networks the local node of the network is dialled using a telephone. The node, usually a mini-computer, switches messages through to the required computer on the network. Some of the networks that are currently used for on-line retrospective searching are:

(a) *ARPA*. This can only be used for experimental work. The National Library of Medicine in Washington is accessible via the network, and there is a node of the network at University College, London.

(b) *ESA*. The European Space Agency's network links many computers in various European countries. The node at the Department of Industry's Technology Reports Centre (TRC) in Kent enables UK users to access the ESA's Space Documentation Service.

(c) *TELENET*. This is a network operated by Bolt, Baranek and Newman in North America. A transatlantic link is planned shortly. SDC and Lockheed can be accessed via the network.

(d) *TYMNET*. This is a network operated by Tymshare Incorporated of the USA. The network is mainly based in North America but there are several nodes in Europe which allow access to SDC and Lockheed. At present a node in Paris, Brussels or The Hague is used to give UK users access to the network.

SEARCH METHODS

Compiling a search request for a batch retrospective search is similar to compiling a user's profile in an SDI system. Boolean logic and/or weighted terms are usually used to express the concepts of the search. However, with on-line systems there are again differences.

Choosing of terms

As with batch or manual systems, this is frequently done by consulting a thesaurus before going on-line. However, once on-line one can usually determine how many times each term has been used for describing documents in the data-base. This can help in the choice of a broad or narrow strategy. The structure of the thesaurus can sometimes be displayed which helps in choosing broader and narrower terms. Terms alphabetically close to the one chosen can usually be displayed to check for any more possible terms. This enables typing errors to be highlighted and so is useful when an exhaustive search is required.

If any relevant documents are known by the searcher these can be retrieved by an author search and the terms used to describe that document can be checked for potential usefulness.

Combining terms

Boolean logic and weighted term searching are commonly used for combining terms into a search statement. Some designers of on-line search systems have tried other methods. The RIOT (Retrieval of Information by On-Line Terminal) system in operation at the United Kingdom Atomic Energy Authority's Culham Laboratory makes use of a specially designed visual display unit.[5] Terms within each row are ORed, then the first three rows are ANDed and finally NOTted with the fourth, e.g.

COMPUTER	AUTOMATION	MECHANIZATION
LIBRARY	INFORMATION	
BRITAIN	UK	
PUBLIC		

This is equivalent to the Boolean statement:

(COMPUTER OR AUTOMATION OR MECHANIZATION) AND (LIBRARY OR INFORMATION)
AND (BRITAIN OR UK) AND NOT PUBLIC.

The QUOBIRD (Queen's University On-Line Bibliographic Information Retrieval and Dissemination) system developed at Belfast also attempts to overcome the use of Boolean operators by referring to the intersection (AND) and union (OR) of terms.[6]

Matching of terms

If terms from a controlled vocabulary have been used to describe the documents in a database, then terms from that vocabulary will be used in the search statement and the query will be matched term by term.

Some on-line systems offer full text searching facilities. In such systems, words from various fields of the record (such as title, descriptor, abstract) are compared against a stop-list and those words which are not in the stop-list are used as search terms. These words can then be linked when choosing terms to retrieve documents that include the words in the same field, or in the same citation or within a specified distance of each other. Examples of linking words for documents on adult literacy in the ERIC database using the Lockheed DIALOG® system are given.

The DIALOG® command for choosing a search term is SELECT and this prints the number of references in which the search term has been used. The ways of finding documents on adult literacy, from the broadest to the narrowest, are:

Command	No. of references	Comment
SELECT ADULT (C) LITERACY	725	C—the words are in the same reference
SELECT ADULT (F) LITERACY	658	F—the words are in the same field
SELECT ADULT (3W) LITERACY	331	3W—the words are in the order shown with up to three intervening words
SELECT ADULT (2W) LITERACY	323	2W—as above but up to two intervening words
SELECT ADULT (W) LITERACY	305	W—as above with no intervening word
SELECT ADULT LITERACY	229	The phrase exists in the controlled vocabulary

String searching, as described in Chapter 10, is also available on some on-line systems.

Command language

When using an on-line system the searcher needs to be familiar with the commands of the system. Although the basic function of these commands is similar, the actual commands vary between systems. Some of the basic functions of a command language for on-line search systems are given and are accompanied by the specific commands of the DIALOG® and ELHILL software systems (the parameters of the commands vary and so the systems offer different facilities):

Functions	*DIALOG®*	*ELHILL*
Choose appropriate database	BEGIN	FILE
Select a term and find out how many times it has been used	SELECT	just enter the term or FIND
Look at alphabetically close terms	EXPAND	NEIGHBOR
Look at related terms	EXPAND	TREE
Form search statement	COMBINE	just enter terms
Look at some of the references on-line	TYPE	PRINT
Have the references printed off-line	PRINT	PRINT
Look at search statements generated so far	DISPLAY SETS	DIAGRAM
Store search statement on the computer for use another time	BEGIN followed by END/SAVE	STORESEARCH followed by FINISHED
Find out how to use a command	EXPLAIN	EXPLAIN
Finish the search	END	STOP

Other features of the command language which need to be ascertained are:

what is the symbol for the universal character?
what is the truncation symbol?
how is a single character erased?
how is a whole line erased?

SOFTWARE AND SERVICES

Software

The designer of a retrospective search service has the same three fundamental questions to answer as the designer of an SDI service:

should an external service be used totally?
are the details of the documents to be internally or externally produced?
is there a suitable software package for the system?

Some of the available packages for retrospective searching are described.

Name	*Details*
ASSASSIN	A general information retrieval package produced by ICI which includes the facility for batch retrospective searching.
BIRD	An on-line information retrieval package, based on the QUOBIRD system, and marketed by ICL.

Name	*Details*
DIALOG®	An on-line search system produced by Lockheed and used by them for their service.
ELHILL	Named after the Lister Hill National Center for Biomedical Communications, ELHILL is a modification of the ORBIT system and is used for the on-line MEDLARS service MEDLINE.
FILETAB	A general purpose package used for the selection and printing of data from files. It is available on a range of computers and is available from the National Computing Centre, UK.
FIND-2	Used by BP Chemicals, Fisons Ltd. and the Wellcome Laboratories for retrospective searching of databases produced by Derwent Publications.
FREESEARCH	An on-line text searching program which is available from Cybernet Time Sharing Ltd., UK and was used for the UK SCISEARCH service and the experimental RETRO-SPEC service.
INFIRS	Inverted File Information Retrieval System. INFIRS was developed at UKCIS and is used there for processing several databases in batch mode. It has been designed for possible use with on-line systems.
ORBIT	A package produced by SDC and used by them for their on-line information service.
RECON	A modified version of the DIALOG® software which is used by NASA and the Space Documentation Service of ESA.
SPECOL	Special Customer Orientated Language. SPECOL was written by the Civil Service in the UK for general information retrieval work. It is used at Bath University Library for running special searches on the library's catalogue.
STAIRS	Storage and Information Retrieval System. This is a package produced by IBM for on-line text retrieval systems on 360 and 370 series computers.
STATUS	A package of programs for on-line text word searching which has been developed at the Atomic Energy Research Establishment at Harwell, UK. It has been used for searching legal material at the Council of Europe.[7]
TEXTPAC	TEXTPAC is used by part of Unilever Ltd. and the Shell International Petroleum Company Ltd. for batch retrospective searching.
THOR-2	A package developed by the National Computing Centre, UK for use on ICL 1900 series computers. THOR-2 is used at the NCC for their on-line information retrieval service.

Some of the above packages, notably BIRD, STAIRS and STATUS, were included in a recent investigation of a suitable computer-based information system for libraries of the House of Commons and the House of Lords in the UK.

Comparisons of searching the same database on different software systems have been reported. Hummel's paper compares searching the toxicology database TOXLINE on ELHILL and RECON.[8] Humphrey's paper compares searching the MEDLARS database on ELHILL and STAIRS.[9]

As with any package, the librarian wishing to use a general retrospective search package should check with the computer centre staff on the availability of the package on the computer.

Services

A brief description of each of the four major international on-line retrospective search systems will be given.

(1) Lockheed DIALOG®

This service is operated on an IBM 360/50 at Lockheed Information Services in California.[2] The service is available via the TYMNET and TELENET networks. At present there are over 30 files covering various bibliographic databases which can be searched. The cost of using the system is dependent on the database used; examples are given in the section on costs.

(2) MEDLINE

This is the on-line MEDLARS service operated on an IBM 370/158 computer at the National Library of Medicine, Washington.[10] The service is available via the ARPA and TYMNET networks. SDC were responsible for providing the software for the MEDLINE service in 1970. AIM-TWX was used experimentally and in 1973 the full service using ELHILL was set up.

Apart from the main files of the MEDLARS database of medical literature, other available files include:

CANCERLINE—which is the machine-readable database formed from *Cancer Therapy Abstracts, Carcinogenic Abstracts* and *Cancer Research Projects;*

CATLINE —which contains bibliographic details of monographs, serials and reports catalogued at NLM since 1965;

SDILINE —which contains the latest month's input to the MEDLARS file;

SERLINE —which contains bibliographic and location information for over 6000 biomedical serials;

TOXLINE —which contains articles on toxicity as well as the database formed from *Pharmaceutical Abstracts, Pesticide Abstracts* and *Environmental Pollution Abstracts.*

(3) SDS RECON

The Space Documentation Centre of the ESA use RECON to offer an information service from several databases to the 10 member countries of the association.[11] The service operates on an IBM 360/65 based at Frascati, near Rome. Users of the system need to link in to the leased line network which links the member countries. In 1976, a dial-up service, known as DIALTECH, was started by TRC. This enables anyone in the UK to dial the node of the network at TRC in Kent and be connected to the system in Rome.

(4) SDC ORBIT

SDC offers a similar service to Lockheed and provides users in 16 countries on-line access to over 20 databases containing more than 8 000 000 references.[3] The ORBIT software runs on an IBM 370/158 computer at Santa Monica and is available on the TELENET and TYMNET networks.

As with SDI services, several organizations offer retrospective search services.

In the UK, UKCIS undertake retrospective searches for users. These are frequently carried out using the Lockheed DIALOG® or ESA RECON services. The British Library Lending Division used to run batch MEDLARS searches but these searches are now carried out using MEDLINE.

In France, the Centre National de la Recherche Scientifique runs a batch retrospective search service on the database formed from *Bulletin Signaletique*. This is part of a general information service known as PASCAL. An on-line search system is being developed.

In Sweden, the Royal Institute of Technology has offered a retrospective search service using ESA RECON since 1972. The Karolinska Institute in Stockholm runs the MEDLINE system. MEDLINE is also run at the Deutsche Institut fur Medizinische Dokumentation und Information (DIMDI) in West Germany.

National libraries also organize retrospective search services. In Canada, the CAN/OLE (Canadian On-Line Enquiry) service forms part of the scientific and technical information service. In Australia, the National Library subscribes to the BIOSIS Previews, ERIC and MEDLARS databases and offers a retrospective search service.

TRAINING AND INSTRUCTION OF USERS [12]

With batch retrospective search systems users are rarely involved directly with the system and so the training aspect pertains only to the intermediary searcher. In many cases (e.g. UK MEDLARS centre) these are the same people who are responsible for indexing documents that enter the system. They are therefore well used to the vagaries of the database.

With on-line searching many more people are potentially involved, and at many levels. The major services usually run training courses for prospective customers. These vary in length, content, cost and accessibility.

Before using MEDLINE, users are required to attend a two to three day course which will be held at the nearest MEDLARS centre. In the UK this consists of lecture sessions explaining:

the concepts of MEDLARS indexing;
how to search using the ELHILL commands;
practicalities of access and logging on and off;
databases available;
the current service and possible future developments.

Ample time is given for individual practical sessions at the terminal, under the guidance of an experienced MEDLINE searcher.

In general there are three levels of training in the use of on-line bibliographic databases.

Terminal usage

Many searchers may not have experienced on-line communication with a computer. It is necessary, therefore, to allow a new user time to get accustomed to on-line interaction with a computer. If a remote computer is used for information retrieval the familiarization can take place on the local computer if on-line facilities are available.

Creating search strategies

General instruction on choosing terms, combining terms and forming broad and narrow search strategies needs to be given. The commands used for searching must also be explained as well as the effect of their use on the various databases.

For example, if using ELHILL on the MEDLARS database a warning is given against using the MESH term HUMAN on its own as a search term. It generates too many entries to be stored in the space available on the computer. It is necessary, therefore, always to AND HUMAN with another MESH term.

Factors associated with the database

These include:

fields of the record;
searchable fields;
coverage of the database;
indexing policy;
availability of a thesaurus;
frequency with which the database is updated;
limitations on the use of commands on the database.

It is obviously necessary for a training course to be aimed at the general level of the participants. The information needed by a new user of an on-line search system is very different from the information needed by an experienced user who wishes to know the peculiarities of a particular system. The method of instruction can vary between:

Personal instruction. This can be expensive and may not be feasible if there are many geographically remote users to be trained.
Audio-visual instruction. Tape-slide programs or videotapes can be made and then played back at any time by the user.
Computer-assisted instruction. This can vary in complexity.

Sometimes all three methods are used.

The BLRDD are currently financing several projects concerned with studying methods of teaching on-line bibliographic searching. At Aberystwyth, one method of training included the student listening to an audio commentary of a search which was being played back locally from a magnetic tape cassette on a Texas Instruments Silent 700 terminal. Any number can be trained by this method, with the costs, apart from the equipment costs, being:

(a) the cost of running the original search;
(b) the cost of the tutor's time in preparing the commentary.

A necessary adjunct to any method of instruction is the written documentation. This usually consists of:

a manual which gives full details about the command language and the databases and is kept up-to-date;
numerous examples of sample searches;
a summary sheet of commands which can easily be referred to when at the terminal.

On-line system suppliers usually produce monthly or quarterly newsletters which include advice on techniques to be used, explanation of amendments to the system, answers to users' problems and plans of future developments.

EVALUATION AND COSTS

Methods of evaluating batch retrospective search systems are similar to those for evaluating SDI systems. The main factors which influence the recall and precision measurements are the indexing policy, the vocabulary, the searching method and the searcher's interaction with the system.

A major evaluation of the MEDLARS batch retrospective service was undertaken in the late 1960s;[13] 302 searches retrieved, on average, 200 references. The average recall ratio was 58% and the average precision ratio was 50%.

The charge made by UKCIS for carrying out a batch retrospective search of

the BIOSIS Previews database is given as an example of costs of a batch
retrospective search service:

Years	Content of output	Price	Postage
1959–1974	Abstract and citation	£110	£6.00 per 100 references
1959–1974	Reference numbers	£70	£0.50 per 100 references

With on-line systems many other factors need to be taken into consideration
when evaluating the system. These include:

access;
communication with the system supplier;
ease of using commands;
ease of using the equipment;
response time;
time taken for delivery of off-line prints;
time taken to do a search.

The response time of an on-line system depends to some extent on the means
by which the system is accessed; for instance, most satellites, being 23 000 miles
high will impose a delay of 0.5 seconds in addition to any other delays. If the
response time is too long, the searcher will become bored whereas if the response
time is too short the searcher may feel harassed.

Some of the above factors are subjective and therefore difficult to measure.
Evaluations of on-line search systems have been undertaken and many are
reported in Chapter 9 of Lancaster's book.[14]

The results of evaluation studies should be considered when selecting an
on-line information retrieval service. Other criteria, apart from those described
in the previous section on supplier communication, are the available databases,
the necessary hardware, the means of transmission and, most importantly, the
needs of the user.[15]

The cost of accessing the large on-line retrospective services breaks down into
four parts.

Database costs

These are normally charged by the hour spent at the terminal. The prices range
from $25 to $150 per hour. Average, minimum and maximum charges for three
services are given in Ref. 16:

	Average ($ per hour)	Minimum ($ per hour)	Maximum ($ per hour)
ESA	49.88	36	64
Lockheed	64.33	25	150
SDC	82.22	40	120

Table 11.1 gives some idea of the differing costs for differing databases on differing systems. The database sizes are based on the latest available information, this being:

ESA	December 1975
Lockheed	April 1976
SDC	October 1975

Note: SDC reduced the cost of accessing some of their databases in April 1976.

TABLE 11.1

Database	Start date	Size	Service	Database cost ($ per hour)	Print costs ($ per ref.)
BIOSIS PREVIEWS	1972	1 030 000	Lockheed	65	.10
CA CONDENSATES	1969	2 005 000	ESA	64	.08
CA CONDENSATES	1972	1 400 000	Lockheed	45	.08
CA CONDENSATES	1972	1 307 000	SDC	60	.12
CLAIMS/CHEM	1950	392 000	Lockheed	150	.10
COMPENDEX	1969	450 000	ESA	53	.06
COMPENDEX	1970	467 000	Lockheed	65	.10
COMPENDEX	1970	420 000	SDC	90	.20
ERIC	1966	242 500	Lockheed	25	.10
ERIC	1966	216 000	SDC	40	.12
LIBCON	1965	672 000	SDC	120	.25
METADEX	1969	187 000	ESA	45	.06
POLLUTION	1970	350 00	SDC	90	.15
PSYCHOLOGICAL ABSTRACTS	1967	230 000	Lockheed	50	.10

Communication costs

This is made up of telephone costs and/or the cost of using the network. For instance, a charge of $22 per hour is made for using the TYMSHARE network. The telephone cost is dependent on the distance from the nearest node of the network.

Equipment costs

This includes the cost of the terminal and the cost of a modem or acoustic coupler.

Staff costs

If an intermediary carries out the search, then this staff time should be included in the costs.

In an evaluation of EARS (Epilepsy Abstracts Retrieval System) the search times ranged between three minutes and three hours. Studies at SDC have shown that the average time spent at the terminal is 19.1 minutes, with 20.7 minutes, on average, spent planning the search and 17.7 minutes, on average, spent in post-terminal work.[17] Thus, using these average figures a search on the Biosis Previews database (going back to 1972) using Lockheed from Aberystwyth would currently cost:

	$	£
Database (19.1 minutes @ $65 per hour)	21.01	11.67
Network (19.1 minutes @ $22 per hour)	7.01	3.89
Telephone (19.1 minutes @ 37p per minute)		7.06
		22.62

(*Notes:* (a) Rate of $1.80 = £1 used. (b) 37p per minute is the cost of an international call connected via the operator to the nearest TYMNET node, which is currently in Paris.)

The total cost would be £22.62 + £5.56 per 100 references plus staff and equipment costs. The comparable UKCIS cost for running on-line searches for a client on this database is £47.00.

Several studies comparing manual and computer-based search systems have been undertaken. Elman[18] concludes that on-line searching of the Lockheed DIALOG® system is an efficient and cost-effective complement to manual searching, and in some cases, especially in special libraries, it provides an acceptable substitute. Goodliffe and Hayler,[19] however, found that searching the experimental RETROSPEC system was more costly than performing manual searches. The RETROSPEC system offered limited search facilities on a database of three years input to the computer and control abstracts part of INSPEC.

FUTURE

Large-scale access to on-line bibliographic information retrieval services has only been available for a short period. Many problems still need to be solved. In the USA a National Science Foundation study is underway. Questions to be answered include:

(a) is on-line searching cost-effective?
(b) do on-line systems require additional staff?
(c) who should do the searching?
(d) what makes a good searcher?
(e) what is the effect of the method of indexing?
(f) what is the effect on the library administration?

Lockheed, NASA, SDC and other large processing centres are involved in this study.[17] Lockheed have set up terminals in five public libraries as part of the experiment. In this way the service is brought to the person in the street.

Preliminary reports of the study are appearing in the literature.[20] Some of the effects on the public libraries' administration during the first year, when the equipment and system costs were free to the library, were:

new library customers;
an increased workload;
an increased awareness of the library's services.

In Europe the governments of the nine countries of the European Economic Community have decided to set up a network for scientific, technical, social, economic and legal information. This is known as EURONET.

The impetus for implementing such a network came from a survey carried out in 1974. As a result, estimates of the demand for on-line searches of scientific and technological information (STI) in Europe were made. The estimates were:[21]

in 1976   60 000 searches;
in 1980   960 000 searches;
in 1985   2 350 000 searches.

A study of alternative solutions to meet these demands was undertaken. If was concluded that a shared network approach with a moderate distribution to host computers would be three to ten times less expensive than individual systems in each country.

Thus, in 1975, the Commission of the European Communities allocated a budget of 6.6 million accounting units (during 1976 1 accounting unit = £0.57) for the development of the shared system, EURONET.

The overall plan of action for EURONET consists of three aspects:

(a) *Providing support for information services in selected subjects.* The Food and Agriculture Organization in Rome is an example of an existing international information service. Input from separate institutes is processed and merged in Rome and then disseminated to other countries. The other subjects to be covered will include the environment, medicine, education and metallurgy.

(b) *Creating a shared physical communications network.* Late in 1975 a contract for setting up this network was signed between the Commission of the European Communities and a consortium of the nine communications authorities. The current plan is for the network to be operational by late 1977. The main nodes of the network will be in Frankfurt, London, Paris and Rome. Initially, about 8 host computers and 30 databases will be linked to the network. INSPEC have recently been awarded a contract to investigate the feasibility of a standard command language, so that searching the various systems could be made easier for the users.

(c) *Training of specialists and education of users.* This is obviously important in any situation but in a multi-lingual system there are special problems to be solved.

Other developments which might influence the effectiveness of on-line retrospective search systems in the future are:

(a) *Telecommunications developments.* This would have an effect on the telecommunications networks making their access and use easier.

(b) *Developments of standards.* Some standardization of the structure of databases is already underway, and, as noted above, so is a study into the feasibility of a standard command language.

(c) *Development in the range of services available.* Some data retrieval systems and shared cataloguing services are available on the current systems and these may be extended. Studies into facsimile transmission of the original document are also being undertaken.

(d) *Development of the databases.* The databases could become more application oriented, more multidisciplinary or could fractionize into narrower subject fields.

Example 1: An example of an on-line retrospective search

Query: Find documents which describe how libraries have helped with adult literacy.

Solution: Choose the on-line system   —Lockheed DIALOG®
Decide on the database   —ERIC
Choose terms from the appropriate thesaurus—libraries, adult literacy
Access the database

The actual search is shown in Fig. 11.1.

Having explored several avenues such as extra terms, relevant authors and places where relevant work is in progress, the full bibliographic details and abstracts of sets 3, 5, 7, 8, 11 would be printed off-line at Palo Alto. This search took 19 minutes on a slow (10 characters per second) terminal.

Example 2: *New York Times* Information Bank [22]

In the 1960s it was decided that the information in the printed index to the *New York Times* should be available from an on-line terminal. It was also decided that the original documents (in this case newspaper cuttings) should be available from the information system and that outside users should be allowed to access the database.

The system was designed during 1969 and 1970. By 1971 the computer and the specially designed terminals were installed and the system started to operate with the *New York Times* database. In 1972 the University of Pittsburgh became the first remote user of the service. In the next year the system became fully operational and the database included items from 66 other publications from the English-speaking world. By 1974 the database contained 850 000 citations and was growing at a rate of 250 000 citations each year.

(1) *Input*

The *New York Times* and other publications are scanned and items that are to

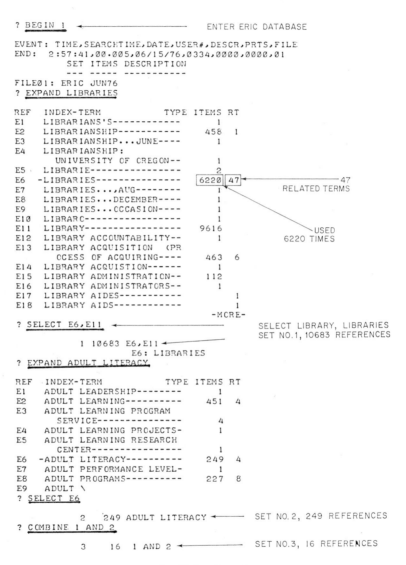

```
? BEGIN 1  ◄──────────────    ENTER ERIC DATABASE
EVENT: TIME,SEARCHTIME,DATE,USER#,DESCR,PRTS,FILE
END:  2:57:41,00.005,06/15/76,0334,0000,0000,01
          SET ITEMS DESCRIPTION
          --- ----- -----------
FILE01: ERIC JUN76
? EXPAND LIBRARIES

REF   INDEX-TERM          TYPE ITEMS RT
E1    LIBRARIANS'S------------    1
E2    LIBRARIANSHIP-----------   458  1
E3    LIBRARIANSHIP...JUNE----    1
E4    LIBRARIANSHIP:
         UNIVERSITY OF OREGON--   1
E5    LIBRARIE---------------    2
E6   -LIBRARIES-------------- 6220 47 ◄──────────── 47
E7    LIBRARIES...,AUG--------    1           RELATED TERMS
E8    LIBRARIES...DECEMBER----    1
E9    LIBRARIES...OCCASION----    1
E10   LIBRARC----------------    1
E11   LIBRARY----------------  9616           USED
E12   LIBRARY ACCOUNTABILITY--    1         6220 TIMES
E13   LIBRARY ACQUISITION  (PR
         OCESS OF ACQUIRING----  463  6
E14   LIBRARY ACQUISTION------    1
E15   LIBRARY ADMINISTRATION--  112
E16   LIBRARY ADMINISTRATORS--    1
E17   LIBRARY AIDES-----------       1
E18   LIBRARY AIDS-----------       1
                              -MORE-
? SELECT E6,E11  ◄──────────────    SELECT LIBRARY, LIBRARIES
                                    SET NO.1, 10683 REFERENCES
         1 10683 E6,E11 ◄────
             E6: LIBRARIES
? EXPAND ADULT LITERACY

REF  INDEX-TERM           TYPE ITEMS RT
E1   ADULT LEADERSHIP--------    1
E2   ADULT LEARNING----------  451  4
E3   ADULT LEARNING PROGRAM
        SERVICE--------------    4
E4   ADULT LEARNING PROJECTS-    1
E5   ADULT LEARNING RESEARCH
        CENTER---------------    1
E6  -ADULT LITERACY---------  249  4
E7   ADULT PERFORMANCE LEVEL-    1
E8   ADULT PROGRAMS---------- 227  8
E9   ADULT \
? SELECT E6

         2   249 ADULT LITERACY ◄──── SET NO.2, 249 REFERENCES
? COMBINE 1 AND 2

         3   16  1 AND 2 ◄──────────── SET NO.3, 16 REFERENCES
```

Fig. 11.1.—Part 1.

? <u>TYPE 3/6/1-5</u>   ←——————————— TYPE 1st 5 titles of set no. 3

1
EJ105396   ←————————————— Reference number to Current Index to
   THE PUBLIC LIBRARY AND ADULT EDUCATION IN INDIA   Journals in Education

2
EJ054866
   RURAL LIBRARIES IN FUNCTIONAL LITERACY CAMPAIGNS

3
ED111952   ←————————————— Reference number to Resources in Education
   MOBRAL--THE BRAZILIAN ADULT LITERACY EXPERIMENT. EDUCATIONAL STUDIES
AND DOCUMENT†J5DLX[J7G\Y\
-1061-04--
PLEASE LOG IN: LMS

PASSWORD: ⌐ PROBLEMS ON THE LINE!
HOST IS ONLINE

          ←——————————— LOGGING IN AGAIN

ENTER YOUR DIALOG PASSWORD
█████████
█████████   RECONNECT @ 3:04:29   ←————————   RECONNECTED.
                                             THE SYTEM REMEMBERS
? <u>TYPE 3/6/3-5</u>   SETS FORMED.

3
ED111952
   MOBRAL--THE BRAZILIAN ADULT LITERACY EXPERIMENT. EDUCATIONAL STUDIES
AND DOCUMENTS NO. 15.

4
ED110722
   THE WAY OUT: A PILOT PROJECT IN ADULT LITERACY. REPORT NO. 1-1974.

5
ED105278
   LITERACY DOCUMENTATION: AN INTERNATIONAL BULLETIN FOR LIBRARIES AND
INFORMATION CENTRES. VOLUME 3, NUMBER 4.

Fig. 11.1.—Part 2.

? TYPE 3/2/4 ◄——— LOOK AT 4th document in more depth

4
ED110722   CE004519
   THE WAY OUT: A PILOT PROJECT IN ADULU LITERACY. REPORT NO. 1-1974.
   COUNCIL OF ADULT EDUCATION, MELBOURNE (AUSTRALIA).
   PUBL. DATE: 74   NOTE: 52P.
   EDRS PRICE MF-$0.76 HC-$3.32 PLUS POSTAGE
   DESCRIPTORS: *ADULT LITERACY/ *ADULT PROGRAMS/ *FOREIGN COUNTRIES/
*FUNCTIONAL ILLITERACY/ GROUP EXPERIENCE/ ILLITERACY/ *PILOT PROJECTS/
SMALL GROUP INSTRUCTION/ TEACHER WORKSHOPS
   IDENTIFIERS: *AUSTRALIA | A USEFUL TERM.

? SELECT ADULT(C)ILLITERACY ◄——— SELECT REFERENCES CONTAINING

         4   312 ADULT(C)ILLITERACY   ADULT AND ILLITERACY
? COMBINE 4 AND 1

         5   18   4 AND 1
? TYPE 5/6/1-6

1
ED111952
   MOBRAL--THE BRAZILIAN ADULT LITERACY EXPERIMENT. EDUCATIONAL STUDIES
AND DOCUMENTS NO. 15.

2
ED110722
   THE WAY OUT: A PILOT PROJECT IN ADULT LITERACY. REPORT NO. 1-1974.

3
ED107919
   A BIBLIOGRAPHY OF MATERIALS: ADULT BASIC EDUCATION: WYOMING.

4
ED105152
   ADULT EDUCATION AND NATIONAL DEVELOPMENT: CONCEPTS AND PRACTICES IN
INDIA.

5
ED099604
   LITERACY DOCUMENTATION: AN INTERNATIONAL BULLETIN FOR LIBRARIES AND
INFORMATION CENTRES. VOLUME 3, NUMBER 2.

6
ED098393
   RIGHT-TO-READ FOR ADULTS. FINAL REPORT.

? EXPAND E6 ◄——— LOOK AT TERMS RELATED TO

REF   INDEX-TERM   TYPE ITEMS RT   ADULT LITERACY
R1   -ADULT LITERACY----------   249   4
R2   LITERACY---------------B   1902 13
R3   ADULT BASIC EDUCATION---R   1221   5
R4   BEGINNING READING-------R   1056   9
R5   READING SKILLS----------R   2803 26
? SELECT ADULT(F)READING SKILLS ◄——— SELECT REFERENCES CONTAINING

         6   53 ADULT(F)READING SKILLS   ADULT AND READING SKILLS
? COMBINE 6 AND 1   IN THE SAME FIELD

         7   3   6 AND 1

Fig. 11.1.—Part 3.

? <u>TYPE 7/6/1-3</u>

1
ED068812
   NATIONAL RIGHT TO READ PARTNERS.

2
ED042960#
   CONTINUING LITERACY.

3
ED017434#
   BOOKS FOR ADULTS BEGINNING TO READ, REVISED 1967.

? <u>TYPE 7/5/3</u> ◄─────────────── TYPE OUT FULL BIBLIOGRAPHIC REFERENCE

3   AND THE ABSTRACT

ED017434#   RE001161
   BOOKS FOR ADULTS BEGINNING TO READ, REVISED 1967.
   MACDONALD, BERNICE
   AMERICAN LIBRARY ASSOCIATION, CHICAGO, ILL.
   PUBL. DATE: 01DEC67
   DOCUMENT NOT AVAILABLE FROM EDRS.
   DESCRIPTORS: *ADULT READING PROGRAMS/ HIGH INTEREST LOW VOCABULARY
BOOKS/ *PUBLICATIONS/ *READING MATERIALS/ READING MATERIAL SELECTION
   IDENTIFIERS: READING LEVELS
   A BIBLIOGRAPHY SUITABLE FOR USE WITH ADULT GROUPS AND INDIVIDUALS
WHO ARE ILLITERATE, FUNCTIONALLY ILLITERATE, OR WHOSE READING SKILLS
ARE LATENT OR UNDERDEVELOPED WAS COMPILED BY THE COMMITTEE ON READING
IMPROVEMENT FOR ADULTS OF THE AMERICAN LIBRARY ASSOCIATION ADULT
SERVICES DIVISION. THIS LIST REPRESENTS A COMPLETELY EDITED AND
ANNOTATED REVISION OF A LIST ORIGINALLY DISTRIBUTED IN THE "WILSON
LIBRARY BULLETIN," SEPTEMBER 1965. FILMS, RECORDINGS, AND PROGRAMED
MATERIALS ARE NOT INCLUDED. THE BOOKS ARE LISTED UNDER ELEMENTARY OR
INTERMEDIATE READING LEVELS. MATERIALS COVER A RANGE OF INTERESTS
INCLUDING BASIC ADULT EDUCATION, FAMILY LIFE, JOB INFORMATION,
PERSONAL AND COMMUNITY PROBLEMS, INSPIRATIONAL AND PLEASURABLE
READING. CHILDREN'S BOOKS ARE INCLUDED WHEN APPEAL, SUBJECT MATTER,
AND FORMAT SEEM APPROPRIATE FOR ADULT USE. A MINIMUM OF INSTRUCTIONAL
MATERIALS, ESPECIALLY WORKBOOKS, HAS BEEN INCLUDED WHEN THE MATERIALS
HAVE SELF-STUDY VALUE. THIS BIBLIOGRAPHY APPEARED IN "THE BOOKLIST AND
SUBSCRIPTION BOOKS BULLETIN," DECEMBER 1, 1967. IT IS AVAILABLE AS A
REPRINT FROM THE ADULT SERVICES DIVISION, AMERICAN LIBRARY
ASSOCIATION, 50 E. HURON STREET, CHICAGO, ILL. 60611. UP TO NINE
COPIES ARE FREE, 10 OR MORE COST 10 CENTS EACH. (JM)
? <u>EXPAND AU=MACDONALD, B</u> ◄─────── SEE IF AUTHOR HAS WRITTEN

REF   INDEX-TERM   TYPE ITEMS RT   OTHER RELEVANT PAPERS
E1   AU=MACDONALD------------   1
E2   AU=MACDONALD-ROSS,
         MICHAEL--------------   2
E3   AU=MACDONALD, A. P.-----   2
E4   AU=MACDONALD, A. P., JR.   14
E5   AU=MACDONALD, ALLAN F.--   1
E6   -AU=MACDONALD, B--------
E7   AU=MACDONALD, B.--------   1
E8   AU=MACDONALD, BARRY-- --   4
E9   AU=MACDONALD, BERNICE---   2
E10   AU=MACDONALD, BRYCE I.--   1
E11   AU=MACDONALD, CATHERINE-

Fig. 11.1.—Part 4.

```
? SELECT E9

         8      2 AU=MACDONALD, BERNICE
? TYPE 8/6/1-2.

1
EDØ17434#
  BOOKS FOR ADULTS BEGINNING TO READ, REVISED 1967.

2
EDØ1Ø855
  LITERACY  ACTIVITIES  IN  PUBLIC  LIBRARIES,  A REPORT OF A STUDY OF
SERVICES TO ADULT ILLITERATES.

? SELECT NATIONAL READING CENTER/CS  ◄─────────── SEARCH BY

         9    Ø NATIONAL READING CENTER/CS      CORPORATE SOURCE ( CS )
? SELECT NATIONAL(W)READING(W)CENTER/CS

        1Ø     18 NATIONAL(W)READING(W)CENTER/CS
? COMBINE 1Ø AND 1

        11      2  1Ø AND 1
? TYPE 11/6/1-2

1
EDØ68812
  NATIONAL RIGHT TO READ PARTNERS.

2
EDØ59Ø14
  READING PROGRAMS: WHAT IS A GOOD READING PROGRAM? NUMBER 6.

? DISPLAY SETS  ◄─────────────── LOOK AT SETS GENERATED SO FAR

SET ITEMS DESCRIPTION
  1 1Ø683 E6,E11 LIBRARIES
  2    249 ADULT LITERACY
  3     16  1 AND 2
  4    312 ADULT(C)ILLITERACY
  5     18  4 AND 1
  6     53 ADULT(F)READING SKILLS
  7      3  6 AND 1
  8      2 AU=MACDONALD, BERNICE
  9      Ø NATIONAL READING CENTER/CS
 1Ø     18 NATIONAL(W)READING(W)CENTER/CS
 11      2  1Ø AND 1
? END  ◄─────────────── LEAVE DATABASE
EVENT: TIME,SEARCHTIME,DATE,USER#,DESCR,PRTS,FILE
END:  3:24:19,ØØ.331,Ø6/15/76,Ø334,ØØ1Ø,ØØØ3,Ø1
? LOGOFF ◄─────────────── LOGOFF FROM SYSTEM
```

Fig. 11.1.—Part 5. A search on the DIALOG® system (reproduced by kind per
mission of Lockheed Information Services of Palo Alto).

be included in the database are marked. The items are cut out, pasted on to a sheet of paper and duplicated. One copy is sent to the indexers and the other is used to make a microfiche of the item.

The indexing is conducted on-line. Trained indexers prepare a full bibliographic record which includes index terms (chosen from a thesaurus) and an abstract. This record is input to the computer via a VDU and corrections are made on-line using a text editing program. Each night a list of the records which were input the previous day is produced on a line-printer. The index terms used which are not included in the on-line vocabulary are indicated. If necessary, records can be amended on-line.

Weights are added to the index terms at the input stage to indicate the relative importance of the term to the item being indexed.

(2) *Searching*

Terms from the thesaurus, combined with Boolean operators if necessary, are used to search the database. In addition, other fields of the record, such as date or type of item, can be used in compiling the search strategy. The number of citations satisfying a search request is given. The searcher can specify that the citations be printed in chronological or reverse chronological order.

(3) *Output*

The citations printed as a result of a search contain the bibliographic details, the index terms and the abstract. In addition, the address in the microfiche file of the original cutting is given. Within the *New York Times* building, the original cutting can be viewed on the same terminal which is used for the search. A hard-copy printout of any item displayed can also be obtained.

The system runs on an IBM 370/145 and the programs are written in PL/1, COBOL and assembly language. The system is designed to support 500 terminals.

The information bank, although designed for the staff of the *New York Times*, can be used by people in industry, government, commerce or indeed anyone. Several public libraries in the USA have been experimenting with the service. Brooklyn Public Library made some 500 searches in five months, of which 310 were answered successfully (62%). North York Public Library processed 217 questions in two months, of which 134 were answered successfully (61.75%). The costs in 1974 for using the system were $45.00 per hour.

REFERENCES

1. M. M. Kessler, The MIT Technical Information Project. *Physics Today*, **18**, 28–36 (1965).
2. C. A. Cuadra, SDC Experiences with Large Databases. *Journal of Chemical Documentation and Computer Sciences*, **15**, 48–51 (1975).
3. R. K. Summit, Lockheed Experience in Processing Large Databases for its Commercial Information Retrieval Service. *Journal of Chemical Documentation and Computer Sciences*, **15**, 40–2 (1975).
4. R. J. D. Johnston, An Experimental On-line Retrieval System Using Ultrafiche. *Program*, **9**, 56–63 (1975).

5. A. E. Negus and J. L. Hall, Towards an Effective On-line Reference Retrieval System. *Information Storage and Retrieval*, **7**, 249–70 (1971).
6. M. Carville, L. D. Higgins and F. J. Smith, Interactive Reference Retrieval in Large Files. *Information Storage and Retrieval*, **7**, 205–10 (1971).
7. N. H. Price, C. Bye and B. Niblett, On-line Searching of Council of Europe Conventions and Agreements: a Study in Bilingual Document Retrieval. *Information Storage and Retrieval*, **10**, 145–54 (1974).
8. D. J. Hummel, A Comparative Report on an On-line Retrieval Service Employing Two Distinct Software Systems. *Journal of Chemical Documentation and Computer Sciences*, **15**, 24–7 (1975).
9. S. M. Humphrey, Searching the MEDLARS Citation File On-line Using ELHILL and STAIRS: an Updated Comparison. *Information Processing and Management*, **12**, 63–70 (1976).
10. D. B. McCarn and J. Leiter, On-line Services in Medicine and Beyond. *Science*, **181**, 318–24 (1973).
11. N. E. C. Isotta, ESRO's interactive system—an aid for development, in *The Interactive Library: Computerized Processes in Library and Information Networks* (ed. S. Schwarz), Swedish Society for Technical Documentation, Stockholm (1975). ISBN 91 7390 000 1.
12. D. Moghdam, User Training for On-line Information Retrieval Systems. *Journal of the American Society for Information Science*, **8**, 184–8 (1975).
13. F. W. Lancaster, *Evaluation of the MEDLARS Demand Service*, National Library of Medicine, Washington (1968).
14. F. W. Lancaster and E. G. Fayen, *Information Retrieval On-line*, Melville Publishing Company, Los Angeles (1973). ISBN 0 471 51235 4.
15. D. B. Marshall, User Criteria for Selection of Commercial On-line Computer-Based Bibliographic Services. *Special Libraries*, **66**, 501–8 (1975).
16. G. Pratt, *Information Economics: Costs and Prices of Machine-Readable Information in Europe*, Aslib, London (1976). ISBN 0 85142 078 8.
17. J. Wanger, C. A. Cuadra and M. Fishburn, *Impact of On-line Retrieval Services: a Survey of Users* 1974–75, System Development Corporation, Santa Monica (1976). ISBN 0 916368 01 7.
18. S. A. Elman, Cost Comparison of Manual and On-line Computerised Literature Searching. *Special Libraries*, **66**, 12–18 (1975).
19. E. C. Goodliffe and S. J. Hayler, On-line Information Retrieval: Some Comments on the Use of RETROSPEC in an Industrial Library. *Aslib Proceedings*, **26**, 177–88 (1974).
20. R. K. Summit and O. Firschein, On-line Reference Retrieval in a Public Library. *Special Libraries*, **67**, 91–6 (1976).
21. M. J. Voigt, Europe's Plan for a Coordinated Information System: EURONET. *Library Journal*, **101**, 1183–5 (1976).
22. J. Rothman, The *New York Times* Information Bank. *Special Libraries*, **63**, 111–15 (1972).

FURTHER READING

C. Wilmot, On-line Opportunity: a Comparison of Activities in America and the United Kingdom. *Aslib Proceedings*, **28**, 134–43 (1976).

BINARY ARITHMETIC

The normal method of numbering is based on the ten digits 0, 1, 2, 3, 4, 5, 6, 7, 8 and 9 and is known as the decimal system. The binary system is based on two digits 0 and 1. Similarly, there is the ternary system based on 0, 1 and 2, the octal system based on 0, 1, 2, 3, 4, 5, 6 and 7 and the hexadecimal system based on 0, 1, 2, 3, 4, 5, 6, 7, 8, 9, A, B, C, D, E and F.

In the decimal system 100 represents

$$0 \times 1$$
$$0 \times 10$$
$$1 \times 100 \ (10 \times 10)$$

In the binary system 100 represents

$$0 \times 1$$
$$0 \times 2$$
$$1 \times 4 \ (2 \times 2)$$

Thus 100 in binary is equivalent to 4 in decimal.

The binary numbers used in Chapter 2 can be converted to decimal in a similar way. 1001 represents

$$1 \times 1$$
$$0 \times 2$$
$$0 \times 4 \ (2 \times 2)$$
$$1 \times 8 \ (2 \times 2 \times 2)$$
$$\text{or } 1 + 8$$
$$\text{or } 9$$

11100 represents

$$0 \times 1$$
$$0 \times 2$$
$$1 \times 4 \,(2 \times 2)$$
$$1 \times 8 \,(2 \times 2 \times 2)$$
$$1 \times 16 \,(2 \times 2 \times 2 \times 2)$$

or $4 + 8 + 16$

or   28

The arithmetic operations of addition, subtraction, multiplication and division can be applied to binary numbers as well as decimal numbers. For example:

(a)

$$
\begin{array}{ll}
101 & (5) \\
+\ 10 & (2) \\
\hline
111 & (7) \\
\end{array}
$$

(b)

$$
\begin{array}{ll}
111 & (7) \\
\times\ 11 & (3) \\
\hline
1110 & \\
111 & \\
\hline
10101 & (21) \\
\end{array}
$$

Decimal numbers are converted to binary by repeatedly dividing by 2 and using the remainder. For example:

$$
\begin{array}{c|cc}
2 & 25 & \\
2 & 12 & 1 \\
2 & 6 & 0 \\
2 & 3 & 0 \\
  & 1 & 1 \\
  & 0 & 1 \\
\end{array}
$$

The resulting binary number is 11001.

GLOSSARY OF COMPUTER TERMS FOR LIBRARIANS

Some of these terms have less specific meanings than the definitions given but these are how a computer person would understand the terms.

Acoustic coupler. A type of modem which is used with an ordinary telephone to link a slow (10–30 characters per second) terminal to a computer.

Alphanumeric data. Data which consists of alphabetic symbols, numeric symbols, punctuation and some other symbols such as / or $.

Assembly language. A representation of the computer's machine code which can be written and read by programmers.

Backing store. A storage device which holds programs and data which are not currently being used by the computer. Discs, drums and magnetic tapes are examples of backing store.

Back-up. The means of providing a service when the main system for providing the service is not operational.

Bar-coded label. A label on which data is coded in the form of thick and thin lines, or bars. The labels are read by using a light-pen.

Batch processing. A method of processing in which the programs or data are accumulated and processed one after another by the computer.

Baud. A measure of the speed of a telecommunications channel. 1 baud is normally the same as 1 bit per second.

Bit. A binary digit. This is the smallest unit of information. It can have only two states which are usually thought of as '0' or '1'.

Boolean. The most important Boolean, or logical, operators are AND, OR and NOT.

Byte. 8 bits. This is the unit of information used by most modern computers to represent a character.

Central Processor Unit. The part of a computer which consists of the control unit and the arithmetic unit.

Character. One of the set of alphanumeric symbols that can be used for communicating information.

Check digit. A number arithmetically related to the rest of the data which can be used to check the accuracy of the data.

Compiler. A program which checks the structure of a high-level language program and translates from the high-level language to the computer's machine code.

Data. Information to be processed by a computer.

Database. A collection of records, or a file.

Data collection device or **data collection unit.** A device, usually used in a computer-based charging system, for automatically collecting data about transactions.

Debug. To locate and correct errors in a program.

Diagnostics. Information printed out by the computer system to assist the user in locating errors.

Down. A description of any piece of equipment which is not operational.

Execute. To process the instructions of a program.

Feedback. The act of using the output from a system as part of the input to the system.

Field. A logical sub-division of a record which can contain a unit of information.

File. A set of records.

Fixed-length field. A field which is always of a specified length.

Flow chart. A graphical representation of the sequence of operations needed to carry out a job.

Front-end. A piece of equipment attached to a main computer which helps in the communication with users. The term is particularly used when the front-end is a minicomputer.

Hard copy. A permanent form of output which can be taken away and read later when desired.

Hardware. The physical components of a computer system.

High-level language. A programming language which has been designed to allow users to write in a notation oriented towards their problems. A program written in a high-level language is often comparatively machine-independent and so can be moved to any computer which has the appropriate compiler with only a small amount of work.

Host. Often used to refer to a computer which is either accessed via a node of a network or via a front-end computer or is being used as part of a system involving other, probably smaller, computers.

Hot borrowers. Used to describe borrowers who need to be contacted by the library for some reason.

Hybrid. Used to describe a mixed system—e.g. an on-line and off-line processed system, an on-line and microfiche search system.

Input. The process of transferring, or reading, data into a computer system. It is also used to refer to the data which is transferred.

Job control language. The language used to communicate commands to the operating system of the computer. In particular this is used to tell the computer what programs to run with what data.

K. An abbreviation for the number 1024 (2^{10}). It is often used when referring to the size of a computer's store.

Kb. Used to refer to the number of bytes in a computer's store.

Key. A group of characters used to identify a record for searching or sorting purposes.

Keyword. A word used to describe a document.

Light-pen. A pen-like device which uses a ray of light and photocells to read special forms of data, such as a bar-coded label, into a computer system.

Live. Used to describe an operational computer system.

Log off. The process of closing down the communication between the user and the computer in an on-line system.

Log on. The process of setting up the communication between the user and the computer in an on-line system.

Machine-code. The basic set of instructions which the computer can obey.

Machine-readable form. A medium used for recording programs or data which can be input directly to the computer—e.g. punched cards, punched paper tape, magnetic tape.

Main-frame. The main part of the computer system—i.e. the central processor unit and the store. It is also used to describe sophisticated computer systems which have extensive software.

Master. Used to describe a basic record (or file) from which other records (or files) are derived.

Microcomputer. A recently developed form of computer which physically consists of only a few 'chips' of semiconductor material.

Minicomputer. A small computer often, but not always, dedicated to a particular task. The number of peripherals and the software available are usually limited.

Modem. A device which is used to link a terminal to a computer via a telecommunications channel. A modem is required at each end of the channel to modulate and demodulate the signal. A special telephone handset is usually required.

Multiprogramming. The process of sharing a computer's resources between several programs which are being executed in parallel.

Node. A branch point of a computer communications network. In particular, the point at which terminals gain access to the network.

Off-line. Used to describe a peripheral which is operating, but not connected to, the main computer system.

On-line. Used to describe a peripheral which is in direct and continuing communication with a computer system.

Operating system. A program which supervises the running of other programs, and allocates storage, input and output devices to programs.

Output. The process of transferring data from a computer system to the outside world. It is also used to refer to the data which is transferred.

Package. A complete program, or suite of programs, written to carry out a type of job which may be common to a number of users.

Parity check. A means of checking data by adding an extra bit which ensures that the data always has the same parity. This can either be odd parity (i.e. there is always an odd number of 1's) or even parity (i.e. there is always an even number of 1's).

Peripherals. Equipment which can be operated under computer control. This includes input and output devices and backing store.

Program. A sequence of instructions which when translated into machine-code and executed will effect the necessary processing for a given job.

Programming language. A language in which programs may be written.

Random access. The process of accessing any record in a file directly and without having to read any other records.

Record. The complete set of information referring to a particular item in a file.

Response time. The time taken for the system to respond to a user's command.

Sequential access. The process of accessing any record in a file by examining every record preceding it, in the sequence in which the records occur.

Software. All the programs required in order for the computer to produce the required results. This includes the users' programs, the compilers, operating systems and the packages.

Stand-alone. A description of a computer system which can operate independently of other computer systems.

Stop-list. A list of words which would never be required as keywords.

Store. A device capable of receiving programs or data, retaining them, and allowing them to be retrieved and used as required.

System. A set of component devices which carry out procedures in a clearly defined manner in order to accomplish a particular job.

Tag. A set of characters or digits which can be attached to a field or any other part of a record.

Telecommunications channel. A means of communicating between one place and another—e.g. by telephone or by satellite.

Terminal. A device used to communicate information to and from a computer system. It may be connected through a telecommunications channel and hence can be some distance from the computer system.

Time-sharing. Used to describe a computer system which, by multiprogramming, can service several terminals seemingly simultaneously.

Trapping store. A store, usually attached to a data collection device, which contains details of books and borrowers that are required by the library.

Variable length field. A field whose length can vary. The start, or end, of the field is usually indicated by a specified tag.

Word. The unit of information for computer operations. The number of bits in a word and the word length varies between computers.

HOW TO COMPUTE A MODULUS 11 CHECK DIGIT

1. Write down the number	0	8	5	5	0	1	2	2	1
2. Write down the position of each digit in the final number (i.e. including the check digit)	10	9	8	7	6	5	4	3	2
3. Multiply (1) by (2) position by position	0	72	40	35	0	5	8	6	2

4. Add these up $0 + 72 + 40 + 35 + 0 + 5 + 8 + 6 + 2 = 168$

5. Divide by 11   15 remainder 3

6. Subtract the remainder from 11 to form the check digit $11 - 3 = 8$

Notes: (a) If the check digit is 10 then X is used.

        (b) If the check digit is 11 then 0 is used.

ACRONYM INDEX

ALGOL	Algorithmic Language
ALS	Automated Library Systems Ltd.
AMCOS	Aldermaston Mechanical Cataloguing and Ordering System
ARPA	Advanced Research Projects Agency
ASCA	Automatic Subject Citation Alert
ASCII	American Standard Code for Information Interchange
ASIDIC	Association of Information and Dissemination Centers
AWRE	Atomic Weapons Research Establishment
BALLOTS	Bibliographic Automation of Large Library Operations using a Time-sharing System
BASIC	Beginners All purpose Symbolic Instruction Code
BIOSIS	Biosciences Information Service
BLBSD	British Library Bibliographic Services Division
BLCMP	Birmingham Libraries Co-operative Mechanisation Project
BLLD	British Library Lending Division
BLRDD	British Library Research and Development Department
BNB	British National Bibliography
bpi	bits per inch
BTI	British Technology Index
BUCCS	Bath University Comparative Catalogue Study
CAIRS	Computer Assisted Information Retrieval System
CAN/OLE	Canadian On-Line Enquiry system
CAN/SDI	Canadian Selective Dissemination of Information
CIM	Computer Input Microfilm
CIP	Cataloguing In Publication
COBOL	Common Business Oriented Language
CODEN	Code Number
COM	Computer Output Microfilm

COMPENDEX	Computerized Engineering Index
CONSER	Conversion of Serials records
CPI	Central Patents Index
DEC	Digital Equipment Corporation
DILS	Dataskil Integrated Library System
EBCDIC	Extended Binary Coded Decimal Interchange Code
ELHILL	Lister Hill
ERIC	Educational Resources Information Center
ESA	European Space Agency
EURONET	European Network
EUSIDIC	European association of Scientific Information Dissemination Centres
FORTRAN	Formula Translator
GEOREF	Geological Reference file
IBM	International Business Machines
ICL	International Computers Limited
INIS	International Nuclear Information Service
INSPEC	Information Services in Physics, Electrotechnology, Computers and Control
ISBN	International Standard Book Number
ISDS	International Serials Data System
ISSN	International Standard Serial Number
KLIC	Key Letter In Context
KWAC	Key Word And Context
KWIC	Key Word In Context
KWOC	Key Word Out of Context
KWUC	Key Word and UDC
LASER	London and South Eastern Library Region
LC	Library of Congress
LIBCON	the name given to a file of Library of Congress records
MARC	Machine-Readable Cataloguing
MASS	MARC-based Automated Serials System
MEDLARS	Medical Literature Analysis and Retrieval System
MEDLINE	MEDLARS on-line
MERLIN	Machine-readable library information system
MESH	Medical Subject Headings
METADEX	Metals Abstracts Index
MINICS	Minimal Input Cataloguing System
NASA	National Aeronautics and Space Administration
NCC	National Computing Centre
NFHS	Newcastle File Handling System
OCLC	Ohio College Library Center
OCR	Optical Character Recognition
ORBIT	On-line Retrieval of Bibliographic Information Time-shared

OSTI	Office for Scientific and Technical Information
PAIS	Psychological Abstracts Information Service
PERDEX	Periodicals Index
PL/I	Programming Language One
PRECIS	Preserved Context Index System
PRF	Potential Requirements File
RAPRA	Rubber and Plastics Research Association
RECON	Remote Console system
RECON	Retrospective Conversion of bibliographic records
RIT	Royal Institute of Technology, Sweden
RJE	Remote Job Entry
SCI	Science Citation Index
SDC	System Development Corporation
SDI	Selective Dissemination of Information
SDS	Space Documentation Service
SLIC	Selective Listing in Combination
SPC	Stored Program Control
SPIN	Searchable Physics Information Notices
SSCI	Social Sciences Citation Index
STAIRS	Storage and Information Retrieval System
SWALCAP	South-Western Academic Libraries Co-operative Automation Project
TRC	Technology Reports Centre
UKCIS	United Kingdom Chemical Information Service
VDU	Visual display unit

SUBJECT INDEX

Notes: (i) Acronyms which appear in the acronym index (pp. 198–200) are not spelled out in full in this index; other acronyms are spelled out in full.

(ii) References at the end of chapters have not been indexed; however if an author's name appears in the text there is an entry for that author in the index.

A

A Computerised London Information Service (ACOMPLIS), 155
Acquisitions systems
  bibliographic record, 72–4
  costs, 79
  example system, 83–5
  general, 1, 65–8
  method of processing, 71–2
  software and services, 74–5
Aircraft Research Association, 138
Alcan Technical Information Centre, Jamaica, 116
ALGOL 60, 30
ALGOL 68, 30
ALS
  at Bromley, 93
  at Newcastle University, 117
  at SWALCAP, 108–9
  cost aspects, 105
  general, 87–9, 94–5
  software and services, 103
AMCOS, 54, 67, 71
Ames Laboratory, US Atomic Energy Commission, 145
Antwerp University Library, 57, 140
Arguments against computer-based systems, 5–6

Arithmetic Unit, 20
ARPA, 167, 170, 175
Articulated subject indexes, 133
ASCA, 145, 156, 158, 159
ASCII, 14, 154
Ashford, J. H., 79, 104
ASIDIC, 153
Aslib, 2, 43, 54, 140
Aslin, C., 104
ASSASSIN
  at RAPRA, 160
  description, 154
  profile construction, 150–1
  software for indexing, 137
  software for scarching, 173
Assembly language, 29, 193
Aston University Library, 127
  see also BLCMP
Australian National Bibliography, 53, 134
AWRE, 54, 87, 91, 100, 118
  see also AMCOS

B

Back-of-the-book indexes, 135
Backing store, 13, 19, 193
BALLOTS, 71–2

Bar chart, 46
Barnet, London borough, 66
BASIC, 30, 31–4
Batch processing, 11–2, 193
Bath University Library
    see also BUCCS
    catalogue record, 73
    catalogue study, 69
    circulation system, 97, 103, 107–8
    use of KWOC, 132
    use of SPECOL, 174
Becker, J., 70
Belgian union catalogue of periodicals,
    121–3
Berkshire County Library, 75
Bernstein, H. H., 39
Bibliographic Information Retrieval and
    Dissemination (BIRD), 171, 173, 175
BIBNET, 56
BIOSIS, 157, 159
BIOSIS Previews, 128, 161–2, 176, 179,
    180
Bits, 13, 15, 19, 193
Blackwell, B. H., 27, 66
BLBSD, 5, 51–4, 75, 128, 134
    see also BNB
BLCMP
    as a co-operative system, 3, 56
    description, 60–2
    implementation of filing rules, 75
    involvement with COM, 70
    serials coverage, 113, 119
BLLD, 76, 143, 157, 176
BLRDD
    see also OSTI
    as a funding body, 9
    funding for BLCMP, 60
    funding for SCOLCAP, 77
    funding for SWALCAP, 8, 108
    funding for teaching of on-line biblio-
        graphic searching, 178
BNB
    see also BLBSD
    co-operation with LASER, 43, 51
    co-operation with LC, 51
    PRECIS, 133–4
    production of printed products, 19, 139
Bodleian Library, Oxford, 72
Bolton Library Service, 94
Book numbers for circulation systems,
    88–9
Books in English, 51
Boolean logic, 148

Borrower numbers for circulation systems,
    89–90
Bournemouth Public Libraries, 89
BP Chemicals, 174
Bradford University Library, 88, 97, 103
Brighton Public Libraries, 55, 89
BRIMARC project, 55
Bristol University Library, see SWALCAP
British Library, 7, 8, 53, 75, 80
British National Film Catalogue, 6
British Steel Corporation, 132, 138, 139
Bromley Public Libraries, 89, 93
Brooke Bond Liebig Services Ltd, 131
Brunel University Library, 89
BTI, 133
BUCCS, 69, 77–8, 140
Buckland, M. K., 87, 100, 104
Building Research Establishment, 132, 137
Bulletin Signalétique, 128, 156, 176
Burroughs
    at Bath University, 103, 107–8
    data collection unit, 87
    general, 22
    software, 137

                            C

CAIRS, 138, 155
Calgary, University of, 158
California at Berkeley, University of, 119
California at Los Angeles, University of,
    117, 119
California at San Diego, University of,
    114
Cambridge University Library, 99
Camden, London borough
    as an experimental system, 3
    catalogue system, 66, 82–3
    circulation system, 89, 92, 95, 106
    use of a minicomputer, 72, 82–3
Campey, L. H., 137
CAN/OLE, 163, 176
CAN/SDI, 155–7
Canadian Institute for Scientific and
    Technical Information, 156, 163
CANCERLINE, 175
Cardiff University Library, see
    SWALCAP
Cataloguing
    bibliographic record, 72–4
    evaluation and costs, 77–80
    example systems, 81–5

Cataloguing—*contd.*
  filing problems, 75
  general, 1, 65–6, 68–71
  method of processing, 71–2
  software and services, 74–5
  union catalogues, 76–7
CATLINE, 175
Central Electricity Generating Board, 158
Central Processor Unit, 13, 19, 20, 193
Centre National de la Recherche Scientifique, France, 128, 176
Chapman, E. A., 38
Charging systems, *see* Circulation systems
Check digits, 59, 88, 112, 194, 197
Chemical Abstracts, 128, 129, 145
Chemical Abstracts Condensates (CACON)
  general, 128, 154, 161–2
  on-line database costs, 180
  SDI services, 156, 159
Chemical Abstracts Service, 128, 157, 161
Cheshire County Library, 67, 71, 75, 81–2
CIM, 17
CIP, 51
Circulation systems
  book numbers, 88–9
  borrower numbers, 89–90
  data collection devices, 93–9
  evaluation and costs, 103–5
  example systems, 105–9
  general, 1, 87–93
  method of processing, 99–101
  records, 101–3
  software and services, 103
City of London Polytechnic Library, 134
Cleveland Library Service, 71
Clwyd County Library, 73
Co-operative systems, 3, 56, 76–7, 101
COBOL, 30
CODEN, 112, 120, 123–4
College Bibliocentre, Canada, 56, 134
COM
  general, 18
  in acquisitions, 66
  in catalogue production, 70–1, 76, 77–8
  in serials control, 122
Commercial computer bureaux, 7
COMPENDEX, 128, 155, 156, 159, 180
Compilers, 33, 35, 194
Computer manufacturers, 22
CONSER, 113, 118, 119, 120
Control Data Corporation, 22
Control Unit, 20

Cooke, M., 74
Costs
  acquisitions and cataloguing, 78–80
  circulation, 104–9
  general, 9
  index production, 140–1
  retrospective searching, 179–81
  SDI, 159–60
Cox, N. S. M., 37
  see also Oriel Computer Services
CPI, 153, 154
Critical path chart, 46
Current-awareness, *see* SDI

D

Dammers, H. F., 160
Data collection devices, 93–9, 194
Data General Corporation, 22, 82, 100, 101
Databases, 128, 152–4, 194
Dataskil, 57
Davison, P. S., 6
Davison, W., 72
DEC, 22
Derbyshire County Libraries, 75
Deutsche Institut für Medizinische Dokumentation und Information (DIMDI) 176
DIALOG®, 167, 172–3, 174–5, 183–8
  see also Lockheed
Digico, 22
DILS, 57, 74, 103
Directory format, 26
Disc, 19, 21
Dorset County Library, 88, 99
Double-KWIC, 131
DRUGDOC, 154, 156, 158
Drum, 19, 21
Dual Dictionary, 127
Dundee University Library, 116

E

East Anglia University Library, 72, 99, 103, 105
East Sussex Libraries, 134
EBCDIC, 14, 154
Education and training of library staff, 44–5
Education and training of users, 45, 176–8

ELHILL, 172~177
Elman, S. A., 181
Engineering Index Inc., 128
ERIC
　costs, 159, 180
　general, 127, 176
　on DIALOG, 172, 183–8
ESA, 163, 170, 174~180
Essex County Library, 112
Essex University Library, 101
EURONET, 182
EUSIDIC, 153, 161
Evaluation of Printed Subject Indexes by Laboratory Investigation (EPSILON), 140
Excerpta Medica Foundation, 128, 154, 156, 158
Exeter University Library, *see* SWALCAP

F

Feasibility studies, 37–8
File conversion, 43–4
File structure, 26–8
FILETAB, 174
Filing by computer, 75–6
FIND-2, 155, 174
Fisons Ltd, 174
Fixed field format, 25
Flow charts, 47–9, 194
Food Science and Technology Abstracts, 154
FORTRAN, 30
FREESEARCH, 174

G

Gallivan, B., 87, 104
GEC Marconi Systems, 169
GEOREF, 128
Georgia, University of, 157
Glasgow Public Libraries, 95
Go-list, 129
Goodliffe, E. C., 181
Goodyear Aerospace Corporation, Akron, Ohio, 117
Gottingen University, 114
Greater London Council, 100, 155
Greenwich, London borough, 66

H

Hardware, 11–23, 194
Havering, London borough, 95, 100, 102
Hayler, S. J., 181
Hewlett Packard, 22
High-level languages, 30–1, 194
Higham, N., 105
History of computer-based library systems, 3–4
Honeywell, 22
Hummel, D. J., 175
Humphrey, S. M., 175
Hunt, C. J., 66
Hybrid circulation systems, 95, 100–1
Hybrid computer/microform information systems, 169

I

IBM
　costs, 9
　data collection devices, 97
　general, 22, 36
　in history of SDI systems, 145
　software for information retrieval, 137, 156, 174
IBM Technical Information Retrieval Center (ITIRC), 156
ICL
　general, 22, 36
　software for acquisitions and cataloguing, 74–5
　software for information retrieval, 137, 155, 173–4
　software for MARC, 57
Imperial Chemical Industries Ltd
　as a computer bureau, 7, 160
　ASSASSIN aspects, 137, 150–1, 154–5, 173
　PERDEX aspects, 120
　SLIC aspects, 137
Implementation of computer systems, 40–2
Index Medicus, 128, 142–4
Index production
　evaluation and costs, 139–41
　example systems, 141–4
　general, 2, 126–7, 138–9
　KWIC-type, 129–32
　machine-formatted, 127–8
　machine-generated, 129–37

Index production—*contd.*
  software and services, 137–8
  string-manipulated, 132–5
Index Thomisticus, 136
Indiana Co-operative Library Services Authority (INCOLSA), 77
Information Dynamics Corporation, 56
INIS, 128
Input devices, 13–7
INSPEC
  general, 128, 162–4, 182
  production of printed services, 139
  SDI services, 147, 152, 156
Installation of computer systems, 41–2
Institution of Electrical Engineers, 128, 156, 162–4
Intel Corporation, 22
Inverted File Information Retrieval Service (INFIRS), 174
ISBN, 59
ISDS, 111, 119, 120–1
Islington, London borough, 74
ISSN, 112, 121
Issue systems, *see* Circulation systems

K

Karolinska Institute, Sweden, 176
Keen, E. M., 140, 147
Kent Automated Serials System (KASS), 116
Kent County Library, 75
Kent University Library, 116
King, G. W., 50
Kingston-upon-Hull City Library, 89, 112
KLIC, 149–50
KWAC, 131, 137, 140–1, 155, 162
KWIC, 122, 129–32, 137, 141
KWOC, 77–8, 131–2, 137, 155
KWUC, 140

L

Lancashire County Library, 55, 71, 94
Lancaster, F. W., 179
Lancaster University Library, 38–9, 97–8, 100–1
LARC, 2, 9
LASER, 43, 51, 76
Laval University, Canada, 114, 117
LC, 50–4, 56, 61–2, 113

Leatherhead Food Research Association, 138, 155
LIBCON, 180
Libra Information Systems Ltd, 138
Library Information System (LIBRIS), 56
Library management games, 39
Lincolnshire County Library, 57
Line-printers, 18, 21, 69–70, 77–8
Literary and linguistic indexes, 135
Liverpool Polytechnic, 57, 132, 141–2
Liverpool University Library, 55
Lockheed Information Services
  evaluation and costs, 179–81
  general, 163, 167, 174–5
  sample search, 183–8
  search commands, 172–3
  studies for future needs, 181–2
  telecommunications access, 170
London, Oxford, Cambridge (LOC) Project, 76–7
London University Library, 113, 118, 120
Loughborough University Library
  cataloguing, 73–4
  circulation system, 93, 101–2, 103
  SDI service, 155–6
  serials control, 114, 115, 119
Luhn, H. P., 129, 145
Luton Public Libraries, 106

M

McGill University, Montreal, 137
Machine Aided Notification Dissemination and Retrieval of Information (MANDARIN), 154
Magnetic tape, 15, 18, 21, 22, 154
Main-frame, 21–2, 195
Maintenance and development of computer systems, 42
Manchester University Library, 66, 72, 88, 99, 100
MARC
  as an externally produced database, 128
  development outside UK, 52–3
  example systems, 60–3
  general, 2, 5, 7, 8, 43, 50–1
  records, 58–60
  records for serials, 118–9
  software and services, 52, 56–8
  UK developments, 51–2, 53–4
  uses made, 54–6, 66, 72, 74

Mason, E., 5–6, 9
MASS, 119
Massachusetts Institute of Technology, 166
Master List of Medical Terms (MALI-MET), 154
MEDLARS
　evaluation, 178
　general, 142–4
　retrospective search systems, 166, 167, 174–6
　SDI systems, 147, 157, 159
　training, 177
MEDLINE
　for SDI (SDILINE), 147, 175
　for serials (SERLINE), 118, 175
　general, 143–4, 175, 176
　software (ELHILL), 174
　training, 176–7
MERLIN, 53–4
MESH, 143, 166, 177
METADEX, 180
Microcomputers, 22, 99, 195
Mills Associates, 97
Minicomputers
　for cataloguing, 71–2, 82–3
　for circulation, 95, 97, 99–101, 107–9
　general, 7, 21–2, 35, 36, 195
MINICS, 73–4, 119
Ministry of Economic Affairs, Belgium, 67, 91
Minnesota Union List of Serials (MULS), 119
Moraine Valley County Community College, Illinois, 118

N

NASA, 153, 167, 174, 181
National Agricultural Library, 113, 153
National Cash Register Company, 51
National computers, 8
National Library of Canada, 113
National Library of Medicine
　as a database producer, 128, 142–4
　involvement with CONSER, 113, 118
　retrospective search services, 167, 175
　SDI services, 147, 157
National Reprographic Centre for Documentation, 70, 77
National Serials Data Centre, UK, 113, 120

NCC, 42, 137, 174
Nested tagging, 129, 142
New University of Ulster Library, 56, 75, 119–20
New York Times information bank, 183, 189
Newcastle University Library
　as an experimental system, 3
　cataloguing and acquisitions, 74
　circulation, 101
　education aids, 45
　serials, 113, 117
NFHS, 74

O

OCLC
　as a co-operative system, 3–4, 8, 56
　general, 62–3
　link with CONSER, 113, 120
OCR, 17, 135
Ohio State University Library, 9
Olivetti RP 50, 99
On-line processing, 12
Operating systems, 35–6, 195
ORBIT, 27–8, 167, 174, 176
Organization for Economic Co-operation and Development, 159
Oriel Computer Services, 57, 66
OSTI, 9, 51, 83, 134, 162
　see also BLRDD
Output devices, 13, 18–9
Oxford City Libraries
　cataloguing, 69
　circulation, 89, 99, 102, 105–6
　education and training, 44

P

PAIS, 128
Paper-tape, 14, 15, 21
Parent body's computer, 6–7, 46
PERDEX, 120
Periodicals Data System (PDS), 119
Periodicals Holdings in Library School of Medicine (PHILSOM), 113
Peripherals, 13, 196
Pfizer Inc., 114
Pflug, G., 8
PL/I, 30

Plessey
  at Loughborough, 93, 101
  at Oxford City, 102, 105–6
  general, 87, 89, 95
  hybrid system, 100
  software and services, 103
  use for serials control, 114
Polytechnic of Central London Library, 134
PRECIS, 56, 133–4, 137
Precision measure, 139–40
Pressed Steel Fisher Ltd, 116–7
Problems of computer-based library systems, 8–9
Profile construction, 150–2
Program packages, 36
Programming, 28–33, 41
Psychological Abstracts, 128, 180
Punched cards, 14–6, 21

Q

Queen's University On-line Bibliographic Information Retrieval and Dissemination, *see* Bibliographic Information Retrieval and Dissemination (BIRD)

R

Rank Xerox, 22, 63, 108–9
RAPRA, 153–5, 160
Reasons for computer-based systems, 4–5
Recall measure, 139
RECON (Remote Console), 167, 174–6
RECON (Retrospective Conversion), 51
Record structure, 24–5
Remote job entry processing, 12
Reorganization of manual procedures, 44
Retrieval of Information by On-line Terminal (RIOT), 171
RETROSPEC, 181
Retrospective search systems
  access, 168–70
  evaluation and costs, 178–81
  example systems, 183–9
  future, 181–3
  general, 2, 166–8
  search methods, 170–3
  software and services, 173–6
  training and instruction of users, 176–8
RIT, 152, 156, 157, 176

Robinson, F., 38
Rontec, 97
Ross, J., 83
Routing serials, 116–7
Royal Library, Brussels, 121–3

S

Saskatchewan University Library, 56
SB Electronic Systems Ltd, 99, 103
  see also Telepen
SCI, 145, 154, 156, 159
Science Abstracts, 128, 162
Scientific Documentation Centre, 6
Scottish Libraries Co-operative Automation Project (SCOLCAP), 77
SDC
  evaluation and costs, 179–81
  file structure, 27–8
  general, 49, 167, 174–6
  studies for future needs, 181
  telecommunications access, 170
SDI
  evaluation and costs, 157–60
  example systems, 160–4
  general, 145–7
  profile construction, 150–2
  software and services, 66, 123, 154–7
SDILINE, 147, 175
SDS, *see* ESA
Search methods, 147–50
Selection of equipment, 42–3
Selection of program packages, 43
Serial printers, 18
Serials control systems
  accessioning, 113–5
  bibliographic record, 118–9
  binding, 115–6
  cataloguing and listing, 112–3
  circulation, 116–7
  general, 1–2, 111–2
  method of processing, 117–8
  software and services, 119–20
  subscriptions control, 115
SERLINE, 118, 175
Sheffield City Libraries, 103
Sheffield Polytechnic Library, 99
Shell Research Ltd, Sittingbourne Laboratories, 115, 160–2
Shropshire County Libraries, 78, 99
Silberstein, S. M., 119
Singer, 99, 105

SLIC, 136–7
SMART, 127
Software, 24–36, 196
Southampton University Library
  acquisitions, 74–5, 83–5
  as an experimental system, 3
  circulation, 87, 97, 101, 103
  MARC, 55, 57
  staffing, 47
SPC, *see* Plessey
Special Customer Oriented Language
    (SPECOL), 174
SPIN, 153, 156
SSCI, 128, 156, 159
Staffing, 46–7
Staffordshire County Library, 71, 99
STAIRS, 156, 174, 175
Stanford University Library, 71–2
Statistics CumIndex, 135
STATUS, 174–5
Stirling University Library, 115
Stop-list, 129, 196
Store, 13, 19
Sunderland Polytechnic Library, 118
Surrey University Library, 79
Sussex University Library, 94, 105
Sutton, London borough, 106
SWALCAP, 8, 79, 101, 108–9
Swiss Department of Defence, 169
Systems analysis, 38–40

                          T

Taylor, N., 6
Telecommunications, 170, 183
Telecomputing, 57, 120
TeleMARC, 57, 75, 120
TELENET, 170, 175–6
Telepen, 99, 100, 103
Teletypewriter, 17
Terminal, 12, 17, 21, 196
Texas Instruments, 22, 138, 178
TEXTPAC, 156, 174
THOR-2, 174
Time-sharing, 12, 196
TOXLINE, 175

Trapping store, 91, 196
TRC, 170, 176
Trinity College Library, Dublin, 56, 69
Tucker, C. J., 79
TYMNET, 170, 175–6, 180
TYMSHARE, *see* TYMNET
Typesetting, 18, 51, 70

                          U

UKCIS
  costs, 178–9, 181
  general, 157, 158
  production of KLIC index, 149
  software and services, 174, 176
Unilever, 154, 174
Union catalogues, 76–7
United Kingdom Atomic Energy
    Authority, Culham, 171
United Kingdom Atomic Energy Research
    Establishment, Harwell, 123–4, 174
Univac, 22, 137, 161–2
Utrecht University Library, 113

                          V

Variable field format, 25
VDU, 17
Vickers, P. H., 46

                          W

Warheit, I. A., 6, 8
Weighted term logic, 148
Wellcome Research Laboratories, 154,
    158, 169, 174
West Sussex County Library
  acquisitions, 55
  as an experimental system, 3
  circulation, 87, 91, 94, 102
Western Australia, University of, 95
Westminster City Libraries, 78
Williams, M., 158
Wolverhampton Polytechnic Library, 120